FROM WILLOW CREEK TO SACRED HEART

"Sometimes you hear someone share their story and you get the sense that they are pioneers, scouts, groundbreakers . . . blazing a trail that a lot of people will hike on after they are long gone. Chris Haw is one of those trailblazers."

Shane Claiborne
Author of *The Irresistible Revolution*

"Because of Chris Haw's beautiful prose, *From Willow Creek to Sacred Heart* reminded me of Thomas Howard's *Christ the Tiger*. Because of Haw's lucid line of thought, it reminded me of G. K. Chesterton's *Orthodoxy*. But the book offers today's readers unique gifts as well, because Chris feels the peculiar challenges of the present moment. He proclaims a catholic faith (big or small 'C') that is simultaneously rooted in history and engaged with our gritty, conflicted, often superficial, and yet profoundly questioning world."

Brian McLaren
Author of *Why Did Jesus, Moses, the Buddha, and Mohammed Cross the Road?*

"This book is really excellent, and reveals the maturity that seems to be showing itself in so many of our churches today. It is an ideal example of 'non-dual thinking,'the contemplative mind that can see 'beyond the shadow and the disguise' of things. Before returning to the Catholic Church, Chris Haw did courageously from the outside what so many of us cradle Catholics seldom do—but need to do—from the inside."

Richard Rohr, O.F.M.
Author of *Falling Upward*

"With an appealing candor and a storyteller's skill, Haw explores here a principal question of contemporary western Christianity: What is the role and proper place of the praxis, traditions, and theology of Inherited Church in shaping the religion of today's Christians? I must add as well that only rarely, if ever, have I seen a more persuasive or compelling apologia than the one he makes."

Phyllis Tickle
Author of *The Great Emergence*

"Chris Haw's journey from Willow Creek to Sacred Heart (and the Roman Catholic tradition) is an important addendum to the story of twenty-first-century American Christianity—not only because Haw's journey is representative, but because he has engaged the questions that come up along the way so well. You don't need to believe that all roads lead to Rome to see that we can all learn something from a faithful pilgrimage in that direction."

Jonathan Wilson-Hartgrove
Author of *The Wisdom of Stability*

"This book is in part about why the Catholic communion is good, but it is not about why the Protestant communions are bad. It is blissfully free from polemics, which we don't need. Haw's book is a gift to a Church too often divided by 'conservatives' who demand submission and 'liberals' who demand freedom. Chris Haw has, through his witness and his words, opened up a broader vision of a truly Catholic life beautifully lived."

William Cavanaugh
Professor of Catholic Studies and Senior Research Fellow
DePaul University

"In an accessible and intelligent way, Chris Haw presents us with the colorful fabric of his faith journey woven together with rich resources, inviting readers on a theological and spiritual adventure of action and contemplation. This book is perfect for those struggling to understand how they fit into the Church and world today, especially those young adults seeking to make sense of their faith in challenging times."

Daniel P. Horan, O.F.M
Author of *Dating God*

"Much more than an already fascinating Chestertonian re-discovery of the Catholic Faith, Chris Haws bears witness to the slow, patient, ideology-busting determination of God. This has brought him, via the dying reefs of Belize and the apocalyptic landscape of Camden, New Jersey, into one of our faith's best-kept secrets: a deep, delighting love for our material, corporal, human life—in all its vulnerability."

James Alison
Author of *Broken Hearts and New Creations*

"Chris Haw's new book is a gem: honest, insightful, funny. With sparkling prose and considerable theological insight, Chris describes his journey from Willow Creek to Sacred Heart—from American Evangelicalism to Roman Catholicism. In this narrative —part biography and part theology—he asks hard questions and refuses to settle for easy answers. Along the way he incorporates insights from Wendell Berry, G. K. Chesterton, and John Howard Yoder, among others. Chris's story will be of special interest to Protestants who wonder about all things Catholic and Catholics who wonder about leaving the Church. To all readers this book is a lovely gift."

Steven Bouma-Prediger
Author of *For the Beauty of the Earth*

FROM WILLOW CREEK TO SACRED HEART

REKINDLING MY LOVE FOR CATHOLICISM

CHRIS HAW

ave maria press AMP notre dame, indiana

Founded in 1865, Ave Maria Press is a ministry of the United States Province of Holy Cross.

www.avemariapress.com

Paperback: ISBN-10 1-59471-292-1   ISBN-13 978-1-59471-292-0

E-Book: ISBN-10 1-59471-350-2   ISBN-13 978-1-59471-350-7

Cover and text design by Andy Wagoner.

Printed and bound in the United States of America.

Library of Congress Cataloging-in-Publication Data

Haw, Chris, 1981-

   From Willow Creek to Sacred Heart : rekindling my love for Catholicism / Chris Haw.

      p. cm.

   Includes bibliographical references.

   ISBN 978-1-59471-292-0 (pbk.) -- ISBN 1-59471-292-1 (pbk.)

   1. Haw, Chris, 1981- 2. Conversion--Catholic Church. 3. Christian biography. I. Title.

BX4705.H3337A3 2012

248.2'42092--dc23

   [B]

2012022178

CONTENTS

FOREWORD

Sometimes you hear someone share their story and you get the sense that they are pioneers, scouts, groundbreakers . . . blazing a trail that a lot of people will hike on after they themselves are long gone. Chris Haw is one of those trailblazers.

His story is personal—about a suburban kid growing up in an evangelical megachurch but winding up Catholic and living in one of the toughest corners on earth. But it's bigger than that. Chris's life is a mirror to the Church. He reflects back to us our blemishes and scars, and our dimples and dazzle. Chris is part storyteller and part theologian. In fact, I'd consider him one of the sharpest young theologians in North America. But here's what I love as much as his smarts—he is also a potter and a carpenter, a dad and a neighbor. He isn't interested in endless debates or stale ideology, unless it has a real impact on how we live, and on how we love. He is not stuck in academia but has his feet firmly rooted in the street, the suffering, the real stuff of earth—for him that is Camden, New Jersey. His hands are not just familiar with books, but also with tools. They have calluses on them. He is not interested in ideas alone but how our theology can actually begin to affect our living choices. Hence, he makes his own coffee mugs and restored his house using scrap wood from abandoned factories. These are the types of theologians we need—for our challenge today is not just right-thinking but right-living.

This is a pivotal moment in Christian history. Young people are leaving the institutional Church in droves. Religious institutions are hemorrhaging. Headlines read of sex scandals and prosperity preachers gone wrong. Bad theology is everywhere. Sick religion is epidemic.

Those things are real and true. But there is something else also stirring, a new kind of Christianity. What we see is a new generation of Christians who love Jesus, love the poor, and want to see an end to war and injustice and other ugly things. Chris Haw is one of the voices of that movement.

And here's where Chris's book is so important and unique. Many of the young, emerging, post-evangelical Christian leaders have jumped ship from the institutional church, choosing instead to form renegade Christian communities and postmodern house churches that want little to do with the big ship. They are like lifeboats—and small is beautiful, but eventually you can run out of food in a lifeboat.

I once heard a pastor talking about folks who wanted Jesus without the Church, and he compared the Church to Noah's ark. He talked about what a mess it must have been inside the ark and how bad it must have smelled. And then he said, "The Church is sort of like that old boat—it stinks inside, but if you get out you're going to drown!"

Chris's journey led him back to the Catholic Church. His story is not an anecdote or an argument. He's not trying to convince us all to become Catholic—but he does celebrate the best and the worst of Catholicism and the best and worst of Protestantism. It seems to me he might help some of us Catholics become better Protestants and some of us Protestants become better Catholics. Many Catholics would do well to protest a little more. And many Protestants have drifted so far from our history that we have forgotten what we are protesting (after all, half the word protestant is "protest"). It is precisely the time to discover a new way of being Christian.

Reflecting on why he ended up Catholic after such a wild ecclesial adventure, Chris once said to me: "At first I thought I was in a kayak, whipping downstream head-on, but then I discovered this thing is more like a rowboat, and we have to look back in order to move forward."

Some of our denominations are like streams that have split off the main river. And some of them have begun to dry up. If we aren't careful, we will find ourselves so far off the main channel that it's tricky to find our way home.

We dare not forget that Jesus' longest recorded prayer was that the Church would be one as God is one. He is coming back for a bride—not a harem. With over 35,000 denominations, we have a long way to go to fulfill that prayer. Perhaps the way forward is by looking backward.

Shane Claiborne

ACKNOWLEDGMENTS

I thank my wife, Cassie, for her endless discussion of my text and its ideas, and her loving support along the journey. For their vetting generosity I thank Dr. James Alison, John McRay, and Rachelle Martindale, my editor Patrick McGowan, Dr. Evan Howard, Logan Laituri, Dr. Robert Daly. For indefinable blessings to my life, I thank my grandma Bindokas for passing on the tradition herein discussed, my mom and dad, Mitch Martin, Michael Doyle, Susan Cedrone, Mark Doorley, Mark Graham, Christopher Roberts, Steven Bouma-Prediger, Brian Walsh, Tim and Cheryl Heatwole-Shenk, Kristin Schrum, Andrea Ferich, Melissa Pacella, Sarah Schmidt, Kim Lowitzki, Jeff Frazier, Jarrett and Jeannie Stevens, Bill Hybels, John Ortberg, Aaron and Shauna Niequist, Rob Bell, Shane Tucker, Brian Zibell, Darin and Meeghan Petersen, Shane and Katie Jo Claiborne, TJ Fuller, David Gibson, Matt Shelton, and Scott Stevens.

INTRODUCTION

While writing this book, I saw a video of a spoken word poem released on the Internet titled, "Why I Hate Religion, but Love Jesus." In it, a young man describes how Jesus hated organized religion for being a dead end of mind-numbing, injustice-purveying, and violence-causing superficiality. Instead of the blind, enslaving, self-righteousness of religion, the young man promoted a Jesus of grace who sets us free. The video quickly went viral with nearly twenty million views.[1]

The lively controversy that followed the video's release assured me that writing this book was entirely worth it, for I had once found myself speaking much like that young man. Experience has since helped me strike a balance between a desperate desire for justice, grace, and depth *and* a respect for that oft-maligned word, religion. It is not an easy or obvious balance to maintain, and in truth it often feels like I happened to come across it by sheer luck.

My "luck" was born of spending the past fifteen years in the midst of a whirlwind of people, places, and spiritual movements. I have been passionately involved in one of the most energetic Christian projects in North America, Willow Creek Community Church—a Church that certainly is attempting a type of Christianity without all the "religious baggage." I have played among some of the spiritual rebels of my generation, loosely known as the Emergent Church. I have attended not a few gatherings of "Christian anarchists." I have been a leader among a curious subset of mavericks known as the "New Monastics." The winds of discipleship have blown me from the tidy suburbs of Chicago into one of America's most dangerous and impoverished cities, Camden, New Jersey.

But perhaps the oddest twist in my spiritual journey occurred on a street corner of this crumbling city. There resides in Camden, on the corner of Ferry and Broadway, a beautiful outpost of what I had once considered a crumbling artifact of Christianity: Catholicism. Upon my arrival in Camden, still full of evangelical fervor, I began worshipping at Sacred Heart Catholic Church—first as a visitor, then as a friend, and finally as a committed Catholic.

Having taken this step, I often feel as though I've walked into an ancient, mysterious world while the current fashion, very often, is to walk out. Sadly, I am convinced that many have walked out of the Catholic Church for good reason, in search of a more authentic and relevant faith. Like many today, I have piled up any number of objections to the Catholic Church, many of which came from my immersion in Protestant evangelicalism. Indeed, beginning hundreds of years before my life, and increasing ever since, reasons for opting out of this Body have existed. The recent pedophilia scandal and the ongoing controversies regarding the Church's teachings on contraception and the role of women in the Church are among the frequently cited reasons people jump ship today—to say nothing of Catholicism's many theological curiosities.

If I did dive overboard today, my case would be common enough. But, for reasons to be explored here, I haven't. I see the Catholic Church as a body whose problems are painfully obvious on the surface, but with gold embedded underneath; conversely, the Protestantism I knew was pristinely appealing on the surface, yet I found that problems emerged once I dug below. I now find myself wishing that those who follow our current cultural fashions had the gift of drawing from the deep well of beauty, stability, and wisdom that still abides in the Catholic Church—despite its problems.

Many of my opinions about the Catholic Church have come as a result of formal academic study. But while I have cultivated a near-nerdy love for theology, this particular book is meant to express theology through the fabric of my own story. Thus any theological *apologia* (defense) here—and there is some of that—is tied into my experience. For readers piqued by controversy, fear not. At times, I stray beyond the boundaries of defense into the more spirited work of *kategoria* (attack). Still, this book is not meant to be an all-encompassing, systematic defense of Catholicism or "takedown" of evangelical Protestantism. There are books out there for those who need to be dragged into the Catholic Church on every point. I was not argued into Catholicism; I first showed up to it as a Protestant partner and co-laborer in the fields of Camden. Along the way, through experience and study, I came to appreciate and even love it. In a way, this book is more of a *self*-criticism—a criticism of the ways my prejudices against Catholicism had blurred my vision—while showing how I risked a vulnerable openness to something I had previously written off.

Borrowing from a pattern promulgated by the Franciscan Richard Rohr, I have arranged the book into two parts: Action and Contemplation. The order is significant for me, since I have confirmed through my own experiments that humans do best by "failing forward." We cannot figure everything out and *then* act. Rather, the more sensible approach is to go about doing what we see needs doing, and, after we run into questions (and failures) along the way, to cycle back to contemplation and begin anew.

Thus, my first section, "Action (With Some Contemplation)," shares my story of growing up Catholic, moving into the world of Protestant evangelicalism at Willow Creek, attending Eastern University, studying in the rainforests of Belize, protesting the war in Iraq (with a short stint in jail), and finally forming what some have called a "new monastic" community in Camden.

The second and larger part of the book, "Contemplation (With Some Action)," reflects on my transition from Protestantism to Catholicism. The tone is more theological, delving into my own questions regarding ritual, hierarchy, the Bible and tradition, corruption and opulence of the Church, and so on. These are the questions that I had to wrestle with.

In addition to considering the more classic Protestant objections against Catholicism (veneration of Mary, believing in the "Real Presence"), I also decided to spend some time paying attention to more current fashions—for example, the above-mentioned sentiment of "Hating religion (or the Church) but loving Jesus," or, that endless echo of our current times, being "spiritual but not religious." I tried these ideas on myself, sometimes quite fervently, but ultimately I found them lacking.

I am delighted to tell my readers that I did not write this book owing solely to my own passion, but rather, because I was *summoned* and even lobbied to write it by friends and people I have met along the way. My last big project, *Jesus for President*, and numerous other speaking engagements at churches and universities, have taken me all around the United States and even to parts of Europe. In every place I have found Christians of all stripes eagerly living out their faith, and often pressing for a more durable and true manner of doing so. Many are seeking to make sense of the border between Catholicism and Protestantism. Cross it? Ignore it? Deride it? Start anew?

Many say that Christianity is going through a revolution now—what some call the "every-500-years-Church-rummage-sale," wherein the Church loses its deadweight and moves into a new era.[2] Even if there is truth to this (especially if there is truth to this), revolutions—however much they excite me—can take some serious turns for the worse; we easily forget that revolutionaries often become just as bad as the dictators they overthrow. Many new blossoms, however vibrant, may find themselves repeating divisive or thin innovations of the past. In my own journey, having traversed the waves of inspiring Christian experiments, I have discovered a paradox that I recognize as freshness in this old Church. We would do well to learn from rowboats—to move forward you must look backward.[3] Instead of "emerging," I have chosen to "converge." It will be up to the reader to decide whether my journey offers inspiration to follow suit.

Given my unique position, I have ventured a risk that another book on Catholicism will not cause the earth to sag to a breaking point. According to the journey thus far, my risks have been worth it; may it be the same for you.

PART ONE:
ACTION
(WITH SOME CONTEMPLATION)

ONE:
FROM MASS TO MEGACHURCH

Once upon a time, without any decent qualifications, and irrespective of my potential to damage the institution, I was baptized into the Roman Catholic Church. My mother, from a Catholic ethnic heritage as longstanding as the family tree, initiated the initiation. My father, from a Protestant background, apparently offered no protest. I was born in the birthplace of aviation, Dayton, Ohio, to a pilot father and a nurse mother. My dad's side is a Scottish, Irish, German mix, some traceable to the Mayflower, whereas my mother's side has the exciting privilege of claiming that elevated category of persons in the Bible, aliens— my maternal grandfather's side became established here via the efforts of a Croatian stowaway.

My impact on the city of Dayton was minimal, but my arrival was a source of scandal to the family dog, Sammy. My parents are convinced that he ran away after I, a second child, signaled a human monopoly on parental attention and affection. Increasing the stray-dog population by one and being frightened of the nearby field of cows is all I'm reported to have done in Dayton, and within a few years my family moved to the suburbs of Chicago, where my father worked out of O'Hare Airport.

Raised Catholic largely by my mother, my early years in the Catholic Church were a mixture of appreciation and boredom. Like many young kids, I often simply did not want to go to Mass. I vividly recall one Sunday morning when I feigned sickness by testing the thermometer-to-the-light-bulb hypothesis. It failed. Arriving at Mass, I would often wiggle among the pews and claim (multiple) bathroom emergencies. And yet I must say that years later, I somehow retained an interest in what I would call, for lack of a better term, the *militancy* of Catholic ritual—its cleanliness of form, its solemn action, the mindful readings and symbols, the slow and serious relishing in one bite of communion and one small sip from the cup. But back in elementary school, those moments were sporadic and were often marginalized in light of other, more pressing events of youth.

Mom taught CCD courses for us kids; CCD stands for Confraternity of Christian Doctrine. It's religious education for Catholics who don't go to Catholic school, but the name did not exactly fit my mother's teaching style. More artistically than doctrinally inclined, my mother would often play music or display art, asking us youth to interpret them. A lot is made today of the problem of mushy catechesis, but in truth, I remember it fondly, though my mom insists it was more akin to pulling teeth. In addition to getting us to CCD, my mom made sure we made it to Mass faithfully, long enough to have the creeds, incantations, and common songs seared into our memory.

One thing about Catholicism that I enjoyed—then and now—was the culture, which at its best is filled with festivals and parties. I recall, around age five, attending an exciting festival in our church's parking lot, held over a period of several days. Every time we visited my grandparents on my mother's side in Cleveland, it seemed there was some occasion for a similar church festival—day- and night-long parties stocked with food and beer, piñatas, volleyball, water balloon (and egg!) tosses. And although no longer fashionable in our society, even among most Catholics, this side of my family tried hard to keep alive a few old folk traditions—for example, an Easter-time breakfast custom of tapping one's hard-boiled egg against the egg of another at the table. The person whose egg didn't completely crack up was the winner. We dueled until the dinner table had found a winner who had at least one side of their egg intact, abiding through the violence.

My Catholic childhood began to fade just before entering the stage at which most young Catholics prepare for Confirmation. Around this time, my mother heard that the local Protestant kids had some really vibrant youth groups. Our Catholic youth group was, to put it mildly, less than vibrant. Appealing to her CCD supervisor, my mother requested to investigate and perhaps import some practices of these other denominations. She was promptly rebuked and reminded of how such Protestant projects were anathema. With concern for her kids foremost, we began to consider a change of ecclesial scenery.

Church shopping because of dissatisfaction with the youth groups might seem a bit extreme, but anyone who has seriously tried to raise middle schoolers to embrace the Faith knows it is a real challenge. In addition, however much Catholicism was a staple in my mom's family tradition, the fact was that we had few deep friendships at the local Catholic church. We were a long way from Cleveland, my mom's Catholic gravitational field.

Around this time, our family caught wind of a very different kind of church. It was called Willow Creek Community Church, and many close friends were inviting us there. No stuffy dress clothes, we were told. No statues, no crosses, no stained glass, no priests, no altars, no rituals (or so we thought), and not even a building that looked like what one might typically call a "church." Gatherings were of an entirely different nature from Catholic liturgy. They supposedly played videos and even clips of popular movies at the services and sang along with songs performed by professional rock musicians. Concert lighting and smoke machines were often employed to enhance the experience. And with legions of staff and volunteers, Willow's youth branch of the church, called "Student Impact," could entertain teens, teach them, summer camp them, mentor them, and exhaust them until they fell over in giddy excitement. Their youth ministry was replete with its own separate services, "relevant" songs, speeches, topics, dramas, videos, games, retreats, and so on. On any given Sunday over one thousand students would pour in. So, we went. And then we kept going.

Upon driving into Willow Creek's zip-code-sized campus for the first time, we viewed a gargantuan complex, a mall-sized, modern sprawl. The parking lot's size necessitated memory markers; volunteers suited with reflective vests directed traffic. I walked through the doors and into the auditorium, awestruck at its thousands of seats, mezzanine levels, enormous stage, and humungous, concert-like speakers. (Their updated building, a $73 million or so project, is one of the world's largest theaters.) The jumbotrons near the stage, listing the song lyrics and showing soothing Christian imagery, would occasionally post announcements mid-service like, "Parents of child #354, please come to the nursery."

I was enthralled. The sheer volume of people worshipping there spoke to me of its inherent goodness. It was successful, doubtlessly. Its sense of joyful volunteer collaboration was perhaps the most inspiring attribute, from the traffic-controllers to the greeters, from the video technicians to the "hospitality team." Everybody was contributing to a mission. In fact, other than sharing the word "Jesus" in common, the experience of Willow Creek made me think I had stepped into an entirely different religion.

Willow had already become so successful that it wasn't hard to catch rumblings around town from suspicious skeptics— "It's a cult," some would say. That accusation only served to intrigue me, prompting even closer investigation. Of course, fourteen-year-olds don't *really* investigate—not all that analytically, anyway. But if by "cult," one meant weird, insane, wild-eyed people looking to capture and brainwash me, this group appeared exempt. I could tell that most people there weren't weird at all. They seemed quite normal by middle-class American standards, in fact, and while they appeared excited about their spiritual lives, they did not seem crazed, pushy, or overly intense.

I should make it clear that while I was undoubtedly impressed, I did not immediately "fall" for Willow Creek. At the beginning, I hung lightly on the fringes. I had jumped from the Catholic to the Protestant world at just the time in life when we develop significant habits, styles, and cliques, according to our own religion or upbringing. I was in between worlds. The pious Protestant pop music, music which virtually all tweens at these churches know and love, was impressive in its professionalism, but it did not do much for me. Too often it seemed to simply ape the music of the secular mainstream—Justin-Bieber-style-but-for-Jesus kind of music. I was not dazzled by the "youth-groupy" culture either, where cultural seclusion or restriction seemed to have socially hamstrung some of the youth there; something about having your own special types of t-shirts, music, and bracelets felt "off."

My real passion at this time was playing in a punk rock band—hence my initial resistance to the Willow Creek music scene. "Shows" and parties where our band could play were my thing. (The band hit it big when we made it in the local newspaper!) I had enough respect and love for my parents that I didn't pursue that whole world of drugs and drinking that people might associate with teenagers into punk rock, though I had a few good friends who did embrace that scene. And that is where I came to a crossroad of sorts. A friend of mine committed suicide.

I had been with her and many friends the night before at an exciting high school football game with our crosstown rivals. At the end of an excruciating game, our school's team, the Central Tigers, squeezed out a tremendous win, and uproarious celebration ensued. We all made our way across the field to the high school dance and enjoyed a long, cool autumn evening of youthful festivity and improvised break dancing.

The next morning I was awakened by a phone call. A friend had shot herself through the head with a shotgun in her basement room. I immediately went over to visit with my friends, talk, and share the shock of the news. She had left a note that I never got to read. Apparently it shared cries of frustration about our social scene and its overwrought drama, abetted by its drinking and drugs.

Any funeral following this type of tragedy is bound to feel wrong, but the ensuing rituals were awkward, to say the least. The oddness of the funeral was punctuated with a playing of the latest fad of pop-dance music amid the mourning service. It was supposed to be a form of tribute, but it felt more like a clown had walked into the wrong gathering. Even taking that into consideration, something simply didn't feel addressed. Somehow it didn't seem that her death disarmed or decentered the affected group of friends. My friend Mitch and I took our acoustic instruments to her burial at the nearby graveyard where we played, for all attendees, an instrumental piece in her honor. Apart from the tears and sorrow, it was subtly yet chillingly obvious that, once the funeral was over, things were going to carry on as before.

In addition to dealing with this tragedy, my own social world was going through changes; a close friend of mine had just moved out of town, leaving me feeling very alone. Coupled with my friend moving, the tragic suicide left me feeling like I had come to a fork in the road. As the ancient eerie phrase goes, "Her blood cries out from the ground." I wanted to heed this warning. Thinking about what had happened, the drinking and drugs path became further sealed off, and a path of mourning and spiritual searching opened.

It just so happened that the week before this tragedy, I had attended Willow Creek's "Student Impact" and met the newest intern youth pastor for our school: Darin, a friend of now sixteen years. I had barely talked to him upon our first meeting, but when he got word of the funeral he came to it, and I still thank him for that.

I didn't quite know what to offer my friends so affected by this tragedy, but I thought inviting them to Willow Creek's youth group was a start. A handful came, and some considerate staff took us aside to have a grief counselor offer solace. More striking was that a popular Christian singer named Nathan Clair came to sing an a cappella song of lament for our group. I don't recall much of what my friends thought of this, but I wept bitterly, each lyric a touching of the wound. Whatever a "Christian" song had meant to me up until that point, it now meant facing reality, openly experiencing grief, letting it reshape me.

From that point on, I didn't see much of my old friends. I gravitated more and more toward the youth group world. I started attending Willow Creek regularly, often brought along by older friends. I continued to play in my garage bands, but I also got excited to join Student Impact's highly skilled worship band. I started to attend parties under the banner of the youth group, sometimes even trying to persuade my secular bandmates to join me. I made friends with more of the older interns, who, being in their twenties, were a great expansion of my social world. We would often go on hiking and camping trips. I borrowed their books, like ones by Dietrich Bonhoeffer, and we discussed them. This was especially helpful for me in that I found theologians like Bonhoeffer more satisfying than the literature directed toward the youth group. I was shifting into a new way of maintaining friendships—what Bonhoeffer called "friendships mediated by Jesus," friendships where a mutual experience of forgiveness and worship of God is the primary connection.[1]

And so, with study and involvement in Willow, coupled with some key mentors who offered me the chance to get to know some theology, my evangelical piety began to build. I started gravitating toward evangelical worship. Throughout the church services, I would find reflections on faith mixed into long—sometimes forty-five minute—sessions of worship songs. I would help lead many of them, often scouring the Bible and other literature during the week, to offer up meaningful "worship experiences" to the attendees on Sundays, retreats, or alternative gatherings. And I got the inside scoop on what it takes to produce effective, inspirational, megachurch services.

Upon arriving at rehearsal, I would be handed the schedule for the service, which was planned down to the *second*. Each song was selected as part of a long flow of elements to make for an inviting and moving experience for the young people. As one song was completed, the lights would change, a light melody would play, and the pastor would walk up; at other times several backstage hands would quietly talk through their headsets and cue a video in a perfectly executed transition; a musician would sing an introspective ballad in dimmed lights; an energetic song would whip hundreds of kids into excitement. And it was all done with professional excellence, on par with skilled public concerts and performances. Periodically, using their stage for all it was worth, Willow put on full-fledged plays and musicals, meant to be attended (and paid for) in the same way one might attend the opera or ballet. Bill Hybels, Willow's talented, long-faithful, and sincere pastor whose passion and leadership I am eternally grateful for, critiqued the oft-slovenly approach to mainstream church services, in which things are hastily slapped together, saying, "Well, it's just for God." Bill would have none of that and consistently aimed for the best.

It is an understatement to say that the services were mesmerizing—especially from the point of view of the stage. Sometimes a service, attended by a thousand teens all fixed on the musical performance, had the energy of a rock concert. Looking back, I see now that it is dangerous to the spirit of a sixteen-year-old to lead a concert-like worship event, to have several girls walk up afterward, saying things like, "You're like our own Dave Matthews up there!" Some of Willow's leaders, aware of the dangers of the crowd-drawing energy at these things, would remind us, "It's not about the numbers." They were careful to advise us against an almost too-effective evangelism, saying the focus should not be on the hype and excitement that an enthralling service can attract; instead, we must stay focused on the spiritual goals of Christianity. But over time, however much I constantly tried to remember, "it's not about the numbers," I also noted how the enormity of Willow's project *required* numbers to pay the bills and fill the seats. If only half the seats were filled in their enormous auditorium, it would somehow deflate the energy of the services, making things feel less compelling and successful.

There was little-to-no mention of "sacraments" at Willow Creek. However, it was customary for worship services at Student Impact to include at least one intense, emotional-breakthrough moment that one might call, at some level, "sacramental"; students who felt so moved during worship would often stand up apart from the rest of the crowd, raise their hands, close their eyes, and express with their face a moment of mystical, spiritual depth.

Perhaps this event filled the void of not having traditional sacraments. But it was a sacrament that only some people received. Other students would either look on, feeling awkward, or some might be moved to imitate—and if most people chose to rise to their feet in praise, even the impious would be compelled to stand. Almost every service had this line-in-the-sand moment of joining (or not) the wave of sanctity. I didn't see this at the time, but no matter how much a Christian community tries to remove stuffy, ritualistic requirements from worship, new forms and structures of ritual come to fill the void.

A truly exciting aspect of Student Impact was its emphasis on mining the unique talents of the group. While I would offer my musical skill on guitar, perhaps a young ballet dancer would do an interpretive dance (these were pretty good, I might add). Others might put on a drama, illustrating a Christian reflection on the pressures of high school life. The whole student ministry would break up into smaller groupings, composed of a hundred or so students from a few neighboring high schools, called teams—almost like smaller "parishes" that all cohere within the larger "diocese." Each team would hold its own separate parties and events. The team leaders would give students "spiritual gifts tests," where their unique talents were sniffed out, beckoning them to offer these gifts to the larger group.

Willow's approach seemed ingenious to me; in many ways, it was democratizing the Church—a wave of inspiration that seemed never to have occurred to the Catholics of my upbringing. In the Catholic world I heard about "lay involvement," but *everything* at Willow seemed *lay*. Even kids with the gift of "encouragement" or "hospitality" were told that they were indispensable parts of a larger body, the Body of Christ, which was on a mission to reach out to and welcome friends. Others with the gifts of "mercy" or "wisdom" or "teaching" could all consider ways that they might help. This sense of purpose was not only pervasive and contagious—it was also dignifying. Any person that you met in the halls of school who had not yet suffered your evangelism was a precious, unique, potential contributor to a persistently welcoming body.

There are, of course, well-known objections to this kind of evangelism. If you have winced your way through the movie *Saved* or the documentary film *Jesus Camp*, you may have pondered the facile and extremely disparaging climate of some youth-evangelicalism. For the record, I too look at such depictions of fourteen-year-olds seeking to "change their generation for Christ" with a pain similar to watching home movies in which I embarrass myself. In *Jesus Camp*, kids who have barely internalized the Christian message and know little or nothing of Christian tradition are recruited to be its zealous evangelists—primed with a dichotomous sense of good and evil, culture war, and the "otherness" of every neighbor not in the congregation. They know nothing of other Christian denominations, but they are prepared to slander them all as falling short.

But to interpret evangelical Christianity only through such critical lenses is to be disingenuous, to miss the more moderate elements which offer solace and meaning to many. To be clear, Student Impact, on the whole, avoided the excesses and the emotional manipulations depicted in *Jesus Camp* and other such documentaries.

Extending beyond my participation at Student Impact, I began joining the adult congregation for its midweek services, which were not for "seekers" but for "fully-devoted followers of Christ." That's right—committed members of the leading megachurches likely go to church events twice a week—and maybe three times if you include small groups or Bible study. "Seekers"—Joe-six-pack and Jane-soccer-mom—were understood to be people who would likely only show up on Sundays—at least at first.

While ministering to the already-convinced, Willow Creek's leaders had long been in discernment about how to attract the "unchurched" into their congregation. They judged that the modern world, in its increasing secularization, had grown weary of the stuffiness of old-school church services (or "Mass" in the Catholic world) and their mystifying religious imagery. People wanted something more accessible, something more "relevant," something without an embarrassingly religious gravitational pull. To that end, crosses and other obvious ritual imagery were rarely displayed. The "seeker" service was designed as a time in which a seeking person could show up without the awkwardness of having to meet and greet everybody. He or she could simply sit back, relax, take in the performance, and walk out with his or her freedom intact. They wouldn't be hounded to kneel, incant any odd confessions or creeds, or hold their neighbor's hand in prayer. Willow confined social contact to a momentary "shake the hand of a person beside you while you sit down." That would keep bodily exchanges to a minimum—business casual, with an emphasis on casual. This cleanliness was upheld even at the midweek services when, perhaps every few months, we would celebrate communion with bread cubes and wine dispensed in super-tiny, plastic, disposable, individual sip cups on a platter. Upon seeing the cups for the first time, I quipped that perhaps Catholics had stronger immunity systems, given their sharing of the cup.

One of the most significant effects my early days at Willow Creek had on me was on my view of other Christian denominations. The community saw itself as "nondenominational," and I accepted that, going so far as to wonder why all of the other Christian denominations in the world bothered with being so sectarian. Why couldn't they just be like Willow Creek—inclusive and "nondenominational"? Why couldn't they give up their silly rituals, dogmas, and traditions for the sake of simply following Jesus—without reference to the past? This sentiment was found, sometimes subtly, sometimes not so subtly, in many of Willow Creek's members. I even began to warm up to the increasingly fashionable language of saying, "I'm not a Christian; I'm a follower of Jesus," or, "I like Jesus, but not the Church."

In my newfound zeal I discovered reason for a newfound Baptism. A photo can be found somewhere on this planet of me emerging from the waters of a second Baptism with an adolescent face shining with an exuberant smile, sparkling with braces. I fancied myself emerging from the waters of old religion and parental obligation into the world of choice, freedom, and self-determination.

Overall, the Willow Creek ethos and mission were very upfront—and it was indeed less churchy or group-oriented than most other churches. It was more focused on the transformation of the individual: "Our mission is to turn irreligious people into fully devoted followers of Christ." (They were also not unfamiliar with the language of "accepting Jesus as your personal Lord and Savior.") Bill Hybels would declare, "Ninety percent devotion to Christ is ten percent short of full devotion." I took this challenge seriously and with eager devotion. For years I would attend virtually all of Willow's events, retreats, and studies. As I entered into my driving years, taking up jobs like pizza delivery, I would listen to countless sermons-on-tape. For Willow had made it a norm that after every sermon—usually forty-five minutes or so—hundreds of tapes and CDs, containing what had just been preached, would be made instantaneously and sent up to the foyer. After the service's conclusion, people would line up to buy the sermon and take it home with them for later edification, or perhaps to give one to their "seeker" friends—an utterly unimaginable scene at any Catholic church I had ever visited.

My first satisfying entrée into Willow's talks-on-tape was a "Christianity vs. Atheism" debate between Dr. William Lane Craig and Frank Zindler—today found posted on Internet video. The intellectual engagement in these talks was thrilling to a budding Christian like me, a sign of participating in meaningful, intelligent, public dialogue. I took to the implied apologetics that comes from thinking on these matters—obviously picking up C. S. Lewis's *Mere Christianity* for starters,[2] and, on more complicated days, an astrophysicist named Dr. Hugh Ross, who pondered the questions of science, the cosmos, evolution, and a Creator.

If apologetics were not to the individual's taste, he or she needed not worry. The Willow Creek audio sermon library was astonishingly diverse. The drive to develop people "fully devoted to Christ" made for constructing services toward the whole gamut of life-topics: psychological health, financial stability, family problems, marital intimacy, forgiveness, faith depicted in popular movies and music, introduction to the Bible, motivational living and leadership, sexuality, addiction, and so on. It seemed that the old-fashioned style of revolving homilies (sermons) around the lectionary had grown useless and wearying, like an old merry-go-round. It was time to get off and freely explore the countless topics affecting us today. During my time there, my ears never heard the word "lectionary." To be honest, I still to this day sometimes wonder about ways in which the lectionary cycle could somehow merge with this more topical approach (and vice versa).

The most inspirational aspect of Willow Creek's leaders was not the voluminous catalog of topics they were tackling, however, but their insistence that members get involved in their expansive service ministries—ministries that went far beyond keeping the church grounds clean, the altar decorated (they had none), or cooking for a potluck. For example, they were proud to talk about their many members, once "seekers," who had been brought into the fold and were now putting their auto-mechanic skills to work in a cars ministry. The idea was to rehabilitate donated cars in the service of poor families and single mothers. With a member base of over ten thousand—and even more who anonymously attended and dropped a check in the basket—Willow Creek's capacity for charitable services dwarfed anything one could imagine in a typical old-fashioned church of two or three hundred families. Their emergency-shelter ministry garnered housing for numerous homeless people; their disabilities ministry intentionally reached out to those normally overlooked. More traditional ministries like soup kitchens were offered as well, but often through an intelligent approach of helping ministries already in place twenty miles south in Chicago. Willow leaders asked the congregation for lawyers who could volunteer assistance for immigrants—in response, *several hundred* gladly stepped forward. Truly amazing!

With such resources in talent as well as treasure, the sky was the limit for serving opportunities—foreign missions assisting entire portions of countries could be expected. I am proud to say my mother has gone with groups of doctors to the bush of Africa and elsewhere, bringing medical assistance and supplies. (I, myself, participated in a mission trip to the Dominican Republic, which certainly fell short of Willow's more formidable medical missions—it was more of a cross-cultural exposure to other Christians, with short stints of being useful.) The sense of being part of a large, exciting group, serving the world for good in practical ways, was intoxicating.

Sharing first place among Willow's inspiring contributions to my life was their placing students in small groups of about six or seven (of the same sex), who met about once a week or two. Over this group presided a youth-group intern, whose prime objective was to compassionately care for and support students.

I remember several whom I counted, and still do, as sanctified older brothers and sisters, people who *really* meant it when they asked, "How are you doing, really?" This was precisely what I, reeling from my friend's suicide, needed. At our meetings we would study the Bible and discuss our personal lives. The word "accountability" was big in these groups, since we were encouraged to share honestly about our struggles, temptations, and problems. It was a form of intimacy and vulnerability that few young Christians, I find, are privileged to have experienced.

Within this abnormal church, I eventually found myself within an even more abnormal subsection. My youth pastor and friend, Darin—who would later be among the seedbed of the "Emergent Church" movement—sought to expand the minds of our "team's" white, privileged upbringing. He took to the habit of bringing a few of us down from the northwest suburbs to the streets of Chicago with the goal of meeting people from different backgrounds, perhaps bringing some food or blankets. And to challenge some students to a greater level of engagement, he would host Bible studies on Saturday mornings at 6:00 a.m.

Also interning at Willow at this time was a young man named Shane Claiborne, who was finishing off his Eastern University undergraduate work with an internship stint at Willow and nearby Wheaton College. With Darin, he was raising questions about economic class, going into the streets, and spurring thought about sweatshops, corporate greed, and war.

I remember going on a retreat one particular weekend, with Darin and Shane as our college-aged guides, where we discussed how the fundamental economic aspects of our lives appeared to be both out of touch with the poor and exploitatively founded upon their backs. As I would later read, G. K. Chesterton expressed this well, saying that many of us earn our living off the sweat of *another's* brow. I remember hearing of the disparity of the average US worker making one-hundredth of the average CEO (a gap which has grown to about 185th since the mid-nineties, when I first heard it.[3]) We heard the statistics about the United States having a minuscule percentage of world population while consuming a huge portion of its resources. We also opened up the can of worms regarding corporations, bursting the bubble of happy trust traditionally placed in them. We began discussing Nike's sweatshops, Nestlé's questionable promotion of baby formula in poor countries, and the car manufacturers that globalized their labor at times of record profits.

We also started talking about gargantuan US military spending —rare discourse in our suburban haven. We talked of our government spending around half its budget on maintaining a military prominence—more than all potential enemy countries combined—and maintaining several hundred military bases around the world.[4] Those vague soundings I had heard about the Gulf War in Kuwait when I was ten were being filled in with context and detail.

One of the most heart-wrenching stories I heard was of the incessant violence raging in Central America and of the role played by a US-funded school that trained soldiers and dictators who returned to places like El Salvador to engage in ruthless repression and torture.[5] Stories of bayonets and babies, of assassinated nuns and priests, and of village massacres were utterly startling to my soft, placid mind. I was startled to read of the United States' "torture manuals," declassified in 1996–97. And worse, the trail of violence could be traced back to our country, our taxes, and, if we dared the admission, our responsibility.

"Why haven't I ever heard of this?" I cried. While I had envisioned "accepting Jesus into my heart" and happily living in a prosperous suburban dreamland—populated not with depleted uranium, poverty, and tanks but rainbows, unicorns, and gumdrops—such fantasies rapidly began to fade. The Gospel, as my friends and I began to read it, was becoming uncompromising, even political.

I sometimes got the impression that the larger Willow community did not exactly favor the particular tack Darin and Shane were taking; but at the same time, I don't remember any signs of vehement opposition, apart from one "parents' conference" held at our house, where the progenitors could ask questions to this rabble-rousing youth pastor. No excommunications followed, but I also recall no soccer moms seriously pondering political radicalism—except for mine.

I eventually hit a point of irreconcilable conflict between my comforts and the uncomfortable world—I looked upon the televised news of the war in Bosnia-Herzegovina as my father returned home from the store with a latest consumer technology. I risked turning into a critic, and asked, with nervous tears peppering my declaration, "Can't you see what is going on in the world? Why not return that and give the money away?" I suppose one might consider this a prophetic breakthrough of sorts. More likely it sounds like the arrogant and naïve plea of an overzealous youngster. Regardless of whether it was more of the latter than the former, it signaled a change in me. I was now uncomfortable with what I felt the Gospel was telling me about the economic and military context in which I was living my life. The Gospel demanded a response.

These conversations, the trips to the streets, and the whole Willow Creek package worked together to destabilize my life trajectory—which up to this time had been to continue my flight lessons and become a pilot like my father. Instead, I now wanted to pursue understanding—about the world, about the Gospel, and about how they related to one another. I decided that studying the state of the world through sociology and Christian theology was to be my focus.

Upon graduating high school, I left the surging vortex of spiritual energy at Willow Creek to go to college at Eastern University. The Catholic Church was entirely off my radar—I had gladly left its theology and tradition in my wake, casually waving them off, considering them guilty of all the popular criticisms: they probably worship Mary, they engage in empty and dead ritualism, they make up doctrines in contradiction with the Bible, they are credulous enough to believe the bread and wine is literally Jesus, they have that silly pile of books called the "Apocrypha," they are burdened with a long list of historical sins, and they are so old fashioned that women are not in leadership. The list went on. Though a fair-minded critic might have pointed out that I had never read a Catholic theologian, I would have insisted that was beside the point. I found myself miraculously capable of judging over a millennium of Church history as entirely corrupt, without knowing any of it.

Why bother even thinking about Catholics? I thought. Just carry on and let the dead bury their own dead; there's a hurting world out there waiting to be improved through faith, hope, and love. At Willow, people were inspired by their faith to make a vibrant community life; women could be seen preaching numerous sermons; people didn't appear morally out of date; they kept rituals to a minimum. In college I would hear a provocative (and at the time, obscure) statement from the theologian Stanley Hauerwas that "God is killing the Church in America, and we goddamn well deserve it."[6] I supposed at the time he was referring to what I considered the virtually dead Catholic Church. Whatever he meant, I knew he was not talking about Willow.

TWO:
FROM CLASS TO STREETS

On a beautiful fall evening at the end of my first day on campus at Eastern University, I saw three folks sitting and talking on a grassy knoll. They had just met. Two of them, Jonathan Hartgrove and Leah Wilson, would get married in a short few years. I looked at them, found them good candidates for spunky conversation, sat down, introduced myself, and asked, "So what is your life story?" And I was serious. At that time I had all the zeal in the world and an unlimited attention span for spiritual conversation. I fully intended to talk to them until we got to the bottom of it. Leah looked at me, saying something like, "That's a kind of funny question for a first meeting." Laughing, I thought her mistaken. "No, seriously. I'd like to know." In part, I was seeing them through that Willow Creek lens—knowing that we all have special gifts and passions, and all we have to do is encourage each other to use them.

Oddly enough, I did not scare them away with my questions, and this grassy-knoll conversation led to friendships that would uphold the four of us throughout college. One of my new quartet's first orders of business at Eastern was to join the YACHT Club. YACHT stood for Youth Against Complacency and Homelessness Today. My friend Shane, just before coming out to Willow, had cofounded this group, in which students visited the streets of Philadelphia on a weekly basis to meet homeless people, and, through study and action, challenged apathy and ignorance (our own and others') about poverty, social problems, and injustice. The group had formed after some Eastern students encountered a group of homeless people who were squatting in an old, abandoned Catholic church in Philadelphia. Shane and his friends at Eastern felt compelled to join this group in solidarity, and the experience marked a watershed shift of focus in his and their lives. In reference to Matthew 25, where Jesus says, "Whatever you do to the least of these, you do unto me," the group pronounced on the campus, "Jesus is getting kicked out of a church in north Philadelphia!" This sparked a movement of people on campus to get involved.

The newly formed student group continued to visit with homeless people in Philadelphia, bringing lunches along after Shane and others graduated. They raised money, awareness, and donated clothing—sometimes achieved through campus events and small festivals. When I arrived at Eastern, my friends and I quickly jumped in, mixing YACHT in with our academic lives. One of the first events I organized was the "Global Feast," in which dinner attendees were divided into economic groups, proportionate to the world population. The largest percentage of those dining received only a cup of rice and a small vegetable. A smaller, "middle-class" group received a half way-decent dinner, while a select few got a multiple-course feast. The point was to catch a glimpse of the world's food inequities in a room.

I had learned about the Global Feast from a visit to a ministry called the Church Under the Bridge, in Texas. There, people underwent a "poverty immersion," the point of which was to cultivate some empathy with the needy by detaching participants from middle-class privileges for the weekend and sending them out into the streets. I remember spending the night in a porta-potty with my friend Josh. The night was uncomfortable, but we didn't care—we fancied ourselves as joyfully imitating the vagrant Francis of Assisi.

I also helped organize HAHA (Hunger and Homelessness Awareness) week and a festival called PAPA (People Against Poverty and Apathy). Our acronyms were quite often "against" things! In one great push of effort, we managed to help Eastern University become the first college to purchase one hundred percent wind energy from its utility company (instead of coal, nuclear energy, etc.).

The spiritual momentum I had brought with me from Willow was quite intense, and not just for activism. I would study hard all the time, and almost every day Jonathan and I would bring a few fellow students to go running through the nearby forest (jumping over its rivers and climbing campus walls along the way) and then conclude with studying the Bible for an hour. On Saturdays we packed bag lunches for the homeless and hit the streets with YACHT (sometimes sneaking a few homeless folks into the dorms for shelter). On Sundays, my grassy-knoll group would often experiment with attending different church gatherings (Episcopalian, Mennonite, Pentecostal) and afterwards go to parks for an intentional "day of rest" together.

After two years of this, the fall 2001 semester began. On September 11, soon after being let out of my Church History class, I turned to a nearby lobby television to see the World Trade Center towers smoking. I saw the news of another plane downed in Pennsylvania, and another that hit the Pentagon. Within a few seconds, several thoughts rushed to my mind: How far will this all go? Will we see attacks erupt all around the United States? Or is this isolated? Will it fade like a shooting star as a marginal act of terrorism? Were these attacks, in CIA-speak, "blowback" for US foreign interventions? Lastly I thought, "Oh my God, that could be my dad piloting those planes! He flies American Airlines

767s out of New York and Boston!" I hurried from the lobby and jumped on my bike to get to the nearest pay phone. My mom answered the phone and assured me that my dad was home and safe. I hurried back to the television, only to be devastated as I watched the towers crumble.

Amid tears and sorrow, acquaintances offered solace, saying things like, "Thank God your dad is OK." As comforting as that thought might have been (and in truth it was), I couldn't help but think, "But among the dead was *somebody else's* dad." Up to this time in my life, I had built a vague but fairly strong notion that God kept loved ones from danger—especially if one asked for this in prayer. Of course, the whole business of God mysteriously protecting and blessing some but not others gets complicated in the face of great tragedy. Why would *my* dad be made divinely safe and not another? Should we just downgrade "God's protection" to meaning a metaphor for good luck? The view of God as Protector-in-the-Sky had been slowly eroding in my subconscious already, especially after having read the book of Job; it crumbled along with the towers.

Worse than having to radically reassess God's protection, however, was the effect the events had on my campus. Within a few hours, after our campus quickly organized blood drives and made calls to offer cleanup assistance to New Yorkers, the collective spirit soon started feeling very dangerous. I could sense it among the student body as well as on the Internet and news sources—there would be vengeance and retribution. As most of the campus gathered in the baseball field for prayer when the day grew dark, my petition was that individual people and our nation as a whole would not irrationally pounce upon this transgression with further violence. Sadly, though, the opposite would be the case; it didn't take much effort, even in the first days after the attack, to see clouds of fear and hatred on the horizon that would quickly bring a downpour. Before we could even finish grieving, only a few weeks later, the United States invaded Afghanistan. Jonathan, always ten steps ahead of me, wrote to *Time* magazine with a small opinion piece that read, "We have pulled the pin on a grenade but don't know where to throw it."

For my part, I knew of no way to confront this bellicose spirit apart from sympathizing with its victims—both here and there. One of the quiet stories hidden under the war reports was that because of US bombing, the homeless population in Afghanistan had spiked. I aimed to gently remind my fellow students—who were quickly returning to business as usual—of this by sleeping for a month or so at the entrance to my dorm with a cardboard sign reading, "Remember the homeless being created by war in Afghanistan." It wasn't protest on my part (yet); it was grief. And though I had never paid much attention to Muslim customs, it often came to my mind, while lying there on the hard ground, that Ramadan was at hand. It was like war at Christmas time.

Opposing, or even questioning, the invasion of Afghanistan was tantamount to terrorism for some of my friends back home. Returning home for a break, over a polite dinner with a suburban mom, I critiqued the shortcomings of the invasion (one of which was lacking any clear plan or analysis of the problems with military occupation, much less any mind to the Christian critique of "loving your enemies"). She boldly asked, "You're not going to go join a terrorist group or something are you?" At the time I had a beard, and perhaps its fuzziness blurred for her the profound difference between my philosophy and Osama bin Laden's—for I was calling into question the redemptive quality of *any* violence. With so many Americans at the time, she could only interpret political critique via George Bush's proclamation, "You are either with us or you are with the terrorists!"[1]

To my deep disappointment, nearly all of my evangelical friends from back home at Willow shared an uncritical acquiescence if not a bold support for retribution and the invasion.

People might rightly accuse me of naiveté, but at the time, I was downright surprised at how quickly my previous guides in the faith—people who had busily and passionately implored us all to worship Jesus with all our heart—found his teaching about enemy love irrelevant in this case.

One woman, objecting to my criticisms of the invasion, shared with me that, "I rest in the knowledge that President Bush is a man of faith, and I trust his relationship with God to lead him in the right direction." The more I learned about atrocities of the past, and how often Christians and their faith fueled them, the less I found solace in such optimistic appeals to trust. Another friend, after I had expressed concern about the deaths of innocent civilians from the invasion, contradicted me with brazen illogic: "Why all of this talk about 'innocent' Afghani civilians? Aren't we all guilty before God and deserve to die?"

I began to see my evangelical world from a different angle. All the rhetoric about being "fully devoted followers of Christ" was being put to the test, and, as I saw it, was unraveling under political strain. All of that worshipful fervor and zeal, what did it really mean, politically? Was it just a cover for patriotic pride—a making of God in our own image? We had been struck hard on one cheek. What were we going to do about it? To heap irony upon the war fever, the countless Christians who implored me to trust in our government about the righteousness of the cause would tell me a few years later—once a president disagreeable to them entered office—that Christians ought to persistently *distrust* the government.

The rhetoric of Americans being the good guys and of all the bad guys being *out there* made me suspicious. I grew suspicious, not only by the irony of Christian calls to war, but by studying. Studying sociology, I learned of the startling Zimbardo prison experiment at Stanford, wherein a dozen students, prescreened for mental stability, were given two mock roles: some to act as prisoners, the others as wardens. They had to call things off after just a few days; even playing the *role* of a warden for a few days was too poisonous to their character, since they soon turned to abuse and evil.[2] This study sparked decades of dialogue about the banality of evil and its propensity to corrupt even the "good guys." It brought new light to interpreting mysteries like the Holocaust and people like Adolf Eichmann, a German in charge of much of the "extermination program"; when he walked into the high criminal court, attendees expected a man with devil horns upon his head and perhaps demonic steam floating about his body. But a curiosity emerged—this was a fairly normal family man who was just doing his job. Plumbing these mysteries, one sociological study on evil chillingly declared, however obviously, "People do evil *out of a sense of right*."[3]

I wondered how much of our "War on Terror" would heed this humbling lesson of history: you don't have to be a monster to do monstrous things. Sometimes you just have to "do your job," feel that you are working on the side of righteousness, and the rest takes over. But the reverse is just as, if not more, important: you don't have to be a saint to do saintly things. One professor, Dr. Sherrie Steiner, told the story of a French village, known for its courageous hiding of Jews during the Holocaust, called Le Chambon-Sur-Lignon. Virtually all the townsfolk here regularly lied to Nazis as they stowed Jews and others being hunted. Risking their lives almost daily, they saved some three to five thousand lives. But after the war, when the story started getting out, a curiosity emerged: this village was not teeming with pious Mother Teresas. Strangely, the people were not strange. They were, in fact, eerily normal.

What accounted for their virtue? Mainly, their community had created a culture where it was easier to be good. While it is true that people must try hard to cultivate virtue, and that a "culture" doesn't maintain itself, it is also true that we partly gain our virtues by passive cultural osmosis, by living near people more skilled at wisdom than us. Evil is contagious, so be cautious; but so is goodness, so take heart. Maybe this is partly what the "wise as serpents, innocent as doves" command is getting at.[4] Another part of the story is that the community was largely composed of Huguenots, who had retained a particular sensitivity to persecution from a keen memory of being persecuted by the Catholic Church centuries prior. Yet another good reason, I concluded, to wave good-bye to Catholicism. If the world is full of war and terrorism, why give any place in our lives to an organization so renowned for creating it?

One day Professor Steiner told me about a studying opportunity in the Belizean rainforest called Creation Care Study Program. It trained students in holistic thinking about the world's ecological crisis, God and nature, and third-world development problems. It sounded like a perfect extension to my growing list of concerns; the more I had heard about the terrorist attacks, the more it seemed the background issues of poverty, natural resources, and development played a part. Going to Belize sounded like a way to wrestle with the issues up close. So, a few months after 9/11, I took off to live in grass huts with fellow students and professors in the middle of the South American jungle.

THREE:
FROM STREETS TO JUNGLE

We drove down a narrow, muddy path as wet palm branches struck the windshield, splashing into water-soaked potholes, until we came to a small campus of grass huts. The enormous cohune palm trees hanging overhead were almost frightening, making it seem as if I had stumbled out of the time-space continuum and ended up in the Jurassic era, about to be chased by a Tyrannosaurus Rex. They seemed on steroids, with branches reaching some thirty feet out from the trunk, dangling low and bouncy.

On our first night in this saturated rainforest, I saw a watermelon-sized armadillo scurrying into the woods, never to be seen again the rest of the semester. When we went to bed, we heard something of a cross between Darth Vader and a lion announcing their presence: howler monkeys. When they howled just outside the door, they made me curl up in my blanket. I was in the jungle.

One morning I awoke to find a bird singing, just outside my window. It was unlike anything I had ever heard. He was

31

chirping a chain of short, five-second melodies, each one a little riff that could have made a full song. I stopped to listen, and I began to melt with delight. For a few minutes the bird did not repeat a single melody. It was playfully improvising! After he was done, I whistled back a few tunes, and he seemed to respond with some of his own.

One warm afternoon in a nearby rainforest preserve, I was walking with fellow students through a field dotted with young, tall trees. Looking up at a nearby tree covered with mosses and epiphytes growing on its enormous limbs, I saw two birds with nearly three-foot-long tails. As if they had noticed our catching sight of them, they flew down from the tree directly toward us, and about fifteen feet in front of us they threw open their wings, halting their flight midair, and proceeded to fly around each other in a small radius of just a few feet, playing tag, or perhaps dancing. It seemed as though they wanted to perform before us. We all watched, awestruck; less than a minute later, they quickly left the stage without a bow for applause, and returned to their tree.

Beauties and wonders such as these were everywhere. But however beautiful a place Belize struck us as, I soon came to discover that it wasn't an untouched, pristine wilderness. After some solid lessons and orientation from an ecologist, I came to see how the rainforest in which we were living had been entirely clear-cut just a few generations prior. Improvised "landfills," ugly and on fire, dotted the few lonely highways with smokes of dangerous dioxins from plastics wafting in the air for miles like demonic incense; Guatemalan refugees could often be seen sifting through the fiery smog and ashes for a few dollars' worth of scraps.

One day our class took an hour-long boat ride, at high speed, seemingly out in the middle of nowhere, to an island to which only marine biologists were allowed access. We snorkeled around with our waterproof notepads, each of us with a different observational task. As I rounded the corner of this tiny island, I peered from the surface through my goggles and saw a beach covered with trash. Our guides told us that the litter was likely from the cruise industry, which has a habit of casting trash from its vessels.[1]

The next day we were scheduled to sit under the tutelage of a marine biologist, flown down from the States to teach our course, and examine several different reefs. Our class jumped into a boat upon the clear, blue water, and while we took off to nearby reefs, I talked to the biologist. He had an unsure look on his face and told me that he was very worried. He said that he had been coming to these reefs for several years, monitoring the fish-school populations. For each of those years he had seen them in decline. He had now been absent from the reefs for two years and was anxious to see if the trend was the same, better, or worse. We dove into the water and went our own way for hours, exploring the reefs.

I dove deep to swim near a large stingray with a thin tail stretching over seven feet long. I found a few straggling parrot fish, creatures that eat coral and poop it out as sand. Nearly all of the coral I saw was bleached out, white, meaning that it was near death if not already dead—a sign of increasing water temperatures. Coral is like the canary in the coal mine in that it can detect subtle environmental changes. Hanging around all this struggling coral were a few fish, each of delicate and minute design.

When we returned to the surface, I saw the professor taking his mask off, weeping. I asked him what he thought, and he said through his tears, "It was worse than I expected. I didn't see a single school of fish. At least two years ago there were a few left." It occurred to me just then that I hadn't seen any schools either, just the few dangling fish. I was familiar with abstract statistics on the warming of oceans and overfishing (of nearly every fishery on the planet), but now I was seeing its effects in person.

The trip out into the oceans was not all gloom, however. Our teacher claimed that all sorts of magic happened underwater at night. So, when the day became dark and the moon came up, we went out on a night-snorkeling adventure. We took a boat out into the deep, stopped, climbed to the boat's sides, and looked down into what appeared to me like a black, infinite abyss. I suspect that even the most stoic and fearless of creatures would find the prospect of jumping into this black ocean at night a bit unnerving. I certainly did. But once I jumped in, I had what can only be called one of the most soul-expanding experiences of my life.

Everyone in the group had a small, underwater flashlight—it felt a bit like a scene from a horror movie where fearful kids walk through a dark house, vision limited to their flashlight's span. After a few moments of warding off the fear of a whale emerging from the dark to swallow me whole, or of a shark to chew me up, I turned off my light and let my eyes adjust to the dim, white glow the moon was casting on the reef.

It was an amazing night. The fear never totally left me, but I somehow redirected it into excitement and even joy. I could now more easily see bioluminescence, the natural glow of tiny marine life. If you struck your hand strongly through the water, you might see a small cloud of tiny lights glow—it was the phytoplankton stirred up for a moment. Small squid, about a foot in length, could be seen changing colors by the second as they floated about. I darted like a playful seal, often turning upward to look through the water at the moon, offering it a wink of appreciation. Engaging the fearful, dark, alien world of the subsea elevated my soul into wonderment.

While I was disappointed about the low volume of fish and dwindling reefs (joined with an awkward feeling that my own ecotourism contributed the decline, watching a few students clumsily hit the reefs with their flippers), I still felt deep affection for it all. After we returned to shore, I chose to sleep out on the rickety, wooden dock because the sand flies were biting in the beach huts. I fell asleep under the stars and over the water, considering both the wonder of the planet in which we live and the tenuous and scary state it was currently in. The contrast between the beauty of the earth and our human footprint upon it began to grow unbearable. Years later, when the movie *Avatar* was released, with its rich depiction of an exotic planet, numerous reviewers affectionately cried out, "I want to live on Pandora!" I too imagined, "If only I could live on a planet with flying beings and creatures that glow at night!" Remembering Belize, I realized that I do live on Pandora.

One of my greatest moments in Belize, and indeed in my life, came as I found myself waiting on a dock for a boat ride into Guatemala. It was just after a long week of studying, not ecology, but theology. In our thatched-roof classroom, we had been discussing how to view *matter*. We discussed whether Christian faith does best to imagine the ultimate human home in an immaterial heaven or if there is something about matter and the universe that is truly "home" to us. It is partly an eschatology question— of some ultimate goal or direction in the universe—and partly a question as basic as how one should view *physicality* itself. The splendid theologian Steven Bouma-Prediger interpreted for our class the few thin scriptures that, in his eyes, had been abused. He began with the apostle Paul's famous "rapture" passage:

> After that, we who are still alive and are left will be caught up together with them in the clouds to meet the Lord in the air. And so we will be with the Lord forever.[2]

This scene is commonly called the "rapture" because the Greek word for "caught up" shares the root from which English derives "ecstasy" or "en*raptured*." It turns out the key words here, "go meet him," are words also used for a first-century Roman procession to welcome a visiting dignitary like Caesar into a town: the villagers "go out" to meet Caesar, *only to bring him back to the city*.[3] Whatever other mysterious meaning the passage has, it doesn't necessarily mean *vacating* the earth.

We also looked at the passage that foretells:

> . . . the earth and everything in it will be burned up.[4]

Bouma-Prediger found this one of the most egregious mistranslations in the New Testament. After sifting through several translations, searching for the best rendering of the Greek, he came to the conclusion that the Dutch translation was best, reading, "the earth and everything in it will be *revealed*."[5] The real crux of Peter's apocalyptic vision of the future is an image, not of total destruction, but of a refiner's fire burning through the chaff and evil of this world to reveal its truly valued elements.

As I rethought my understanding of eschatology, which he was directly critiquing, I read a startling proclamation:

> [A]ll evangelical eschatologies anticipate significant degrees of *continuity* between our present earth and the future world. To be sure, this contrasts greatly with what seems to be believed in some evangelical churches: that our ultimate destiny is an immaterial, spaceless heaven, and that our present earth will be wholly destroyed. Wherever these views may come from, they have no sound foundation in either evangelical theology or Scripture.[6]

A real showstopper to a person drenched in evangelicalism! Apparently numerous church communities had been teaching and thinking in ignorance or contradiction of their theological roots—a discrepancy I was also seeing in the popular evangelical posture toward the Iraq war. While I had always viewed the human soul as bearing the mark of the divine, it had still been my habit to imagine an afterlife through the usual cartoony images of disembodied souls flying into clouds, or some other immaterial realm beyond the stars. Sure, I had been constrained by the rules of Christian language to call the universe "creation," but I had little sense of *connection* to it, of being *part* of, tied to, the universe. Instead, I viewed the world merely as God's begrudging waiting room, or perhaps God's training facility, a proving ground where we practice while we wait to go to the "Real Place." It had never struck me to view bodies, physicality, and *matter itself* as coming directly from the hand of God. Coming to see this while living in the jungle, I felt like I was experiencing a breakthrough like Jacob in the book of Genesis: "Surely the Lord is in this place, and I was not aware of it!"[7] Always looking to the future through the lens of an immaterial heaven, I had never stopped to wonder how the heavenly was already embedded in our midst.

I found an exciting metaphor for resurrection in the apostle Paul's image of a planted seed (1 Cor 15), which illustrated the hopefulness of this more earthy reading of matter: though the tree is immensely greater than the seed, it still retains some *continuity* with the seed. Paul speaks of a hoped-for *spiritual body*, apparently harmonizing his vision with the accounts of Jesus' resurrected body—which was reportedly both physical and yet somehow *more* than that.[8] But it still wasn't *less* than physical. Paul's vision is that the perishable is not to be wiped away, but is to be "*clothed with the imperishable.*" How exciting to picture ourselves as walking acorns—who knows what kind of grand, mysterious, and magnificent future we and our world hold inside?

Given this renewed sense of wonder for the universe, I underwent some deep shifts in my attention and affections in Belize. I had previously found myself magnetized toward "spiritual" matters, articles of "belief," and "afterlife" issues to the detriment of concern for people's bodies and care for this world. You might say I was uncovering an unnecessary separation, in myself at least, between a "social" Gospel and a "spiritual" Gospel. But that wasn't the real core of the change. The greatest change of mind was in my view *toward matter itself*—I came to be surprised by the fact that we exist at all, that life is such an extraordinary wonder. Matter is surprising and miraculous, if only we can see that. A certain reading of Christianity had obscured that from my mind.

With such seeds of thought planted and germinating in my mind, I began to look with new eyes upon ants, monkeys, trees, and water. Waiting on the dock for the boat into Guatemala, we looked to the horizon to see an ominous and truly gigantic storm, deep black and blue, crawling over the sea. Looking upon this looming giant, growing by the minute, I felt strangely comforted. Previously bound for some immaterial heaven, I now warmed up to my surroundings, even loved them, in all their good and ugly parts. When the boat arrived, we all jumped on, since the driver hoped to beat the storm. I took a seat on a pile of luggage and delighted in the sight of the dark, impending wall of clouds, thousands of feet tall, casting upon us the cool winds of a coming storm. As the boat hastily bounced to its destination, I saw breaks in the clouds, windows for beams of light to filter through. The rays streamed onto the green canopy of trees on the mainland, dotting it with color. The lighted spots now became a bright, light green, and the darkened spots a deep shade. Far over the forested hills of our destination, sprinkling over a bright, blue sky, as yet untouched by the storm, were cotton-ball clouds.

I almost couldn't handle the beauty of it. I could no longer call the earth simply "the earth," some lump of material, a place I disdained on my way to heaven. Why had I ever imagined a God—whoever that is—that would create two places for humans: one a physical earth, and the other a nonphysical spiritual playground in heaven? *This* place is a creation; it comes from the very hand of God, each molecule proceeding from the Great Mystery.

It is not merely some boring pile of matter—it is a miracle. Existence itself, every quivering atom and its mind-bending innards, is an improbable marvel. How on earth had I ever considered the cosmos merely *normal* or *natural*? It turns out that this turning of my mind upside down—or right side up—in great wonder for creation prepared the ground for my later appreciation of a more sacramental worldview that I would find later in Catholicism.

If that weren't enough to refresh and reorient the mind, while in Belize I was introduced to the writings of the poet-critic-farmer Wendell Berry. He served to connect this deep appreciation for the earth with a concern for the way humans are currently destroying it. He afflicted me with a passage I can scarcely let die in my mind:

> "The sense of the holiness of life" is not compatible with an exploitive economy. You cannot know that life is holy if you are content to live from economic practices that daily destroy life and diminish its possibility. And many if not most Christian organizations now appear to be perfectly at peace with the military-industrial economy and its "scientific" destruction of life. Surely, if we are to remain free, and if we are to remain true to our religious inheritances, we must maintain a separation between church and state. But if we are to maintain any sense or coherence or meaning in our lives, we cannot tolerate the present utter disconnection between religion and economy. By "economy" I do not mean "economics," which is the study of money-making, but rather the ways of human housekeeping, the ways by which the human household is situated and maintained within the household of Nature. To be uninterested in economy is to be uninterested in the practice of religion; it is to be uninterested in culture and in character.

> Probably the most urgent question now faced by
> people who would adhere to the Bible is this: What
> sort of economy would be responsible to the holiness
> of life? What, for Christians, would be the economy,
> the practices and the restraints, of "right livelihood"?
> I do not believe that organized Christianity now has
> any idea. I think its idea of a Christian economy is no
> more or less than the industrial economy—which is an
> economy firmly founded upon the seven deadly sins
> and the breaking of all ten of the Ten Commandments.
> Obviously, if Christianity is going to survive as more
> than a respecter and comforter of profitable iniqui-
> ties, then Christians, regardless of their organizations,
> are going to have to interest themselves in economy—
> which is to say, in nature and in work. They are going
> to have to give workable answers to those who say we
> cannot live without this economy that is destroying us
> and our world, who see the murder of Creation as the
> only way of life.[9]

Hearing these words eventually led me to the decision that
it was time to start facing the destructive elements of the nation
and economy I came from, to start paying attention to "the ways
of human housekeeping" in the "household of Nature."

I needed to consider the ways I might return to my home
country and contribute to the betterment of one of the world's
largest producers of waste and pollution. Return to the belly of
the beast, as it were. After all, the warming of the world's ocean
temperatures was traceable not just to Belizean wastes, but to the
spewing exhausts of my own country. The waste that the cruise
industries were discharging upon the beaches, for example, is
kind of thing that *my* family would easily overlook. The increasing desertification of Africa, adding to a pile of tensions there
(caused largely by European colonization), comes partly from
the billions of tons of carbon that come from *my* homeland. I was

coming to see the problems of the world as interconnected, that *I*, not "everybody else," am the cause of them. I could no longer placate my conscience by saying that the destruction of our planet was somebody else's fault and somebody else's responsibility to solve. I understood better why G. K. Chesterton, when the *London Times* requested from him a reflection about "what's wrong with the world," wrote in response, "Dear Sirs, I am. Yours, G. K."

On the other side of the coin, I recognized that I was a beneficiary of much of the exploitation of our world—through slavery and deforestation in the nineteenth century, or sweatshops and industrial plumage in the twentieth. In a modern twist on John Donne's popular poem, I thought, "Don't ever ask who the factory stack's smoke spews for; it spews for you." No longer separating myself from the world at large, I realized that I had to confess that *I* am a part of "the system," and I felt that whatever ecological solution to the world I might imagine, it had to start with me.

I soon began dreaming of starting a small community with friends. Defying the maxim that the grass is greener on the other side, I instead pictured myself among no grass, but in a concrete "jungle" of the city—even as I finished my studies in the green jungle. Such an urban community, I envisioned, would be a circle of support and accountability in helping us becoming better stewards of our planet. I wished to cultivate a small culture of renewal amid the deterioration of our world—a culture, as Dorothy Day said, in which it is easier to be good. A culture where it becomes more common to be mindful of water usage, to eat a diet more in tune with the earth's resources, to take up abandoned lots and use them for gardens and growing some veggies, to move into abandoned houses and restore them to beauty, to collectively act on the social problems around us, to go against society's natural currents of class and race segregation and meet people different from us, to share our money and food, to intentionally connect with a few others to support each other along the journey. And instead of constructing this as some newfound church or denomination, I imagined starting this community in connection with an already existing church, hopefully not reinventing the wheel. For I had seen numerous church divisions and many energetic Christians starting new "church plants"; meanwhile older churches withered from dwindling resources and young energy. By creating these pathways of life, I hoped it would become normal, not exceptional, for my future kids and family and me—or whatever my future life would look like—to be conscientious in our way of life and for our habits to more naturally act for the good of the planet.

The more I discussed the idea with friends, the more I found it was a conviction already floating about in the world. Indeed, in the Christian tradition, it is a desire as old as the early Church, monasticism, and religious orders. Granted, I didn't envision something quite as intense as taking vows of poverty, chastity, and obedience. I saw something not as rigorous as a monastery, but more involved than a Willow Creek small group—something for "normal" people, and for families. My friend Shane and his community, the Simple Way, in Philadelphia, had been experimenting with this kind of community for a few years. I took inspiration from them—along with the Catholic Worker movement—and wanted to start my own initiative.

Oddly enough, one such incarnation of this vision was hidden in plain sight, right down the dirt road from me in the rain forest. While in Belize, I encountered a community of Anabaptists. Never having met these renegades before, I quickly came to regard them as a hidden gem among Christian denominations.

Starting back in the Reformation era, Anabaptists objected to infant Baptism, and have traditionally been known for their great adherence to the nonviolence of Jesus, communal lifestyles, and simplicity. They have been experimenting with "new monasticism" since their split with the Catholic Church, a rift suffered with much persecution. Their communities sometimes look a lot like family-monasteries—just the creative way of life I had begun dreaming about.

Our Belizean group visited some Mennonites (a branch of the Anabaptist movement) who dwelled and farmed in the jungle. Some had found themselves there since they had been kicked out of Germany because of their pacifism during World War II. I couldn't help thinking, "That's what good Christians should have been doing in Nazi Germany—getting kicked out!"

I listened to them tell stories of working together to carve out a living, virtually from scratch, in the jungle. They told of encounters with armed bandits and how they creatively found ways to overcome violence and theft. On one occasion their entire community, in something akin to an Amish barn raising, built a notorious thief a house as a gift—and thereby found a redemptive alternative to violence. A very risky and courageous people these Anabaptists are!

Back in the States, I would soon come to meet a similar Anabaptist group known as the Bruderhof. While its members will deny altogether that their communal life is either easy or ideal, it is not a stretch to conclude upon visiting that they look very "utopian." It is not uncommon to arrive at one of their rural communities to find children playing and running barefoot through fields, wearing handmade clothes with flowers tucked in their hair. With communities sizing sometimes into the three hundreds, they share large collective meals, dances, and songs, all finely orchestrated in a way that reflects their inheritance of German orderliness.

Like the German-Mennonite exiles, the Bruderhof were kicked out of Germany, since they would not allow the Third Reich in their classrooms. They ended up living in the jungles of Uruguay and even spread out to parts of the United States. I visit them in the mountains of New York annually, and they continue to impress me with their continual awareness of the ecological state of the world and their need to reform their community's habits. Here are some of the ecological-economic experiments I've seen:

- They have turned off all the hot-water spigots on their hand sinks, using hot water only for needs.

- The last time I visited, 90 percent of their food was produced on their own land.

- They teach their kids skills in building energy-efficient homes, explain to them how to raise chickens and other farm animals, and sometimes tell them they cannot get their driver's license until they build a car that runs on something other than fossil fuels. They have even started using sheep to counteract the need for gas-based mowing.

- They incorporate solar heating systems for their water.

- They actively remediate the ecosystem in which they live by cutting down phosphorus fertilizer in their watersheds, increasing wildlife habitats, bringing more oxygen into eutrophic lakes, etc.

- They organize their community in such a way to create shared jobs (even communal businesses) in which individual commuting is almost fully eliminated.

- They take care of their elderly until they pass away.

- They manage their own sewage systems with reed-bed technology.

- They procure their own heat for buildings with the wood waste from a nearby sawmill to power high-efficiency furnaces.

- They even experimented in getting rid of all of their beds, attempting to stave off some luxuries, for a time.

Communities like the Bruderhof make their resistance to the destruction of our fragile world more than a personal choice (or a legislative tug-of-war). They see their religious communities as viable places to enact economic and ecological change. Just like the Mennonites, they are forming themselves into *a disciplined people, a vibrant and capable culture.*

That sounds nice, but it is in fact very scary to modern people—for these are frightening instances of people's religion infiltrating their politics, culture, and economics. Often when modern people see this, they may be tempted to summon a denunciation that "it's a cult"—for religion has taken over the lives of those who have made such drastic changes. At this time, I preferred to say, "I'm spiritual, not religious," for this was a way for me to avoid the fact that my *culture* (my way of life, my politics) had nothing to do with my *cult* (my religious convictions, my worship). But I soon began to hear of the trinity of thought that Peter Maurin and Dorothy Day spoke so often about: cult, culture, and cultivation all affect one another. If your economics is exploitative and unbalanced, your culture and religion will be deformed. If we refuse to be religious and just be "spiritual," we will leave our culture and economics up to whatever television and dominant culture offer.

Sometimes you cannot see a problem until you see a solution —and by the Mennonite's strong connection between their religion and culture, I could now see how religion and culture were divorced in my evangelicalism back in the States. I could now see a bit more clearly why my Protestant culture saw no disconnection between their knee-jerk response to September 11 and Afghanistan and Jesus' Sermon on the Mount. For, alive at Willow was a suspicion of "organized religion," of "cults," and of cultural religion. In that immensely difficult balancing act between religion and politics, many evangelicals I know chose the extreme that the two can say little to one another. Given that, it would soon make sense that, when President Bush hastily summoned troops for Iraq, Willow uttered little more than that this war was a matter of individual conscience. At the war's cusp, Pastor Hybels gave a sermon titled "Why War?" and outlined three traditional options of realism, just war, and pacifism, stating that he personally preferred the latter.[10] (To be sure, this was better than the hawkish rhetoric from many other evangelicals at the time. But, while this sermon might be regarded as courageous given the war-time evangelical groupthink at the time, it left much to be desired, as I saw it, for the Iraqi.) Meanwhile, the pope himself was pontificating that the invasion was an unjustifiable "defeat for humanity,"[11] and numerous other denominations weighed in with direct condemnation of the war.

Having met some very inspiring communities down in Belize, I returned to the States with a more communal and cultural way of thinking about living out the Christian faith. Nevertheless, I knew that I still owed much of my momentum and excitement about the Faith to Willow's influence. Though I felt somewhat betrayed by evangelicalism, largely through their silent consent for post-9/11 bellicose patriotism, I now had some positive alternative models of a religious community dangerously practicing peace, redeeming enemies, and living more ecologically and sustainably.

FOUR: FROM JUNGLE TO WAR

Sadly, only a few months after my return, war rhetoric was escalating again, this time toward Iraq. Back at Eastern, Jonathan and I organized campus debates on the war; for hours he and I debated two supporters of the war in front of an overcrowded dorm lobby. I once again had hard conversations with my evangelical friends. This time around, proponents offered more religious justification for the invasion, making their previous justifications for Afghanistan seem simpler and comparatively straightforward. Some friends still presented the deplorable argument that, because there is no such thing as "innocent" civilians, we ought to worry less about bombing them. But scripture was now being employed in even more creative ways to justify the war. Bogus interpretations of Romans 13 were used to convince us to "trust the government," since they probably knew a lot of secret information about Iraq that we didn't.[1]

On Eastern's campus, I led Sunday-night worship in the evangelical style I had learned at Willow Creek; at the end of those sessions, replete with a dozen praise songs, it was customary for the leader to share a reflection. I often took those times to read from the prophets, with their incessant critiques of ancient Israel's wastefulness, militarism, and apathy. With a desperate eagerness to undo the sense of inevitability of the looming Iraq war, I quoted Isaiah and his vision for a world where we study war no more, following after the child who will lead us in the way of peace.[2] I also quoted a good deal of Wendell Berry, whose voice had grown ever stronger for me since my first introduction to him in Belize; his words shed light upon the political contradictions I was finding among my evangelical culture:

> I feel no hesitation in saying that, to the extent that a government is secret, it cannot be democratic or its people free. . . . Thomas Jefferson justified general education by the obligation of citizens to be critical of their government: "for nothing can keep it right but their own vigilant and distrustful superintendence." An inescapable requirement of true patriotism, love for one's land, is vigilant distrust of any determinative power, elected or unelected, that may preside over it. . . . The present administration has adopted a sort of official Christianity, and it obviously wishes to be regarded as Christian. But "Christian" war has always been a problem, best solved by avoiding any attempt to reconcile policies of national or imperial militarism with anything Christ said or did. The Christian gospel is a summons to peace, calling for justice beyond anger, mercy beyond justice, forgiveness beyond mercy, love beyond forgiveness. It would require a most agile interpreter to justify hatred and war by means of the Gospels, in which we are bidden to love our enemies, bless those who curse us, do good to those who hate us, and pray for those who despise and persecute us.[3]

I added another passage to my public reading, one Berry wrote in criticism of the first Gulf War, but its words echoed toward us in time with a heavy truth, and I quote them at length:

> In times of war, our leaders always speak of their prayers. They wish us to know that they say prayers because they wish us to believe that they are deeply worried and that they take their responsibilities seriously. Perhaps they believe or hope that prayer will help. But within the circumstances of war, prayer becomes a word as befuddled in meaning as liberate or order or victory or peace. These prayers are usually understood to be Christian prayers. But Christian prayers are made to or in the name of Jesus, who loved, prayed for, and forgave his enemies and who instructed his followers to do likewise. A Christian supplicant, therefore, who has resolved to kill those whom he is enjoined to love, to bless, to do good to, to pray for, and to forgive as he hopes to be forgiven is not conceivably in a situation in which he can be at peace with himself. Anyone who has tried to apply this doctrine to a merely personal enmity will be aware of the enormous anguish that it could cause a national leader in wartime. No wonder that national leaders have ignored it for nearly two thousand years. We have made much of Saddam's tyranny, which logically would imply some sympathy for his people, who were the first victims of his tyranny. But we have shown them no sympathy at all, have regarded them not even as human beings but as "fish in a barrel" or as the targets in a "turkey shoot." Having killed thousands on thousands of them, virtually without seeing or thinking of them, we have hardly spared for them a word of regret or for their families a word of sympathy. In fact, we have no sympathy for them. For our leaders and much of our public, the appalling

> statistics of death and suffering in Iraq merely prove the efficiency of our military technology. Ignoring the Gospels' command to be merciful, forgiving, loving, and peaceable, our leaders have prayed only for the success of their arms and policies and have thus made for themselves a state religion—exactly what they claim to fear in "fundamentalist" Islam. But why God might particularly favor a nation whose economy is founded foursquare on the seven deadly sins is a mystery that has not been explained.[4]

After reading even more of that sharp essay and a passage from the prophet Amos during one night of worship at the university's dining hall, I was chided by a zealous evangelical. He said that I was making worship "too political." The critique was hard to swallow, since it appeared to me that, among the throngs of evangelicals, worship seemed to cloak a profoundly more political posture underneath—a posture of unilaterally and preemptively invading Iraq.

War preparations continued into March 2003. My closest friends, Shane, and Jonathan and Leah Wilson-Hartgrove, among others, had been planning a trip to Iraq with Christian Peacemaker Teams (CPT) to bring medicines, hope, and love—as they said, "offering a human face to the American people, assuring them that not everybody over here wanted to invade their country." CPT is an initiative started by Mennonites, inspired by exhortations like this from Ron Sider:

> Unless we . . . are ready to start to die by the thousands in dramatic vigorous new exploits for peace and justice, we should sadly confess that we never really meant what we said, and we dare never whisper another word about pacifism to our sisters and brothers in those desperate lands filled with injustice. Unless we are ready to die developing new nonviolent attempts to reduce

conflict, we should confess that we never really meant
that the cross was an alternative to the sword.[5]

The CPT team destined for Iraq received a letter from the
Department of Agriculture, of all places, declaring that they
would face fifteen years in jail or one million dollars in fines
if they entered Iraq with medicines, defying the sanctions. The
night before they left, I met with Shane and we prayed in silence,
exchanging almost no words in the visit, able only to weep, in
anticipation of us possibly never seeing each other again and in
dread for the onslaught about to hit Iraq.

After they left, I kept close tabs on war deliberations and on
CPT's advances, from their long wait on the Jordanian border to
pass blockade, and finally into Iraq. I had been meeting for weeks
with a large group of mostly older Quakers who had all signed a
War Resistance Pledge. This pledge stated that if the United States
invaded Iraq, we would place ourselves in front of federal authorities in civil disobedience, declaring, "If you are going to go to
war today, you have to walk over us." The sentiment, I was told,
came in part from a circulating quote: "When they come for the
innocent without crossing over your body, cursed be your religion
and your life."[6] This civil-disobedience group was largely filled
with grandmothers and grandfathers. With that in mind, someone
made a keen observation: in some Native American tribes, their
"war council" was comprised, strangely enough, of *elderly women*.
The tradition developed likely because it is the women who suffer
the effects and aftermath of a war perhaps most gravely; while
they might not fight, they indeed have a larger social, economic,
and familial perspective on the costs of war. So, among the friends
of mine who shared in the protest, we all found it poignant that
we were surrounded with grandmothers, who, were they sought
for wise council, would have strongly advised greater caution and
patience than our government granted.

During this time of preparation—for both warriors and resisters—I joined a small group of—yet again, elderly—people for civil disobedience at the weapons contractor Lockheed Martin. The Brandywine Peace Community in the Philadelphia area had been hounding these makers of weapons of mass destruction for years, declaring that there is scantily any sacred distinction between our country making WMDs and foreign countries making WMDs. Berry again came to mind in support of this claim:

> The difference, as our leaders say, is that we will use these weapons virtuously, whereas our enemies will use them maliciously—a proposition that too readily conforms to a proposition of much less dignity: we will use them in our interest, whereas our enemies will use them in theirs.[7]

With this in mind, and given that fear of weapons of mass destruction was publicly rampant at the time, it only seemed fitting that the United States was due for a visit from some teams of weapons inspectors. So I joined the peace community in a very geriatric arrest, on the Martin Luther King Jr. Day of memorial. It was entirely nonviolent, far too harmless and symbolic for some of my anarchist friends, since we all simply transgressed onto their facility until arrested—none of that more respectable work of hammering on warheads or pouring our blood upon them.

On February 15, 2003, many of us students made our way down to Washington, DC, to join a day of the largest global protests in world history. An estimated six to ten million people gathered in over 800 cities to declare their opposition to the war. One of them was a woman I was falling in love with. Her name was Cassie, and we would wed in a short while. She, myself, and other students wanted to add a positive tone to the protests, aware of their often-vitriolic character. So, we brought loads of free water and donated artisan bread to hand out to people, for no other reason than we wanted to spread good will and support for the event. We all found it uproariously funny that a young man had joined us that day as a "spy" and later divulged our traitorous activities to the school newspaper. Bless his heart—he was unfamiliar with Jefferson's posture on patriotism and presumed we must have hated America if we were choosing to critique it. I never had the pleasure of following up with him after his grand revelation to the public.

In March, diplomatic patience came to an end. President Bush had told the UN weapons inspectors to leave Iraq and had given Saddam Hussein a deadline to leave as well. He declared that he had ordered "an attack of opportunity"; and the invasion began. I called my parents as President Bush finished his remarks. I let them know that I would be arrested the next morning. We planned to peacefully surround the federal building and, sitting down, block its entrances—all to the end of shutting it down, if only for that day. That morning's chilly rain added to the lament. A crowd of several hundred gathered, mostly in silence, a few blocks from the federal building. We slowly walked toward it, accompanied by the sound of a bell tolling.

It was especially important for me to keep in mind that, for me at least, this protest was not to be filled with vague resentment toward "the system," or a disdain for the police officers that would soon enforce the building code against blocking entrances. A rare few in the group took on such a posture. But overall, the protest was about a specific act of the federal government, not the government itself. We would peacefully submit to arrest. I had just read Thomas Merton's suggestion to "activists":

> The tactic of nonviolence is a tactic of love that seeks the salvation and redemption of the opponent, not his castigation, humiliation, and defeat. A pretended nonviolence that seeks to defeat and humiliate the adversary by spiritual instead of physical attack is little more than a confession of weakness. True nonviolence is

totally different from this, and much more difficult.
It strives to operate without hatred, without hostility,
and without resentment.[8]

As we sat out in the rain, my mind centered upon the stories of death in Iraq from the United States' first Gulf War, back in 1991. I had been hearing about the deaths of hundreds of thousands of children over the years caused by the economic sanctions. With the weight of considering more loss like this, I was in tears as the officers came over to me to pick me up. Stumbling past the grief, trying to speak clearly through the tears, I told the officer who grabbed me by the arm, "We don't hate you. This is about the war and the people that will be affected by it. We love you guys too." He said, quite solemnly, to my surprise, "I know."

After waiting in cells in handcuffs to be processed, we were released "on our own recognizance" until the trial. We returned home to find that our friends with the Christian Peacemaker Teams had left a phone message, calling all the way from Iraq. They had dodged the "shock and awe" campaign in Baghdad, and, while squatting under a table, managed to place a call. They expressed their gratitude, knowing that, even over this distance, we shared a special connection. They said that many people in Iraq with whom they spoke were very encouraged to hear that some people back here were expressing solidarity and opposing the invasion. One Iraqi approached their team with eager appreciation and desperate grief, saying, "I can't believe it. I thought that all Americans wanted to invade our country."

Proving the video of jubilant people tearing down Hussein's statue an unrepresentative minority, CPT found many Iraqis referring to the invasion as executed by "Christian extremists." That should not come as a shock when one considers the religious language that was often used to justify the military action. And as Eugene McCarraher says, "An Iraqi killed by a US Marine is just as dead as if she were dispatched by a jihadist."[9]

Months would pass before we saw our court date; many of the arrestees, along with me, refused to pay the fine—each offering their own special reasons during the court proceedings. Such a refusal would land us in jail for a week. I took the week to read as much of the Bible as I could and to pray for all affected by the war. I was lucky enough to share a cell with a friend, while my now-wife, Cassie, took the week in solitary—a very difficult experience for her. On the other side of my wall, sharing a ventilation shaft with our room, was a man who had been there for fifteen years. He said he was there for having been caught dealing drugs three times. I asked him how long he was in. He said, "Life." I asked him if I could write him or visit after I got out; he said, "No." The bleakness of his life weighed on me, and remains with me today. Five times a day, I would hear Muslims chanting their daily prayers, and virtually all day, I heard men breaking out in random arguments—there was scarcely a moment of quiet. But there were also times of profound grace, like when the chaplain priest brought us some letters and literature (Tolstoy and Thoreau—how fitting, I thought), and snuck therein was a letter from Cassie, a smuggling that surely could have landed this priest in trouble.

On the fifth day I was allowed visitation with an older Quaker woman, who was part of a larger group of dissidents. I sat down in the fortified meeting room, waved to her with my handcuffed hands, and we smiled. She was a welcome and gorgeous sight, wearing a whole spectrum of bright colors—especially purples and reds—all hand-woven materials, shiny earrings, and with a grey mane of wisdom upon her head. A wide, lipsticked smile complimented a warm face shaped by the wrinkles of joy. Having seen virtually no color all week except my orange jumpsuit, I found her like rain in a desert of angry men, concrete blocks, and terrible food. She was like an angel, a sacrament of sacred presence, and I welcomed her visitation.

In between the arrest and jail hinged my graduation from Eastern and a road trip around the country to invigorate and expand my thoughts about Christianity. A friend and I drove west, visiting some well-known exponents of faith, at least in the evangelical world—people like Dallas Willard and Rob Bell. Willard, who had inspired me with his *Divine Conspiracy*,[10] imagined Christianity as a movement to change the world from the inside out by rehabituating people in the skills of forgiveness and the manners of the Sermon on the Mount. We enjoyed a long breakfast with this wise man—who, I might add, besides his very generous and loving spirit, also picked up the bill. Back in 2003, Rob Bell was just beginning to enter the public scene, preaching Jesus as a cutting-edge rabbi. I spent a month living in Grand Rapids, studying both with Rob and in solitude. I digested much of the Bible and a diversity of authors from Mennonite John Howard Yoder to St. Benedict (reading his *Rule*). I also visited a fearless, sharp, and jovial Christian, Mark Scandrette, who had stubbornly dropped anchor with his family in the Mission District of San Francisco, starting a creatively titled "Jesus Dojo" where people trained in the habits of Christian discipleship.

Altogether, I was blending the lessons of my national road-trip with my Belizean-bred vision for a fresh way of living Christianity in our ecologically-abused world. Before the trip, I had dropped off all my possessions in Camden, New Jersey, the place where we had decided to begin our post-collegiate life; during the trip, Cassie called to say that the house had been broken into and virtually all my things had been stolen. I was upset, but I decided that maybe this was providential humor for not getting rid of it all in the first place, according to Jesus' suggestion in the gospels. Upon completing the trip, I would move into the scene of the break-in.

FIVE:
FROM WAR TO CONCRETE JUNGLE

Camden, New Jersey, first came to my attention during my final year at Eastern University. On an early Friday morning in December, a few months after my return from Belize, a professor-friend of mine had planned a seminar in a remote part of campus at a time too early for most college students. This particular professor was not entirely popular on campus, since she, along with a small cohort of fellow students, was frequently to be found publicly opposing, through pamphlets or demonstrations, the war in Afghanistan. Knowing that few people, if any, would show up to the seminar, I chose to roll my carcass out of bed mostly out of sheer pity. As I dragged myself across campus to the seminar room, I tried to console myself with the fact that

I had heard the speaker was quite intriguing and from a nearby city reputed for its acute poverty and sociological problems.

Joining about three or so other students at the presentation, I walked into the empty dorm lobby and was quite surprised to find our presenter to be a Catholic priest, and an Irish one, no less. I must admit that, born of the typical urban-suburban stereotypes I carried, I had more than half-expected our presenter to be a black Baptist pastor.

Fr. Michael Doyle of Camden, New Jersey, gave a talk about "environmental racism," a topic I had been learning about in my sociology studies. This type of racism is so named because of a sociological force commonly known as "not in my backyard," or NIMBY. The NIMBY mentality pushes polluting industries and other dangerous or unwanted but "necessary" urban evils into somebody else's backyard, usually the backyard of people who do not have the political, economic, and social clout—factors intimately tied to race—to keep them out. In a small Camden neighborhood of a few hundred people known as Waterfront South, a dark cloud of polluting industries had descended. Within a few blocks of each other were nineteen "brownfields"—sites that can only be reused with significant and costly environmental remediation. There were also some "superfund" sites in Waterfront South, places so hazardous they necessitate a "supersized" fund from the federal government to clean them up. Many American cities with real pollution problems don't have *any* superfund sites; within just a few blocks, this one neighborhood had two.

Fr. Doyle further shared that the manufacturing industries that had long abandoned the city for cheaper labor in southeast Asia and Central America had dumped a great deal of pollution that still scarred Waterfront South. (I have an old typewriter in my basement that says, "Made in Camden." It was fabricated just a few blocks from my house.) Added to the superfund sites were a dozen abandoned factories; a cement-production facility with piles of cement ingredients and slag (a grainy byproduct of steel production, imported from England) sitting out in the open, wind stirring it about; a sewage-treatment facility that funneled down waste from forty-seven different municipalities into one mega-poop extravaganza (you can drive a VW bug through its intake valve); a massive bacon-frying industry (mingling creatively with the sewage smell); a licorice-root mulch transport facility (imported from Afghanistan—the processed root apparently helps keep the weeds down. It smells something like burnt peanuts); an outdoor metal-crushing plant; several metal-scrap yards rusting their ways out into the streets and storm drains; and an enormous trash-burning facility transforming the county's voluminous waste into a burnt solid that must still be buried somewhere, and releasing a vapor from the fuming stacks that the company admits includes traces of mercury and other toxins.[1]

Fr. Doyle shared stories of kids in the parish school vomiting from the smells of a nearby sewage-treatment center—scenes I would later see repeated as I would teach physical-education classes there the next year.[2] But the real icing on this "turd-cake" was the hundreds of thousands of diesel trucks running through the neighborhood every year, with their fumes being the most harmful to young lungs.

It sounded like hell. Surprisingly, I thought to myself, "I should move there." Throughout my youth I had driven past cities like this, particularly Gary, Indiana, on my way out of Chicago to visit family in Cleveland. On the freeway, flying over this sad, postindustrial city, I would see its droves of abandoned factories and houses. "Come on, really? You gotta be kidding. This actually exists?" I wondered. Had civilization collapsed there? The rotting and rusty factories still functioning spewed plumes of smoke or vapor reminiscent of the dark scenes of Gotham City from the *Batman* comics.

I'm convinced that one's mind cannot routinely be shocked at such sights and have a stable psyche; we all find ways to soften or bury the sadness. But mentally diverting the pain of seeing a hurting world—from the high perch of upper-middle-class coziness—was beginning to grow more untenable to me, both before and during college. Years with Darin and Shane, years with YACHT Club, going down to the streets of Philadelphia, handing out food and forming friendships with the homeless, the Belizean revelations, and hosting public discussions about poverty and war had reshaped my view of things.

Now, with that background in place, I had come to hear an Irish priest give a talk to a few desolate students on a cold morning. I had not yet chosen where to go after graduation, but when he spoke of a New Jersey neighborhood in need, it seemed a perfect fit for the kind of community I had imagined in Belize—perfect in all its imperfections. I asked him if they could use some help, and he said yes. He had been hoping for years to fill an abandoned house across the street with a "Catholic Worker"—a community movement begun in the early twentieth century by Dorothy Day and Peter Maurin. My friends and I joked that we would probably only qualify at the time as a "Protestant Slacker" community, but you had to start somewhere. After deciding to start the community, and garnering some like-minded deviants who shared the vision, I went down to Camden for a short visit to Fr. Doyle's church.

As my car neared the church, I passed an entire block of burnt-out houses, dilapidated and abandoned. It is no exaggeration to say that much of the neighborhood looked like a war zone. In many parts of the world, to live in a "dangerous" city is to live in an overcrowded one. But here the streets had an eerie feeling of abandonment. Many of its homes and factories had grown so derelict that they had been bulldozed, and much of what remained standing looked like it could qualify for demolition as well. When

I did see people roaming these streets, I couldn't help but take a look—which made for awkward results. It turns out that if a woman in my part of Camden is on the street, it often means she is a prostitute, and looking at her means that she approaches (sometimes even runs) to your car, ready to cut a deal. Looking at the men conjured shouts of "Yerp!" meaning, "Over here, I've got drugs."

Then there were the sewage smells. I could certainly confirm this part of the priest's lecture—this was indeed the backyard where all the other "not in my backyards" ended up. (Thanks be to God, we have seen the plant's smell slowly improve over the last decade.) It felt portentous that, as I was pulling up to park in front of a laundromat, one of the rare businesses left in the neighborhood (next to the liquor store), a moving van was being loaded—they were going out of business just in time for my arrival. Coupled with that portent, I was notified that a few days prior to my arrival, one of the most loved and essential workers at the church, Sr. Peg, who organized the rehabilitation of houses for the poor, had been killed in a car accident. The other driver, high on crack, swerved and killed her. Apparently, Fr. Michael later told me, I had arrived at the worst time of loss and hopelessness in the neighborhood's history. With the death of an essential servant and frequent scares that the entire neighborhood might be bulldozed in an act of political abandonment of the troubled region, things looked terrible.

I got out of the car and crossed the trash-strewn street to the large, stone rectory, next to a grand, old church that evoked a long-gone era. After a conversation about my intentions with the priest and a tour through the discussed abandoned house, I was, to my surprise, given a key. I was also given a job working at their parochial school (K–8), teaching physical education and health classes, tutoring in literacy, and coaching the sports teams. Quite a bit of trust this priest had granted me.

Fr. Doyle was not a stranger to taking risks. His bishop had exiled him to Camden to stifle his public intrigues, since he had been a war protester during the Vietnam conflict. It turned out he had been a secretive resister to the war: he, along with twenty-seven other pastors of different denominations and friends, broke into a nearby federal draft building to steal the draft cards and burn them—a charming form of "ecumenical" interaction.

It turned out an FBI informant in the group betrayed the activists, arranging their capture at the scene of the break-in. After a lengthy trial lasting over a year, the defendants were declared, to everyone's surprise, not guilty. The jury, like much of the public, greatly opposed the war, and the proceedings revealed the FBI to be so overreaching in enabling their informant that they were considered aids in the break-in.

In a sad turn of events, during the course of the trial the FBI informant's son suffered a fatal accident, falling from a tree onto a fence. Amazingly, Fr. Michael was asked to do the funeral. He says that one side of the church was filled with FBI, while the other was piled up with a bunch of defendants and war resisters. Quite a sight! I hadn't heard such stories before moving to Camden, but as time would pass, I would hear many.[3]

On my first night sleeping in the old house Michael had offered to me and my friends, I felt like I was perched on the edge of the world, in a dark and windy storm, with not even stars as comfort, struggling to hold on. I had slept on the streets of Philadelphia before, with my friend Jonathan, shivering as we entertained thoughts of solidarity with the homeless. But this was different. On the streets of Philadelphia one had a sense of being moderately protected by the vibrancy of the nearby downtown—you could see the ends of alleys, spot a car driving around, and find security in the encouraging glow of a street lamp.

In Camden, however, there seemed to be no glow of civilization around, only the noise. Car alarms and house alarms went off in the middle of nowhere with no response. Street lights were often broken or flickering. Across the street from the abandoned house I was moving into was a liquor store with a seriously maimed security alarm. It went off for hours on end with twisted, choppy, contorted sounds. On my first night, however, an alarm was heeded—with my freshly cut key, I unlocked my door only to set off an alarm that seemed to blast right at me. After twenty minutes of unsuccessful attempts to stop it, cops came to the back door, guns drawn, to find a shabby, post-college kid adorned with too much hair, sweaty from running around to find an alarm breaker. It was hard for them (or me) to understand what I was doing there. If that were not enough, later on that night I experienced for the first (and, hopefully for the last) time something extraordinary—several gunshots fired *from my front porch.* Oddly, no shouts and arguments surrounded the shots. They came out of nowhere, startling me from sleep, with a sound that was deeper and heavier than what I had thought came from guns. Since then I have heard numerous shots down the street or a few blocks over, but nothing that close.

Four others and I moved into this house, each with our own way of approaching the neighborhood. One was a physical therapist, who biked to every house visit as his own act of ecological and political mindfulness. Another turned to urban farming, another to after-school programs and assistance to street people, and I to teaching at Sacred Heart's school. Regularly eating, praying, and attending Mass together, we set about, more or less, enacting the vision I had written up in Belize. We quickly became known as a respite to kids in the neighborhood. And with a closet of donated clothing, we found folks from the streets frequently stopping by.

I often found myself driving people on the streets to where they needed to go. (We would not give money, and so we often responded with gifts in kind, like food or rides, to anyone who asked.) Perhaps the most awkward of them was taking a woman from the streets, Shana, multiple times to a hospital, or to her parents' house—who sometimes refused her entry. A difficult feeling emerges when I drive through our neighborhood, pedestrians look into my car, and they see a prostitute in the seat next to me. Ignoring the subsequent voices in my head—of gossip, of what others might think—has put my feet closer to the fire of the Sermon on the Mount. After five years of welcoming Shana into the house for milk and PB&J sandwiches (she was twenty-seven years old and had no teeth left) and offering her rides, she was found dead, beaten and naked in a dumpster.

Fairly dark events like this seemed disproportionally packed into our beginning years. After having moved in all our things and being away for a bit, we returned to find the house broken into with much of our stuff stolen. We found it ransacked and strewn with garbage, pornography, drugs, and such. One couch was particularly maimed, and we promptly cleaned it. It took us a few months to ever sit on it, however, until one day a visitor bowled into the room and casually threw himself down on it. We all sat silently, looking at him, with a look of surprise and wonder. "What?" he said with a confused face. "Uhuh . . . nothing," we said, and we erupted with laughter. Thus the couch was finally christened back into public use.

We had a car stolen. Hoodlums in passing cars egged a housemate and me while we were biking on separate occasions. Things like that could be laughed off (or at least that's what I told myself), but it was more difficult to laugh off having a baseball bat thrown at my wife Cassie and me while we were biking. Though we avoided anything worse than swerving our bikes (the kids who threw the bat didn't seem interested in investing real effort in an assault), it felt pretty dangerous.

On another occasion we welcomed a woman from the streets into our kitchen for some food and drink, but things got complicated. In a desperate plea for attention, she started proclaiming that she had a gun in her purse. As she became more riled up and irritable, a friend attempted to divert her attention for long enough to get her purse from her. The moment he reached for it she punched him in the throat. It turned out that she did not have a gun, and a woman in our community fixed up some food and took our throat-puncher out back to eat and talk on lawn chairs.

On yet another occasion, late one night, I was talking in the living room with my friend Jeremy when we heard a woman screaming out into the empty, dark streets. We both ran out to her to find she had been stabbed in the side and was stumbling her way across our block—on which our house was only one of two occupied residences. We wondered who would have come to her aid in this emptiness? We hurried to call her an ambulance, and I waited with her on the stoop of an abandoned house as blood soaked her shirt. We managed to share a few words as I asked what happened. She winced out a half-answer. And that was it. The ambulance came—end of story.

Perhaps one of my more awkward interactions was with a man on the street with whom I had become friends. On multiple occasions, he would come to the house to vent his frustrations about life on the street. Coming from such a different background, I couldn't do much more than to sit out back under a tree with him and offer some water and a listening ear. Despite my inability to help him in any immediate, concrete way, he nevertheless found these times a breath of fresh air. He'd often say after talking that, "I feel like I'm not in Camden anymore"—and by that, he meant the street culture of argument, anxiety, and posturing. Sitting under a tree was also a treat, since it often feels that Camden has only a few.

But one night, around 2:00 a.m., I heard a fervent, loud knocking at the back door. I rose from bed and went to the door, opening it just enough to see it was my friend. He was agitated and heaving with sweat. I had become familiar with what drug-induced states looked like, and it seemed very likely that he was high on crack. He kept saying that he wanted to come in as he had soiled himself. (I did not inspect and verify that particular claim.)

It was a very difficult situation, given Jesus' rather unambiguous (and let's face it, somewhat spooky) declaration, "Whatever you do to the least of these you do unto me."[4] What to do? He insisted on coming in, all but threatening me to open the door. It was a very tough call, and after sifting between selfish laziness and a concern for my housemates' safety, I chose to tell him I was sorry, and I closed the door. In the ensuing weeks he was reported to have voiced many threats against me for my lack of hospitality. I can't recall a time I felt so on edge, wondering if I would see him on the streets and what conflict might come of it. As it turned out, he left the neighborhood for a while, but upon his return we reconciled—we went out back beneath our tree again to talk things through.

Growing up in the relatively serene suburbs, I was prone to appraising myself as the Pharisees did, "Thank God I'm not like these other people." I had gladly counted myself above the fray of the world's violent offenders: its addicted, its prostitutes, its drug dealers, its gang members, its racists. In my easy, safe circumstances, my soul was never challenged into wondering how I would respond to anxiety, fear, hatred, depression, racism, and violence. Today things are more complicated, since a grittier world has agitated complex emotions and brought them up from the hidden parts of my soul. I now see the murderer in myself, the addict, the violent offender, even the racist. Years before, I had read Henri Nouwen's *The Wounded Healer*, wherein he writes,

> Through compassion it is possible to recognize that the craving for love that men feel resides also in our own hearts, that the cruelty that the world knows all too well is also rooted in our own impulses. Through compassion, we also sense our hope for forgiveness in our friends' eyes and our hatred in their bitter mouths. When they kill, we know that we could have done it; when they give life, we know that we can do the same. For a compassionate person, nothing human is alien.[5]

I thought I had fully understood this when I first read it. Now I *experienced* it as true. Whether I liked it or not, Camden's social environment has forced me to know myself as a darker person than my optimistic self-appraisals.

Nine years have passed since we first moved to Camden, and in that time things have not been quite as intense and difficult (not for us, at least) as they were in the initial years. In fact, so many positive and inspiring things have happened amid the mess, that we have found it hard to imagine ever leaving; we often forget those odd stories. What dominates our minds today is that we've become part of a fledgling, and hopefully durable, renaissance. I suspect it will sound strange, but there is something hopeful about being amid the hopeless rubble of the world—there is always something creative to do, something to improve and be hopeful for. One can see the ghosts of productivity flying about abandoned factories, or imagine a potential patio in a pile of bricks from a burnt-down house. At times the eyesight to pierce through the darkness wanes, but one can often look past the repulsion of an abandoned house and envision its windows lit once again.

One of the greatest blessings of having moved to Waterfront South is that, when walking down the block, you invariably run into someone you know. Most of the folks we are privileged to know are from backgrounds very different from ours. They are people we would normally have never gotten to know—and I don't just mean the lost, the addicted, or the mentally ill. A beautiful family of Nigerian immigrants lives down the street, and our community mingles with them through ride-shares, parties, working with their kids at school, and worshipping together at our church. It is an amazing thing that even from such divergent backgrounds we can all go to daily morning Mass, as we often do, and connect over the shared Eucharist. And across the Communion table from us sits an old Vietnamese widow, whose husband served the Host and cup faithfully every day, though he couldn't say but a word in English. (He died during the writing of this book, God rest him.) She rarely says a word, as the grief of her loss has piled atop her painful scars from when my country invaded hers. And yet in Mass we are all given a space to connect, beyond words, around the humble "broken body and shed blood." It is an amazing thing to have found myself attending this global Catholic Church, where people who might not even share the same language can share a space at a table of prayer and thanksgiving.

Two doors down from us lives another Vietnamese immigrant family who just recently moved in. They speak not a word of English. One cold day, the family's grandmother came over to my house and started gesturing toward her house and making the motions that she was cold and shivering. I gathered her house was cold, and so we walked over. No family members were around to help figure out the thermostat, and thankfully, all that was needed was to turn the furnace on, which I did. Ever since then, we've been wordless friends. She often brings over gifts of Vietnamese food and pastries, knocking loudly (completely out of proportion to her small size!) and then silently lifting to our eyes a plate of something delectable, accompanied with a smile implying, "Here, take this!" My wife Cassie and I have since reciprocated with plates of chocolate chip cookies.

Every once in a while, I'll look out my window to see her watering the plants in front of her house, and then turn to water ours. The crisp cleanliness and efficiency of her vegetable garden out back makes our poor excuse for a garden and small chicken coop, however quaint, look derelict.

Besides some great neighbors, Sacred Heart parish—where Fr. Michael is pastor—has a beautiful and vibrant core to it. We were lucky enough to move in right across the street; when the bell rings, we can roll out of bed and saunter right in (we try not to). A number of other parishioners, previously commuters, have recently moved into the neighborhood with a similar spirit of revival, taking up abandoned houses and lots too, planting and watering as a public proclamation of faith, hope, and love. Some have engaged in "guerrilla poetry," wherein they go to boarded up houses and paint their boards with poetry, signaling and hoping for a time when the boards will be removed and people move back in. One board reads a statement from Archimedes (third century BC), "Give me a lever long enough and a place to stand, and I will move the world."[6] Countless other parishioners regularly come to serve in the neighborhood, either at the church's thrift store, its regular grocery-bag distribution, its weekly soup kitchen, or its house rehabilitations.

One woman who moved with us into the neighborhood, Andrea Ferich, also a fellow Eastern and Belize alum, has taken up a full-force effort in urban farming, replete with a greenhouse, chickens, a large community garden, a small, weekly farm stand on our block, a weekly firing of a clay bread oven to teach kids how to cook veggies from the garden and make little pizzas, and a small apprenticing program to teach youth the craft of urban farming. One of our shared loves is "urban wood splitting" where we find ourselves swinging an axe and making firewood in the middle of a concrete jungle—if the pleasure of exertion isn't enough, the irony of the urban-bucolic-picturesque brings a smile of delight.

On one especially fun occasion, my wife Cassie and I were celebrating the news that we would be acquiring an abandoned house across the street. My mother had sent us some bulbs to plant in its backyard in expectation for the coming move. As we walked back there with bulbs and tools in hand, through a garbage- and needle-ridden alley, we found the yard was darkened from a dense overhead canopy of vines that had crawled up the back of the house and covered anything in reach. Next door was an abandoned house that was halfway burnt to the ground. I got my hands on a machete and went to work on the vines. Cassie put on her pink gardening gloves, grabbed a small planting shovel, and began to find a good spot for the bulbs amid the garbage. It was quite a comic scene, with its combination of exertion, desecrated ground, fear of the unknown, and an innocent—if ignorant—and stubborn effort to renew.

As I continued hacking away, my cell phone rang. It was Shane, who was stopping by. I told him we were across the street from our home and that he should meet us there. Shane, who—God bless him—often looks like he lives on the streets with his dreadlocks and homemade clothes, must have been spotted by the police as I greeted him and took him down the alley to our tulip-bulb-planting-and-machete-swinging shindig. It likely looked a lot like a drug deal—and one significant enough to necessitate my large, bladed weaponry. A few moments later, we heard sounds coming down the alley. Shane wondered, "I think we have some company," and two policemen emerged from an opening in the dense vine-wall with their guns drawn on us. "Put your hands up." I hefted my machete in the air, and Cassie hoisted her pink-gloved hands in the air. One cop demanded, "What's going on here?" "We're planting bulbs, sir." That didn't quite make sense to him—until, of course, we showed him the bulbs, which were indeed neither cocaine nor heroin. As they lowered their guns we talked about our experimenting with hopefulness—humdrum chitchat about whether we should give up on the planet or not.

Several people have lived with us for a time, and we have learned and benefitted from them all. We have lived for several years now with a young Mennonite couple with two kids. Their own journey brought them to our community with similar hopes. Even as Mennonites they worship with us at Sacred Heart, and their persistent attendance there is a testament to ecumenical engagement. Mennonites have a special memory of Catholic persecution during the sixteenth century, but most modern Catholics probably don't even know Mennonites exist. Cassie and I came from the Protestant world and, despite our many shared critiques of Catholicism, have opted to embrace it. They are in their own discernment process, and, very importantly, any "ecumenical dialogue," wherein we discuss the difficulties of denominations, is seen in light of our shared call of discipleship to live as a community of hope in Camden.

My first paying job in Camden was teaching at Sacred Heart's parochial school—most of our community members work or have worked there as well. I did this for a few years, encountering the challenges of urban, disaffected youth. Some days I would break up fights; some days I would enjoy breakthrough success; other days I would find myself tutoring a twelve-year-old that couldn't read *at all*, but who had new shoes every month. It was challenging and enjoyable, but ultimately not for me, and I looked for other creative ways of work. Taking walks around the neighborhood, I often spotted old wood from destroyed houses and demolition dumpsters, and I thus became engaged in the sport known as "dumpster diving." Taking the hauled wood into my basement, sanding and planing it, I found ways to make it into something special, like furniture, doors, or picture frames. Nothing I can purchase from a store looks nearly as good as this ancient, virgin-growth wood, cut in the late 1800s while our city was first being built. Living in a crumbling city, it has only made sense to add remodeling and repairing houses to my list of vocational activities. So after apprenticing with an electrician and learning from some carpenters, I set about running my own business—now several years going.

One of my biggest learning spurts came when Cassie and I moved from the original community house into the house across the street. We gutted and remodeled every inch of it, making the house a combination of fresh renewal and old wood. Such a satisfying experience of rejuvenation has led me to frequently get dirty with gutting abandoned houses, hanging doors, tiling bathrooms, replacing windows, remodeling kitchens, painting houses, and generally fighting the forces of entropy. In one particularly exciting project, I have been working with the late Sister Peg's housing-development organization, Heart of Camden, on a nearby firehouse, built in 1889, hoping to soon turn it into workshops and artist studios.

Not long after moving into Camden, my friend Shane introduced me to an urban hermit—a gentle, gem of a man, Richard Withers—who was getting rid of his potter's wheel, kiln, and a thousand pounds of clay. I said I would love to learn pottery, and he thereby hefted all that into my possession. And so, with virtually an entire potter's studio on my hands, I asked a knowledgeable friend to teach me how to use it all. We arranged for my teaching him theology for summer college credit in exchange for his teaching me pottery.

In many cases, we hear of artists moving into rough neighborhoods to revitalize them. This was in no way the case for me—I had not a single skill or craft, and could not even work a caulk gun. Rather, I moved into this rough neighborhood having little more than faith, hope, and love to guide me (and the training of a liberal arts degree in sociology and theology). The neighborhood revitalized *me*—it forced me to attempt to become a skilled laborer. Moreover, it has turned my mind, evermore, toward an affection for *matter*, for the created world, for crafting things of beauty, for building homes in ways so that we *love them*, not just dwell in them. Building on my Belize experience, I was coming down to earth, enlarging my thoughts about "salvation" to embrace the physical realm.

Growing up playing soccer and video games, rarely bothering to sweat for work, and on the trajectory for a white-collar job, I've often been mystified when I find myself doing something like crawling through the rafters of that old firehouse to tear out a plaster ceiling, covered in dirt-made-mud and sweat, and breathing heavily through a dust mask. I often step out to find cops' cars littering our street, arresting a pile of drug dealers. I walk by, looking suspect, quite like a metal scrapper or heroin addict, and hope not to get pulled over and questioned about my motives. From such a scene, I step back to wonder to myself, in comic tone, "My, what a different world you now inhabit." Often getting dirty in this neighborhood, I remember from my lessons in Belize that humor is related to the words for "humus" (dirt) and "humility." The humbling symbolism is too deep for words when, on Ash Wednesday, Fr. Michael mingles the ashes from burnt-down and abandoned houses into the palm ashes.

Our "intentional Christian community" is not a big thing; we are not a registered organization, and our "ministry" largely consists of latching onto things already happening in the neighborhood. We have no plan of becoming big. We have moved into Camden, work at the school across the street, swing hammers, tend gardens, eat dinners together a few times a week, share (to some extent) our cars, homes, and money—altogether making ourselves ready to participate in what feels like, in the words of Wendell Berry, "practicing resurrection."[7] We are trying to live normal life in what often feels like an abnormal place.

For readers still confounded by the apparent irrationality of moving into Camden, I turn to a quotation from Chesterton, who gave me words to describe how to best improve the world. He uses a neighborhood of central London, Pimlico, which, at the time (circa 1908) had degraded into a slum, to illustrate. Paraphrasing, I replace Pimlico with Camden:

> It is not enough for a man to disapprove of Camden: in that case he will merely cut his throat or move to Chelsea. Nor, certainly, is it enough for a man to approve of Camden: for then it will remain Camden, which would be awful. The only way out of it seems to be for somebody to love Camden: to love it with a transcendental tie and without any earthly reason. If there arose a man who loved Camden, then Camden would rise into ivory towers and golden pinnacles; Camden would attire herself as a woman does when she is loved. For decoration is not given to hide horrible things: but to decorate things already adorable. A mother does not give her child a blue bow because he is so ugly without it. A lover does not give a girl a necklace to hide her neck. If men loved Camden as mothers love children, arbitrarily, because it is *theirs*, Camden in a year or two might be fairer than Florence. Some readers will

say that this is a mere fantasy. I answer that this is the actual history of mankind. This, as a fact, is how cities did grow great. Go back to the darkest roots of civilization and you will find them knotted round some sacred stone or encircling some sacred well. People first paid honor to a spot and afterwards gained glory for it. Men did not love Rome because she was great. She was great because they had loved her.[8]

PART TWO:
CONTEMPLATION
(WITH SOME ACTION)

I have waited until this second part of the book to describe the dilemma of finding myself, a fervent evangelical, in the midst of a Catholic community. To be sure, the hopefulness and the zeal cooked up at Willow are what fueled my move to Camden. But after moving here and coming into tight proximity with the Catholic Church, I was forced to grapple with my Protestant criticisms. But before this flurry of reflections, I must mention something that I will not discuss in detail, but which will act as a sort of backdrop throughout. It came late in college; and it wasn't insights about the Church. Instead, broadly speaking, it was the demolition of all of my previous notions of "God."

One book that catalyzed some real demolition was *Honest to God*, by John A. T. Robinson.[1] Robinson explored ideas like Bonhoeffer's notion of "religionless Christianity"—that our world had "come of age," no longer believing in some transcendent God—and Paul Tillich's notion that God is best understood not as *a being* but *the ground of being*. And he explored Rudolf Bultmann's idea of "demythologizing" Christianity, attempting to separate the core of Christianity from its pre-modern worldview. Robinson was trying to put to rest some picture of a God "up there" or "out there," encouraging us all to let it die. For a world that, at times, appears to be going atheist with a vengeance, he was promoting a "secular theology"—a Christianity without theism.[2]

A tough sell, to be sure, but it certainly prodded some serious investigation for me.

One might broach the problem by looking at the common claim, "God exists." If the word "exist" means some *thing* that *stands out* from something further behind it, like chalk on top of a chalkboard, one might say that God does not "exist." Even if we say, "God is like the chalkboard," we can only say it knowing it is a very imperfect metaphor—for, behind the chalkboard is the wall, and even more lurks behind the wall. Whatever "God" means, it cannot mean a being that stands out from something further behind—for, by conventional definition, the whole notion of God is to go as "far back" as you can go. Before considering this, I had tended to see God as some obvious and final *answer* to all life's questions—that we, whenever plagued with questions, could somehow assume that some Being up there was the answer to them. In a way, God was no mystery to me, but an answer, a solution, to mystery. But from this different angle, I was challenged to see God as a *never-ending question.*[3]

This whole God-demolition process, which evolved over a few years, is hard to summarize here. But Robinson, putting the problem most sharply, stung the most. His theology made my view of God feel like a crumbling house of cards. It caused a few spells of weeping, one in a professor's office as I narrated the demolition. God had been for me that Being "out there," that comforting construct, the great Other. I already mentioned how the crumbling of the World Trade Center had challenged any of my sugary ideas of God as some "Protector in the Sky." And I also already knew that "G-d" had been understood for ages as ineffable, that mysterious YHWH,[4] whose name reverential Jews insist on not pronouncing, referring only to "the Name" (Hashem). But Robinson and others challenged me to go further, to risk letting go of this "Being" that made the universe feel more comfortable. One might say that the challenge stung so much because I hadn't yet heard a warning like this:

> Woe unto them who keep a God like a silk hat, that believe not in God, but in a God.[5]

Something about the "a" there makes a universe of difference between a Being and Being Itself. But there is a problem: even if we become more open-minded and destroy our limited God-language, the Christian idea of the Incarnation appears to set some very serious limits on God. There, all the sacred mysteries come to a definite point: *God is like this person, Jesus*—or, for the more adventurous, *God is this person.* Likewise, the claim "God is Love" is a big language risk; for all of the vast, unimaginable mystery implied by the word "God," "Love" is a *very specific* and definite claim. For many, there is no reason they couldn't just as well say, "God is a dragon," or "God is an enormous tangerine," or "God is indifferent." For, to me at least, there is no *obvious* reason to associate the Strength that sustains the stars with Love, or a Baby in a manger, than to associate gravity with kittens.[6]

But however much I became aware of the risk in speaking about the Great Mystery, I still experience some joyful adventure in risking it. Robinson, despite any problems with his book (and I found some), both ruined and improved "God-talk" for me—I cannot hazard uttering a theological word without feeling like I'm going skydiving, night snorkeling without a light in a Belizean reef, or picking a fight with a professional boxer. I'm perilously jumping into something that might not end well.

It is delightful that just as I would move into Camden and be forced to engage that gargantuan thing, Catholicism, I gained this extra dimension to my theology. For some, demolishing ideas of God might point them *out* of the Church; for if we can imagine a God without boundaries, why be part of a Church *with* them? Some therefore disengage the Church or any religion, proclaiming, "God cannot be boxed in!" or, the most familiar, "God is too big for any one religion or denomination!"

A key difficulty for any spiritual person, then, is how to marvel at the mysterious question of God, how to proclaim something like, "The Ground of Being is greater than anything we say or imagine!" but not cut the head off a neighbor who utters the word "God" or enacts a religious ritual. Some iconoclasts, for example—with their staunch insistence, drawn partly from the prohibition of "graven images" in Exodus 20:4, that God is too unfathomable for our images—cannot tolerate anyone painting an image of the Imageless Enigma. They are thus their own enigma—their open-mindedness makes them close-minded. An erudite philosopher once said, "What we cannot speak about we must pass over in silence,"[7] and this makes all the sense in the world. But, I imagine that an uneducated Christian peasant whittling a Nativity scene in wood might quietly chuckle and reply, "Yes, if God is sleeping in a manger, it is best to walk by quietly and respectfully," and then continue shamelessly carving his God in wood who had once been in flesh.

It is a curious case that many mystics have adventurously plumbed the boundlessness of God *and* stayed connected to the bounded Church—just to name a few, Gregory of Nyssa, Teresa of Avila, Catherine of Sienna, John of the Cross, Julian of Norwich, Meister Eckhart (all his challenging rhetoric and controversies notwithstanding). These people gloried in the profoundly unfamiliar, in "the Cloud of Unknowing" we might say, and yet remained part of a family. Sometimes they were even persecuted by their family (the Church), but they did not walk away. They persisted in participation. Perhaps their model came from the Incarnation—they assumed that two profoundly different things (God and Human) could mysteriously be one. They didn't pit the universal against the particular, the infinite against the finite, the metaphysical against the physical, or spirit against flesh. They understood that even the profound Shapeless could take the shape of the mundane—that God, at least once, had been "boxed in" and defined, with flesh.

When Thomas Aquinas was on his deathbed, he reportedly sighed and said that all his theology—which, piled high, could sink a ship—was "but straw." Hearing this, I became distraught at how unending (and potentially futile) the project of theology could be. I complained to my friend Jonathan, asking why we ever bother saying things about God. He, in his wisdom said, "But this 'Dumb Ox' [Aquinas's nickname] knew that we still need straw—for straw is quite useful." However much "straw" the following theological reflections might be, I do think it inescapable that, even if God is beyond language, the average human lives in a world of flesh, finitude, and language; and so we are naturally drawn to construct symbols, metaphors, rituals, and art, to describe That "in which we live and move and have our being."[8]

I say this all because letting go of my "God up there" didn't usher me out of the Church but prepared me to *enter* it—to view the symbols, language, art, and rituals of the Catholic Mass with a greater margin for mystery, with new eyes. I would be more prepared to put on hold my anti-Catholic impulses, with an awareness that "God-talk" (and God-ritual) is a very tricky thing, not as clean and clear as I sometimes experienced in the evangelical formulas. It soon became absolutely necessary for me, besides learning to allow for the mystery of the Church's Gospel, to allow for the mystery of Camden, in its own befuddling cloud of darkness. Living in a devastated place messes with your ideas of God. Your faith needs to become deeper and hardier than just ideas about God. You must learn to crawl into dark tunnels (or abandoned basements) with no light at the end of them. You might even say that by moving into a place that sometimes feels godless, I needed to find a faith that was durable enough to live through godlessness.

So I have wondered whether it might do Christians some good to humor the atheists a few moments every day, asking, "Let us grant for a moment that God is not 'out there.' But still, what system of words, symbols, architecture, ethics, ritual, culture, and art would you want to invent that is worthy of our station in this mysterious universe?"[9] I frequently entertain the thought of whether many might construct, over the trial and error of centuries, something like Catholicism.

Part two begins, not with broad theological principles on which I begin a general assessment of Catholicism, but with my experience of Catholic worship at Sacred Heart. Camden (and the Iraq war) imposed upon me a lens for experiencing Catholic rituals from a different perspective: an impoverished world at war, violence on the streets and in homes, and despair lingering as a real option for us all. And so I reflect upon the Mass in reference to the murder and nonviolence at which we are so often at a crossroads (chapter 6). I know many readers might not share that darker lens—but that may be precisely the reason to look through it. The next chapter (7) outlines how I have attempted to work through the ostensible paganism of Catholicism, the question of Jesus' relationship to pagan dying-and-rising gods, and that the Mass is called not just a meal but a "sacrifice."

Following those two chapters, I describe my struggling with questions about denominations, the Bible, and tradition, and how I could no longer honestly hold to Willow's notion of being "nondenominational" (8). I then wrestle with the questions of the apparent corruption and insufficiency of the Catholic Church and its history (9). And then I end on a three-dimensional problem:

how do we make sense of Jesus' simplicity and the Catholic Church's wealth—and, how does this simplicity-luxury question relate to the Christian tradition of envisioning the end of the world (10)?

Unintentionally, I find I have formed these chapters roughly along the pattern of the Paschal Triduum: I begin with Good Friday and the crucifixion, and I end with celebration of resurrection. In between (the "Holy Saturday") is filled with many dark questions, problems, and mysteries (about which my readers may conclude I should have, in the spirit of Holy Saturday, passed over in silence!) and end with the joy of the celebration of resurrection.

SIX:
MURDER AND THE MASS

After over a decade of absence, my first time back to the Catholic Church was at Sacred Heart Church in Camden, on Good Friday 2003.[1] The occasion both startled and comforted me. I was still at Eastern, but had decided to soon move to Camden. The world around me had been pounding with the drums of war. The United States had just invaded Iraq and had been fighting in Afghanistan for just over a year. I had witnessed many Christians in America turning a blind eye to, if not cheerleading, these invasions. It looked to me like Christians were dressing their faith up in a political theology that was little more than a justification of vengeance.

In the midst of all this, I had to come to a Catholic church to memorialize the murder of God in a murderous city. (As I penned this work, a young woman was tragically shot and killed at the end of my block by a shooter who had misidentified her. Two hundred neighbors gathered for a sizable peace walk through our streets. Weeks later, a nine-year-old boy's eyes were shot out by a stray bullet, blinding him for life. At another time, a four-year-old—the grandson of a community mate's boss—was killed by a stray bullet. One time, two people were found in a car in front of my friend's house, shot in the back of the head. Later that week, there were ten shootings in four days. The darkness is heavy here.)

The Good Friday liturgy, held in an old, stone, semi-Gothic church, began in utter darkness and silence. I looked from the array of pews and silent parishioners up at the dim, vaulted ceiling to find it covered with frescoes from the late 1800s—images of Christ raising Lazarus, of Abraham laying down his weapons in the presence of Melchizedek, of Mary bearing Jesus, of the multiplication of loaves and fishes, of Jesus' Baptism, of Herod's slaughtering of the innocents.

While viewing Herod's carnage on the ceiling, I imagined Herod, even though we think he lived in a more brutish era, would marvel at the immense slaughtering of innocents in our day. Media coverage, along with footage and stories from CPT, had been streaming in about the carnage from the war—more Iraqis than Americans—even though the policy from Washington was, "We don't do body counts."[2] In earlier American wars, we had to see their costs, at least for our own sons and daughters, as caskets returning from Vietnam were aired on television. Anticipating the grief and protest that come from such images, no such revelations of this war were permitted.

At the front of the church, above its altar, was an enormous purple shroud covering a ten-foot-tall, cross-shaped object. From the dark front of the church, the priest emerged with the creak of a door and said nothing. He turned to the shroud and prostrated himself, lying in complete silence, with his entire body flat upon the ground. The gathered body responded by kneeling. You could hear only the shuffling of shirts, pants, and kneelers. For some reason, I had not seen anything so silent and dramatic in my young days at Mass; it wasn't simply that the liturgy was "reverent"—like most Americans, I was pretty well-seasoned at revering things from the flag to the constitution, from football players to movie stars. But this appeared to me as a reverence of mourning and of suffering, and it was done largely in silence. If I had ever seen some semblance of this as a child, it struck me now as entirely new and fresh, given my growing experience of the violent world around us.

After a few minutes, the priest slowly rose from the floor, and the congregation followed. I might have been the only one thinking this, but I could not help but notice that the liturgy that followed exalted everything contrary to the fervor outside its doors; the music was slow—beautiful without being sentimental—evoking a solemnity that moved not toward a frown but to tears and lament. The chants, written appropriately to the mournful context of Good Friday, drew the mind to simple but profound meditations. How stunning that we sang, between the cantor's verses on suffering, "my God, oh my God, why have you abandoned me?"

The gospel reading was John's Passion account—the *entire* Passion account. It took nearly a half-hour to proclaim. This was striking to me, as the relentless complaint from my Protestant friends—and often me—was that Catholics don't read the Bible. With apologies to my fellow Catholics, I can now confirm that the biblical literacy of most serious Protestants should probably make Catholics blush. But I can also say that, until that day, I had never sat through a half-hour reading of scripture during worship. So much for crude generalizations.

Near the end of John's account of the crucifixion, the priest read, "and Christ *gave up his spirit.*" With that, the entire congregation and the priest, without prompt, fell to their knees in silence. Perhaps this moment is revered for being the dramatic epitome of his death, and/or because his "spirit" is one with the Holy Spirit. (The Holy Spirit "proceeds from the Father and the Son," as they say in the Western creed.) At the moment of someone's death, especially God's, it is only right to stop, to grieve.

After a long pause, we rose from our kneeling veneration, and the readers finished the story.

The events that followed have nearly destroyed my entire Protestant formation and theology. The priest and a woman assistant proceeded to wield a long stick to unveil the purple shroud hanging from the crucifix. The woman struck me as symbolizing the presence of the women at Golgotha; Luke highlights women as escaping the lynch-mob trance of the jeering crowd, staunchly remaining present, even as others barked their taunts. The priest and woman removed just one portion of the shroud, and the nailed hand of Jesus was unveiled. Combining this sight with the violence and wars raging outside, I started to cry—seeing even just a *part* of his body. In silence, again, his other hand was slowly unveiled; and then finally his whole body was revealed. And all returned to their knees in silence.

The church's crucifix depicted blood dripping from Jesus' thorn crown and nailed hands; his exhausted face revealed his having been tortured to death. As I gazed on the crucifix, my mind merged with it the images of Iraqi civilians bleeding to death, images my friends had brought back from the invasion in photos, stories, and film. I was viewing a scene of torture. I then turned my eyes to the side to see statuette scenes depicting the Stations of the Cross, dotting the surrounding walls of the church. With sights of violence at the front and to my sides, I called to mind the doubtlessly prevalent instances of torture that were taking place, at that instant, in a not-so-distant war zone. In the coming years, as I would repeat this liturgy, the billowing accounts of torture from Abu Gharib would come to mind, mingled with the countless defenses for the "necessity" of torturing detainees in Guantanamo Bay and elsewhere. This imagery has continued to startle me as a kind of anthropological oddity—Christians weekly walk into a space devoted to recalling, and repenting of, the day we collectively tortured and murdered God.

Years later, after Cassie and I had our first son, I would carry him around during Mass. He had begun to point to everything and cutely murmur something like, "And what's that?" One time, he pointed to one of the statuette stations, in which Roman soldiers were whipping Jesus to the ground, and cooed again his question. What fascinating and honest imagery Christians have to answer for here! What do we say? "Well, Simon, that's when we were killing God and didn't understand what we were doing." Is that questioning not, at least in part, a description of what is happening at Mass, in the stories and imagery passed down to us?

In the face of the Cross, we are invited to adore and worship "not only the God of the sufferers, but the God who suffers." Nicholas Wolterstorff, grieving over the death of his son, says it well:

> The pain and fallenness of humanity have entered into God's heart. Through the prism of my tears I have seen a suffering God. It is said of God that no one can behold God's face and live. I always thought this meant that no one could see God's splendor and live. A friend said perhaps it meant that no one could see God's sorrow and live. Or perhaps his sorrow is splendor. . . . Instead of explaining our suffering God shares it."[3]

Instead of exalting the image of some "mega-God" in the sky, who, like Zeus, casts down thunderbolts of vengeance upon transgressors, this crucifix represented a God being killed by transgressors—and, even more importantly, willingly entering into it. We hear it emphasized in the Mass, while the priest consecrates the bread and wine, that he was "given up to death, a death he freely accepted."[4] To whatever extent the Cross retains any sense of God's power and omnipotence, it becomes all the more exquisitely paradoxical and intriguing to hear of the God-Man crying from the cross, "My God, my God, why have you forsaken me?" Despite all those thoughts about a Christianity without God, about a "secular theology" from Robinson, I saw something very grave here:

> And now let the revolutionists choose a creed from all the creeds and a god from all the gods of the world, carefully weighing all the gods of inevitable recurrence and of unalterable power. They will not find another god who has himself been in revolt. Nay, (the matter grows too difficult for human speech) but let the atheists themselves choose a god. They will find only one divinity who ever uttered their isolation; only one religion in which God seemed for an instant to be an atheist.[5]

The liturgy on this special and terrible day revered this suffering God by having worshippers walk up to the feet of Jesus, at the crucifix, and kiss them. As I approached, even though my Protestant, iconoclastic alarms were sounding (denouncing statues as idolatry or "graven images"), I looked up with reverent affection, and then kissed his feet.

In what followed, there was no long sermon about how an angry God needed this sacrifice to placate his blood lust. Having looked intently upon the cross, we saw that no Father would want their son tortured to death so that he might summon a hidden forgiveness. In fact, the one demanding blood in the Passion was not God, but *us*:

> God is propitiating *us*. In other words, who is the angry divinity in the story? *We are.* That is the purpose of the atonement. *We* are the angry divinity. *We* are the ones inclined to dwell in wrath and think we need vengeance in order to survive. God was occupying the space of *our* victim so as to show us that we need never do this again. This turns on its head the Aztec

understanding of the atonement. In fact it turns on its head what has passed as our penal substitutionary theory of atonement, which always presupposes that it is *us* satisfying God, that *God* needs satisfying, that there is *vengeance* in God.[6]

There were no calls to war with God on our side, as the impassioned pleas of the mob to "crucify him!" were still ringing in our ears; we had just read aloud a story of the murder and lies of violent groups.

The numerous Masses I have since attended at Sacred Heart are not nearly as sober and dark as was the Good Friday liturgy, although our dryly humorous Irish priest is more at home with melancholy. He can barely handle the exuberance of the Carnivale Mass or the rambunctious songs of Children's Day! And yet, whatever the tone of a Mass, the Cross is always the sober, central image, as it was for Paul.[7] At Sacred Heart, every Mass begins with a confession, an absolution, and a lengthy peace sharing, and it then breaks out into a grand procession—at the front of it, the crucifix of the suffering Messiah is held high and slowly paraded down the middle of the aisle. Have you ever stopped yourself to wonder what you are looking at? Apparently, we are all supposed to look upon it and say to ourselves, "*That's* who we worship. The one nailed to that tree, dying, nailed by *us*." I had heard not a few times, and probably parroted myself, the critique against Catholics, that "they leave Jesus hanging up there on the cross, when in fact he is off the cross, resurrected!" But, having mingled the violence of the Cross with the violence of our own day, I could now see at least one reason why they keep the crucifix with its dying Lord upon it. After we have just confessed and been granted God's mercy, the crucifix opens our eyes to see, "*I* am prone to nail him to that tree. See what we do!" Until every last ounce of our proclivity to murder one another is dried up and gone forever, we cannot prance with glee into the promised land. We need to remember who we are, and who we were. We must heed the warning of Luke and Matthew[8], where we are cautioned about our tendency to decorate memorials and tombs for a prophet we would have killed. The crucifix is the anti-memorial, the anti-whitewashed tomb. Imagine a memorial of Martin Luther King Jr. that, instead of depicting a sacred aura of respectability, instead depicted in carved bronze police dogs biting at his leg with him struggling to stand, or an intricately shaped scene of fire hoses blasting him and fellow marchers over. Though such statues might offend more than memorialize, they would at least refuse to paper over the messy truth.

Christianity is no cheap utopianism—it will cry out in worship of the greatest ideals of heaven, hope, and love, but it does so in reference to the violence and evils humans are currently mired in, which need remedy.[9] Depictions of resurrection without the Cross make for cheap happiness, bought at the cost of reality.[10] Even if Jesus is resurrected, the wounds and scars still remain, just as our violence still remains to this day. The one who truly sees Christ crucified is, however joyful in his experience of forgiveness, always tempered and humbled as one who has witnessed the torturing and execution of another human, killed from our own betrayal or indifference. Far too often, instead, our theologies of atonement and pious patriotism can dress up or obscure the painful lament at the sight of the Cross. It didn't seem coincidental, then, that many people from the evangelical community in which I heard this disdain for the crucifix's imagery, who had removed the Cross but kept the flag, were also often overlooking or rationalizing the deaths of civilians in our current wars.

When the cross bearer reaches the front after a Mass's opening procession, the cross is planted down in full view, and will stand there all Mass, as if to reiterate, "*This* is what the liturgy is about here. Dare to look at it." The anthropologists and psychologists have a point when they sum up religion as ornamental totem poles, ultimately a comforting projection of ourselves. We think ourselves strong, and so we place a bull head on the pole; we think ourselves perceptive like an eagle, and place one atop the pole. But do we have the eyes to see when a startling object ends up on our pole, marking an alarming halt to worship-as-usual— one of us, strung up, beaten, and bleeding? *This* is our totem pole. If our projections are meant to comfort us into a false and elevated version of ourselves, this had to be a reversal of the most curious sort. *I*, at least, am not comforted by the sign of someone being tortured to death. We can reserve the "opiate of the masses" criticism for other problems and contradictions in the way Christians live their faith—but it does not apply on Good Friday. Here, the fullness of human ugliness is on full display.

The Good Friday songs, readings, and homily all pointed me toward remembering the one whom we unjustly tortured to death and who, in turn, forgave us. The injustice was a sign of a global disease we are all susceptible to, but the forgiveness of it was an act of cosmological immensity, of constructing a new world not founded on violence, but mercy. And yet the harvest of peace is sown through suffering. I had not expected the theology of Mennonite theologian John Howard Yoder, whom I had been reading since Belize, to be incarnated in the liturgy so intensely:

> Here at the cross is the man who loves his enemies, the man whose righteousness is greater than that of the Pharisees, who being rich became poor, who gives his robe to those who took his cloak, who prays for those who spitefully use him. The cross is not a detour or a hurdle on the way to the kingdom, nor is it even the way to the kingdom; it is the kingdom come.[11]

In one symbol an entire politics is summed up. Instead of trusting in the wisdom of smart bombs or the insight of military intelligence, Yoder counterintuitively insisted that it is the "slain lamb" that truly "moves world history." Yoder reminds us to trust the wisdom of the foolish Christ, and most importantly to do so in our politics. So, sitting in this liturgy in the context of a "War on Terror," I recalled his reminding us about the "war of the lamb"—which is no war at all. For the Lamb of God "conquers" by suffering; his throne is the Cross; his crown is made of thorns.[12]

At later Masses, I also took new notice of how the old-fashioned ritual of "crossing yourself," an action invoking the Trinity upon yourself, can be understood in reference to our own politics, as if to say, "God's nature is cruciform; and I stamp that pattern upon myself." During the reading of the Gospel, Catholics cover themselves in this symbol even further by making the Cross upon their forehead, lips, and heart—again, as if to say, "May the way we think, talk, and feel be shaped in the form of the Suffering Servant."[13] You can't get away with merely saying, "Thank God he suffered for me." No, you must take that very passionate, active, serving, and dangerous nature on yourself. As I carried on this signing habit over time, I imagined the Cross as the "sword" which divides not just "father from son, and mother from daughter," but that cuts our own self in two; I even imagined in this gesture the piercing scalpel of forgiveness slicing open our hardened selves for surgery, to be operated upon by the merciful hands of grace.

The ultimate performance (and remembrance) of the Cross is found in giving thanks to the Lamb of God in the Eucharist. There, we eat the Victim who lovingly offered himself to all, and we receive with affection his broken body and poured-out blood. This, I think, is one of the reasons why the word for the Communion wafer, the "host," means *victim*.

The liturgy's phrase, "May all of us who share in the body and blood of Christ be brought together in unity by the Holy Spirit," struck me in a fresh way that Good Friday. For it is a claim about what best unites people. The force that should unite us all is

not some bloodlust for vengeance, which is all too good at band-
ing people together, as we saw in much of that post-9/11 "togetherness" our nation experienced. Our circled wagons spoke not
of a community prepared to rationally end the cycle of violence,
perhaps through forgiveness. Rather, that culture of unity soon
showed itself to be coalesced around the bonfire of vengeance.
In the remembrance of Christ's death, however, something else
brings people together: instead of shared passion to destroy
the evil terrorist, and thereby "improve" the world, sharing the
Body and Blood of Christ marks a solid and profound strategy,
which we might even call a *lack* of strategy. In the bloodied face
of Christ, we see none of the political calculations of how much
evil and collateral damage is an acceptable cost in my mission to
do good. No—God is Love, and Love, while eagerly healing and
bettering this hurting and angry world, gets killed. The repeated
proclamation in preparing the Eucharist, "Lamb of God, you
take away the sins of the world," now meant to me, not merely
a claim about heaven, but about earth. It was a claim that the
Christ's suffering love, which we mistake for weakness, *actually*
takes away more evil from our world than any military invasion
or ousting of a dictator ever could. By kissing the feet of Jesus
on that statue, I was enacting my affection and allegiance to the
one who brings peace but not as the world gives peace—as he
was audacious enough to bring peace by a most curious method,
being peaceable.[14]

Instead of seeing the eucharist as my own private portion
of sacredness, I came to see them as drawing me into Christ's
profoundly different way of living in the world. The scholar William Cavanaugh, who studied the Eucharist in light of instances
like Chile's murderous regime under Pinochet, summarized:
"If torture is the imagination of the state, the Eucharist is the
imagination of the church."[15] When we eat together the Bread
of Heaven, the Eucharist is a performance of *uniting*—both the

people gathered locally and globally—and of making ourselves one with the Victim. In this—the words are almost too grave to write—we become the Body of Christ. You are what you eat, after all. We might even say it is the other way around: that, in the Eucharist, we are "digested *into* the Body of Christ." Lest this be confused for a badge of pride, Cavanaugh clarifies the ultimate point: "The fact that the Church is literally changed into Christ is not a cause for triumphalism, however, precisely because our assimilation to the body of Christ means that we then become food for the world, to be broken, given away, and consumed."[16] The liturgy, which means "work of the people,"[17] leads out of this beautiful chapel into a hurting world, into justice and service to others. Fr. Michael would often declare this at Mass—that "liturgy leads to justice."

Punctuating this solemn liturgy, two women silently walk to the altar and begin to strip it of every adornment. Every candle, blown out, and removed to a back room. The table cloth on the altar, pulled off in silence and walked off. Each time, they return to seal the finality. Every vase, every plant, taken away. We are left with nothing but Christ hanging on the cross. And then, even the light is taken away from us, as they are turned off in a silence so complete you hear the click of the switch. No benediction, no conclusion. We are left in silence to rise and walk out, and this starkness, this pressing force of emptiness on my heart brought a well of tears to my eyes.

What a performance in the middle of a world of terrorism, vengeance, and war! In experiencing the liturgy this way, I had seen something old in an entirely new way. The ancient liturgy was as fresh and progressive as the morning sun, and the current pattern of our world obsolete and regressive.

SEVEN:
PAGAN
CHRISTIANITY

I suggested recently that people would see the Christian story if it could only be told as a heathen story. The Faith is simply the story of a God who died for men. But, queerly enough, if we were even to print the words without a capital G, as if it were the cult of some new and nameless tribe, many would realise the idea for the first time. Many would feel the thrill of a new fear and sympathy if we simply wrote, "the story of a god who died for men." People would sit up suddenly and say what a beautiful and touching pagan religion that must be.[1]

Kissing the feet of a statue on Good Friday was just one startlingly unmodern thing among many; as I continued going to Mass, I couldn't help but notice how *pagan* it all appeared. I recalled all the Protestant critiques of "ritualism"—that Catholic liturgies were really lemming factories, blasphemously recreating a culture of superstition. Catholic Mass was dripping with what some might call "cult-like" activities, like chanting Latin, sprinkling holy water on attendees, kneeling, bowing, participating in extended silences of contemplation, lighting incense, to say nothing of eating flesh and drinking blood. In fact, seen from an alien's perspective, Catholics might appear as humans who worshipped bread and wine, elevating them into the air three times—as the priest did—and solemnly consuming it. Stained glass wherever you turned enshrined some ancient figure who was gesturing what looked like a type of gang sign or cryptic, secret hand-signal. There were men walking around in white robes, swinging incense; they did so in slow "processions." One parishioner walked down the aisle with a bible held above her head—with the four creatures of the gospels gilded in gold on its cover—another with the aforementioned crucifix lifted high on a pole.[2] Statues stared at you, patiently waiting for you to contemplate, with a silent stillness akin to their own, the Great Mystery. Unlike Willow Creek, this Church had "priests" who seemed like magicians incanting words to make God physically appear. Candles littered an *altar*. Willow Creek had done away with candles (except for rare occasions), and they certainly had done away with priests, altars, and statues. After all, aren't altars about sacrifice? And don't Christians refrain from primitive participation in sacrifice?

Like the pagans of old, Catholics had merged their worship calendar with the moon calendar and the seasons. In ancient custom, partly taken from the Celts, Catholics take autumn as a time of remembering the dead. Starting on the hallowed eve of All Saints Day, Catholics set up a "shrine" in their church with pictures of beloved deceased ones—mirroring the dying and falling leaves outside, which we would rake back into the community. For this time of "harvesting" or gathering-in, an extensive list of saints' names are sung—from Abraham and Sarah down to "holy mystics" of recent decades—and the chorus response sung is "pray for us." I found that Catholics pray for the dead as comfortably as they or I would pray for any of our friends; and, even more oddly, they ask the dead to pray for us as we would ask any of our friends to pray for us. (They might cite in their defense Jesus' claim that, before the eternal gaze of God, *all* are alive. And as long as asking the living to pray for us makes sense, there seems to be no problem here.[3]) Like our ancestors hundreds of years before even the Exodus, Sacred Heart remembers the slaughtering of a lamb at the start of spring (with the key difference of not ritually sacrificing one, though nonetheless eating one); they hold a long, elaborate feast, during which they dip parsley in salt water—to acknowledge the tears and sweat we encounter on the way to liberation—and eat bitter herbs to recall the bitterness of hard labor we endure under slavery (if to no obvious master, then to our own sins). They worship the "Light of the world" tantalizingly close to the winter solstice, the darkest day of the year. I wouldn't have been surprised to find Catholics swinging their incense at Stonehenge, as some planets and stars aligned, lofting their prayers like druids in the direction of shimmering constellations.

At Sacred Heart, those who wish to be inducted into this seemingly pagan ritualism, "catechumens," are dressed in robes at 4:30 a.m. on the first Sunday following the full moon of the spring equinox and are ritualistically initiated by being dunked in water that the priest has blessed, renouncing Satan, death, and darkness. Holding an enormous, lit candle in water, our priest incants these words on Easter morning:

> We bless you, water, by the living God, by the true God, by the holy God, who in the beginning separated you from the dry land, whose spirit moved over you, who made you flow from the fountain of paradise and commanded you to water the earth in four rivers, who changed your bitterness into sweetness in the desert, and who produced you from a rock for the thirsty people. We bless you by our Lord Jesus Christ, who in Cana of Galilee changed you into wine by a

wonderful miracle, who walked with his feet upon
you, who was baptized in you by John in the Jordan,
who made you flow out of his side together with his
blood, and who commanded his disciples that those
who believe should be baptized in you. We bless you.

Also, while not everyone would dress up in suits, the parishioners of Sacred Heart, like many liturgical congregations, had
retained some semblance of the old pagan custom of, before
entering into whatever ritual, putting on fresh, new, and fancy
clothes—symbolizing the notion of "putting on the better self."
Who thought that "dressing up" had such pagan roots? At Willow we had emphasized a contrary informality and anti-ritualism, of wearing everyday street clothes at church.

Willow Creekers—and I a few years prior—wouldn't have
been caught dead doing any of these "dead rituals."[4] But now
living within the fold of Sacred Heart, I attempted to withhold
knee-jerk judgments. Over time I began to question the rejection
of ritual I had cultivated at Willow Creek and as an evangelical
worship leader. For starters, I knew as clear as day that many of
these rituals were not strictly "biblical"—that they had developed by custom and invention over time. But I also knew that
the strict requirement for everything to be "biblical" wasn't in
the Bible. I also knew that much of what other denominations
do, even the so-called strict, fundamentalist ones, are not in fact
"biblical"—and that this is unavoidable, and, in many cases,
just fine. Most churches I know that fancy themselves "biblical,"
refrain, for example, from sharing "holy kisses" or from insisting
women remain silent in church or wear a head covering—and
these indeed are biblical commands. Some churches are so brazen
as to allow their members to wear clothes woven of two fabrics
or to eat shellfish.

In my study-visit with Rob Bell I remember him saying,
"When I talk with 'biblical' fundamentalists as to why they don't

keep these commands, I say they are either intentionally defiant of them, or they have a hidden Bible-interpreting method that they are not telling me about." Furthermore, the early Church did not use a cross as a key emblem of faith, or the Trinity as a key term for God, but most Christians do today. They didn't celebrate Christmas or place a tree in their house, but today most delight in it. The early Church, largely, did not worship separately from other Jews, but I know few Christians among those who speak of "returning to the early Church" attempting to remedy the current rift with the Jewish community. And though no evangelicals I knew mentioned that Christmas suspiciously appeared super-imposed over the date of Saturnalia or the Syrian Unconquerable Sun, or Easter over pagan holidays celebrating gods like Eostre or Tammuz, they still celebrated Christmas and Easter on the same old Catholic schedule.

Nevertheless, it has still taken me a while to warm up to the "extra-biblical," since being strictly "biblical" was a big thing back at Willow. Though in the past I had lodged many critiques against these "pagan influences" in Catholicism, I tried to let my guard down, and even take some pleasure in them. In fact, I felt there was something profoundly human about the rites and rituals. Once I gave Catholic liturgy a chance, something seemed quite "normal" about celebrating the seasons with symbolism and ritual. Something was distinctly human in solemnly blessing the bodies of the dead or bowing when entering a "sacred space." Something was just "right" or "appropriate" in lighting incense and candles to give glory, not just to the "Universe"—a popular term used by those who, seemingly embarrassed by the word "God," feel their alternate word is an expansion of the mind—but to that which is even *beyond* the Universe, undergirding it in silent majesty. In fact, if one were to walk into a Catholic Mass with knowledge of Christianity momentarily blurred, one would find there, if nothing else, a fascinating blend of rituals, built up by centuries of cultural synthesis, beckoning for interpretation—or, more boldly, participation.

Though I didn't know "pagan" was originally just another word for "peasant" or "country folk" when I first started attending Sacred Heart, I did have some vague sense that, in joining in with these rituals, I was coming back to common humanity, returning to some basic human impulse toward ritualistically celebrating both the transcendent and our mysterious life on earth. Andrea, that urban farmer I previously mentioned, though not initially from a Catholic background (she became Catholic later), also found something earthy in Sacred Heart's liturgical cycle:

> Seamless intimacy with the ecological seasons and the liturgical seasons unites the practices of the church and the earth into seasons of the eco-liturgy as one rotation of seasons. . . . Many of these traditions are like umbilical cords that nurture us with the wisdom of our ancestors deeply connected to the earth.[5]

The more I observed the Mass, the more I suspected that a time was coming and perhaps had already come in which people would see that the materialistic view of the world—with its pessimistic and exploitative treatment of the planet and living beings, its universal ban on miracles, and its humorless disdain of rituals—has only fragments of the truth. I began to suspect that people might eventually grow weary of atheism, demythologized Christianity, and modern anti-ritualism. Perhaps the environmental and social crises the world faces would lead people to take on a more enchanted view of the universe, treating it with reverence, ritual, and awe instead of utilitarian domination. Many people might conclude that paganism is the best answer, as it is renowned to revel in the rhythms of seasonal festivals, the worship of life, and the sheer extraordinariness of existence. Perhaps, though, after some long period of experimentation and attempts at rehabilitating paganism, people will then come to realize that paganism died for a reason and that, as Chesterton observes, perhaps overstating, "Christianity is the only frame that has preserved the pleasure of paganism."[6] He states:

> All that genuinely remains of the ancient hymns or the ancient dances of Europe, all that has honestly come to us from the festivals of Phoebus or Pan, is to be found in the festivals of the Christian Church. If any one wants to hold the end of a chain which really goes back to the heathen mysteries, he had better take hold of a festoon of flowers at Easter or a string of sausages at Christmas.[7]

When Chesterton penned those words a century ago (though not Catholic at the time), he was coming to appreciate the Catholic synthesis of ancient rituals, purified and resurrected in Christian form. There is a fine ring to the sound that Christianity is paganism resurrected. I had long critiqued the hubris of missionaries in not honoring the culture they proselytized—and the critique still rings partly true—but I had entirely failed to see the immense historical fact of Christianity's blending with paganism, for it was so woven in I almost couldn't see it. And instead of viewing the blend as a terrible problem, as is customary in many evangelical circles,[8] I was beginning to see it as a delightful advantage.

A Dying and Rising God

Most of the above elements of Mass, though they derail many an evangelical, I have come to see as fairly superficial encounters with paganism. But there are some deeper and more mysterious encounters that cannot be so easily digested. Not long after moving into the neighborhood and regularly attending Mass, I needed to look beyond the delights of smells and bells, the liturgical calendar and robes, and consider the Mass in its more profound intersections with paganism. I have found at least two difficult intersections.

One is that the Mass is called a "sacrifice." One of my key complaints that I parroted against Catholicism back in my Willow days, like my complaint about the crucifix, was that Catholics believe Jesus is sacrificed again and again at each Mass. And this sounded dangerously too pagan.

Second, that Christianity in general appears to elicit worship for a "dying and rising God"—one of those mythological deities studied in ancient anthropology. This is not just a Catholic curiosity, but a problem for any Christian whose eyes have landed upon a history book of ancient culture or religion. Besides having many cosmetic trinkets borrowed from pagan cults and myths, I wondered, how does one accept a Christianity that appears to *be* another pagan myth?

If you wander around the edges of the Christian world, you might hear a faint rumor about how Christianity can be discounted—if not proven unremarkable—by showing how "dying and rising gods," and the groups that worshipped them, were prevalent in ancient culture. Jesus, then, is just another product on the shelf that the latest advertiser is pitching you—no different from the resurrected gods Dionysus/Bacchus, Persephone, Osiris, Pan, Quetzacoatl, and the others. As the stories go, all of them died (or were killed) and rose in their own ways; (e.g. some gods "descended into Hades" only to return later—sound familiar?); and so some modern people think it a matter of course that another ancient religion, Judaism, eventually formed their own version of this mythology by inventing Christianity. You won't find these critiques reverberating far into the center of the Christian community, since such sounds are usually blocked from Christian ears—for they, if they were true, would threaten the uniqueness and "absolute Truth" of Christianity.

Some liberal Christians seemed to resolve the problem by changing the common meaning of "myth" to no longer mean "false," but a more neutral "sacred narrative." That way Christianity could be for them a special myth, their own sacred fable which, in political correctness, plays well with other religions, which are also deemed "myths," perhaps still worthy of their own respective celebrations. But a problem lingered for me; something about Christianity seems averse to this solution. And as I have searched, it seems there is another creative way to use the word "myth."

I am becoming evermore convinced that Christians should not be the least bit afraid of engaging this Christianity-mythology problem. It is perfectly fine, if not advisable, to know very clearly how Jesus is like the other dying and rising gods—*and, more importantly, how he is profoundly different from them.* One of the most exciting ways I've come to understand the difference is through the contemporary philosopher René Girard and his clashing with the thought of Friedrich Nietzsche. Both unpack the meaning of resurrection-gods, pagan religion, violence, and sacrifice, but each with a different spin. Girard's thought, introduced to me years *after* my becoming Catholic, gave me a fascinating perspective for interpreting not only this dying-and-rising-god question, but also the oddness of "the sacrifice of the Mass," of ritual symbolism, and of "eating the Body and Blood of Christ." His insights helped me see in the Mass something profound, not some meaningless ritual; and he offers one intelligent way to see Jesus as something besides another mythical fairy tale. I elaborate on his insights below.

Fredrick Nietzsche, a philosopher of the late nineteenth century, was among those who studied how Jesus and especially his crucifixion resemble other violent stories in ancient mythology. Nietzsche, apparently having seen a common meaning in all mythology, used "Dionysus"[9]—a dying and rising god—as a sort of overarching reference to all mythological cults.[10] He often interpreted Jesus and Dionysus in tandem. And it is *the differ-ences* between these two figures that proved most interesting to Nietzsche. He saw that the Bible, and particularly the crucifixion and resurrection of Christ, was unique among other myths in its sympathy toward the suffering victim. This is a visible scriptural thread, seen in stories like Abel's murder, the rejection of Isaac being a human sacrifice, a sympathetic telling of Joseph being scapegoated by his brothers, the psalmists' cry about oppression, the prophets' railings against sacrifice and oppression, and ultimately—for Christians—in *God becoming the victim* in Christ.

Indeed, the martyred Dionysus and crucified Christ were both "dying and rising gods," but the profound difference was in what the stories *meant*. Especially in the stories that involve bloodshed and murder, the difference is enormous. Girard narrates Nietzsche's insight:

> In the case of Jesus, the emphasis lies on the innocence of the victim and, as a consequence, on the guilt of his murderer. . . . In all of [the Dionysus stories, however] the god is not the victim but the instigator of the mob lynching . . . Nietzsche saw clearly that Jesus died not as a sacrificial victim of the Dionysian type, but against all such sacrifice . . . he understands that the Christian passion is a rejection and an indictment of everything upon which the old pagan religions were founded and with them all human society. . . . Since all human culture is grounded in this collective violence, the whole human race is declared guilty from the standpoint of the gospels. Christianity slanders and compromises life because life cannot continue and organize itself without this type of violence.[11]

Nietzsche therefore thought that the Judeo-Christian prefer-ence for the victim endangers the world by removing its sense of sacred violence and sacrifice. Mythology found ways to justify, play down, or divinize certain forms of violence; and Nietzsche thought this, at times, necessary. But the gospels explicitly depicted the violence as terrible, arbitrary, and tragic; and Nietzsche thought this a disgrace.

The gospels disgusted Nietzsche as exalting weakness, since the sympathy and praise for victims engendered in the Bible stood for everything counter to the strength and surging life of the Dionysus cult—a god whose agenda he supported. Judeo-Christian praise of meekness appeared to Nietzsche nothing more than the weak party's jealousy of the strong, their alternative form of vengeance—what he called "slave morality." "The Crucified One" continued to irritate Nietzsche, and he could not bear its disgusting victimology—and (by Girard's reading) this is largely what drove Nietzsche to a mental breakdown.[12] In his madness he would sign his letters as either "Dionysus" or "the Crucified One." But, for all his madness, he could see one thing clearly: in the Christ story, we had murdered God. We've all heard Nietzsche's famous phrase of the village madman, yelling in the streets, "*God is dead!*" But so much of fashionable atheism, often parroting these words, has missed Nietzsche's point. He is not saying the world has "come of age," or that the "God-out-there" is growing out of style, or that we are ready to move past a childish need for God into a secular world of demythologized modernism. No, Nietzsche knew what Chesterton knew: even atheists must choose their god. And he chose Dionysius, not Christ. Nietzsche saw something more grave and immense than the mere absence or death of god; he saw something that has echoes of Christ's crucifixion: "God is dead . . . *and we have killed him!*"[13]

René Girard, on the other hand, invites readers to see Christianity as provocatively as Nietzsche did (with some tweaks in understanding, to be sure), *but still love and embrace it*. Girard is a French literary critic, philosopher, and anthropologist. He was teaching literature when he decided to study what all great stories have in common. His studies thus took aim at everything from archaic religions and ancient origin-myths, like Gilgamesh, all the way to Shakespeare and contemporary literature. From the common trends and themes in these stories he derived a theory of human desire and violence. It offers an understanding of Christianity that we don't normally hear; although, as I unpacked it, it came off to me as common sense. It goes (something) like this:

1) We unconsciously imitate others' desires—our desires are "mimetic." Consider two kids in a room with one hundred toys. If one kid picks up a toy, which toy does the other child now want? Chances are, the first kid's toy. We don't just want toys, we *desire other people's desire* for toys.[14]

Take, for example, how one is prone to find a person more attractive when he or she is committed to another lover, or how jealousy enflames desire that may have been waning. Or consider the advertiser's exploitation of this—you want the soda more when the pop star is holding it; the sneakers pique interest when the celebrity is wearing them. In economics we say a thing's worth is largely dependent *on what others would pay for it*—its desirability is dependent on . . . well, how much *others* desire it. Girard describes our mimetic desire as the *triangulation of desire* because desire works between a "subject," a "model," and an "object."

The scriptures address this kind of desire. We might recall the great command, "You shall not covet (desire) your neighbor's things." That command warrants elaboration *ad nauseum*—"don't covet their house, wife, their farm, slave, ox, ass . . . oh, everything!"[15] It's as if everything becomes desirable *simply because the neighbor has it!* And this runaway desire warrants a most stern warning. And while desire is one of humanity's most dangerous skills, it is also one of its most helpful and essential ones. We could not learn and grow, for example, without this force unconsciously compelling us to imitate models. The mind is inescapably mimetic. Mimesis is the basis of all culture. The question is whether we can become conscious enough to see if we are imitating healthy people (like saints) or sick people (like lynch mobs). The tenth commandment is thus a profound psychological insight—in telling you not to desire any of your neighbors stuff, the author sees that you only want it *because they have it or want it.*

2) It is a matter of course that when desires converge—like two men fighting over a woman, or two kids for a toy—conflict and quarrels ensue. A rivalry escalates as people claw for their desired person or object. And each person's clawing mutually assures the other person that they should be clawing evermore aggressively. Rivalry is not only started, but also fueled, by the mimicking of the other's desire. Consider the apostle James's observation: "What causes fights and quarrels among you? Don't they come from the desires that battle within you?"[16]

In most stories depicting mimetic rivalry, gaining the desired person or object remains elusive. We want something but cannot have it, and we continue stumbling and failing in an effort to get it. The biblical word for such stumbling is "scandal," or "stumbling block."[17] Scandal, failing to get what we desire, tends to increase desire and intensify rivalry, leading them toward a "boiling point" or crisis.

3) Virtually all the great stories and religions address *how people resolve the tensions of mimetic rivalry.* And the most common form of this solution, by Girard's insights, is what we know as "scapegoating." This is the act of "letting off steam" to keep rivalries from boiling over into all-out war and vengeance. Be it the rival, a third party, or even a group, a relief is felt by casting out, sacrificing, or murdering a scapegoat. Girard sees this "scapegoat mechanism" as the origin of religion and sacrifice—even human sacrifice.

We humans have this ancient habit of rounding up the evils, tensions, and rivalistic desires in our community or ourselves and redirecting them onto a victim, demonizing them. The only way this becomes effective is by people remaining blind to the arbitrariness of their transference and *actually believing* that the victim is the source of evil or problem in society. It could be that a drought is caused by the presence of gypsies, or German economic hardship by Jews, or the attacks of 9/11 by the United States' tolerance of homosexuals.[18] In such cases people tend to become blinded by the mimetic desire of groups.

Consider the blind zeal of lynch mobs or the heinous collective stonings that are still happening around the world (with even videos posted on the Internet); perpetrators in such mobs will stomp or stone to death an accused person, likely a woman, casting cinder blocks upon her head until she is dead. And in an odd twist, while the mob is jostling, kicking, and filming with their cell phones, some person who just stomped on her head takes a moment to cover an exposed body part of the victim. Sacred taboos are mysteriously observed, but justice is not—just as the mob who instigated Christ's death had their sacred qualms about killing on the Sabbath. What can be said about the *shared blindness* that obscures the mind in such mobs?

A dreadful truth is that these acts of "sacred violence" bring people together. Having cast out the source of conflict or disease in a relationship or community, if this victim is effectively expelled or murdered, people become reconciled, experiencing relief or relative peace until the next crisis arises.[19] Take, for example, how Pilate and Herod, formerly enemies, "became friends" through the crucifixion events.[20] We become friends through our violence; war is indeed a force that gives us meaning, even friendship.[21]

For all of the demonic viciousness of scapegoating, it can ultimately result in a curious twist—the victim is divinized, perhaps "resurrected." We can see this in stories about Persephone, Osiris, Dionysus, Tezcatlipoca, and others.[22] A once-demonized person can quickly become divinized because of *how they, after being victimized, served to resolve rivalry and crisis*. The victim is perceived to be both the source of the community's problems and also the community's solution, and is thus divinized.[23] Consider how the gospels take the time to point out how Herod thought that John the Baptist, whom he had been seduced into murdering, was resurrected in the form of Jesus.[24]

For Christians, troubled by Jesus' seeming commonality with pagan gods, it seems to me a meaningless shortcut to say, "Well, Jesus' resurrection wins out above these others for the sole reason that he *actually* rose, whereas the others didn't." Merely emphasizing that *it happened* we gloss over the supremely important matter of *what it actually means*: does the Resurrection mean that Christians are merely more prone to believe in biological oddities? No, it means a culture-shaking reorientation toward victims and sacrifice. The Resurrection means that the poor and outcast, instead of being distrusted for their deserved state of humiliation (as in the caste and karma ideas of reincarnation), may in fact be God incarnate. And a king (or the rich), far from being trusted for good karma, may in fact be another blind oppressor, like Pilate.[25] The Resurrection surely means more than this, but not less.

Similarly, should we think the empty tomb merely means that Christians are more likely to believe in zombies and surprises from the underground? No, it means that Christians should have no tomb to whitewash, no monument to make the violent truth look pretty, no plaque which can read, "Here lies Jesus, avenge his death." If tombs—which Girard argues originated from the piles of rocks left upon stoned victims—often served as ground zero for concocting new myths in sanctified violence, like the tomb of the unknown soldier, the Resurrection is the anti-tomb.[26] That, perhaps, is at least one reason why the tombs of many holy people were evacuated at the moment of Christ's death—the tombs would no longer serve as "Crock-Pots" of the sacred.

All this is to say that resurrection had a *meaning* greater than its mere occurrence. And this meaning speaks to our long and blind history of bloodshed and killing victims.

Curiously, the Greek word for a scapegoat was a *pharmakon*, from which we get the word "pharmacy." It could mean both "poison" or "medicine/remedy."[27] This double meaning describes how scapegoating, rituals, and murders, if not done "effectively," will fail to appease tensions, and instead poisonously inflame a community. Girard identifies this word of scapegoating as an example of "Satan casting out Satan"—that is, rivalry, accusation, and lies, themselves poisonous effects of the "devil," are remedied by the Satanic "solution" of murder.[28] We also see this in humanity's habit of "solving" the problem of violence with redemptive violence. Homer Simpson's analysis of his problems is a fair analogy: "Alcohol is the cause of and solution to all of humanity's problems."[29] Seen from this social sense, we might see "Satan" with new eyes—a figure who, in our demystified day, has become increasingly unfashionable to speak about with a straight face. But, seeing as Satan is referred to as the "accuser," the "father of lies," and "a murderer since the beginning,"[30] Girard regards Satan not as some being, a ghost with horns and pitchfork, floating about our world—however much Dante-ish images might have their creative and imaginative place in art and rhetoric—but as the name for this entire process of mimetic violence and casting out victims.[31] If you watch the movie *The Stoning of Soraya M.*, which painfully depicts an Iranian community's stoning of a woman, you might be prone to call the entire process "demonic," even if you don't believe in demons. This also sheds some new light on the Holy Spirit's name, the "Paraclete"—the *defender* against the accuser.

In sum, while mythology and the Bible both portray mimetic desire, rivalry, scapegoating, and in many cases "dying and rising gods," the Bible is unique in that God is not on the side of the mob, of the accusers. God is on the side of the victim. Or, by Christian proclamation, God *is* the victim. The Cross, then, is a grand revelation, a breakthrough in the social sciences—it is like an enormous flashlight shining in darkness, "unveiling things hidden since the foundation of the world"[32]—a foundation laid by Cain and his founding murder. Through the light of the Bible, the scapegoating process, which had been at the foundation of religious sacrifice and even the maintenance of civilization itself, is seen in all its injustice, its unjustified groundlessness. We see Christ's forgiveness from the Cross not just as an act of mercy but as a psychological *fact* that tends to remain hidden to us: "Father, forgive them, *they don't know what they are doing.*"

We have long been prone to unconsciously transfer our evils and conflicts onto victims, in things as small as kicking the dog or as big as genocides. In mythology, the victimization was normally embroidered and concealed, making it harder to identify and condemn the murders and lies that cover it up. This is why the root words for mythology (*mu* and *muo*) are "to close," "keep secret," "close one's eyes or mouth," "mute the voice," or "remain mute," and one biblical word used to combat myth was truth, *aletheia*—which means "to stop forgetting."[33] This may be the reason that Chesterton hazards an oversimplification of history since Christ: "Since that hour [of Christ's birth] no mythologies have been made in the world,"[34] and no new gods have been created since his resurrection.[35] Or, we might say, any attempts at reviving gods and myths, in light of the Cross and Resurrection, cannot last long. We are beginning to see. It may take aeons to fully open our eyes, but the news has gotten out.

✦ ✦ ✦

I've begun to see the crucifix, the imagery of the Mass, and indeed the whole trajectory of the Bible conveying that we are so prone to blindness, that, even if God were to come among us in the flesh, we would respond with torture and murder. And we did. We are habituated to mimetically follow along with the crowd and pursue violent solutions (through scapegoating, war, or revolution). We see this in the Passion's mob chanting for an insurrectionist, "Release Barabbas!" And of the man who, in hindsight we know as morally innocent, the crowd chants, "Crucify Jesus! Crucify him!"[36] Coming to see this propensity in myself, I remembered an old Catholic custom from Good Friday as a child: the attendees at Mass were actually supposed to participate in calling *"Barabbas!"* out loud during the gospel reading! In the Mass, we are given space to see that we are all capable of being the terrorist, and killing the innocent.

Beyond what I felt personally in Camden, like my visceral anger and judgmental attitude toward drug dealers or men picking up prostitutes, it seemed that the Mass was plunging even deeper—echoing Nouwen again, "When they kill, we know that we could have done it. . . . For a compassionate person, nothing human is alien." At Mass, even the act of murdering God cannot be alien to you. The Good Friday ritual, where we step into the role of the mob, urges us not to ignorantly say, "If *we* had lived in Jesus' time, we would have not killed him." If we proudly claim this, we show our blindness, and thus become susceptible to shedding blood ourselves. Jesus, when he encountered people who could not own up to their propensity to kill the innocent prophet, said,

> What sorrow awaits you teachers of religious law and you Pharisees. Hypocrites! For you build tombs for the prophets your ancestors killed, and you decorate the monuments of the godly people your ancestors destroyed. Then you say, "If we had lived in the days

of our ancestors, we would never have joined them in killing the prophets." But in saying that, you testify against yourselves that you are indeed the descendants of those who murdered the prophets.[37]

Even the claim *"We* wouldn't have joined in killing" *is itself a scapegoating of the ancestors*, a false separation that proves the cycle of blame and accusation is still alive in their hearts.[38] And so we enter into the Passion liturgy with a sober awareness of our weakness, our proclivity to chant with the crowd, our likelihood to betray or deny an innocent person the moment a group begins to press upon us. *We* killed Christ. No one is above that—that's at least *one* way the Cross dissolves the walls and boundaries between Jew and Greek, slave and free, male and female. At Babel, uniformity kept them from seeing the victims of their culture; but in the diversity of Pentecost, and with the telling of the crucifixion and resurrection of Christ, each culture comes to see what all cultures share: we not only all share grace, but we also share in the complicity of murder and making victims.

The Good Friday "Barabbas" ritual also puts its participants in the place of two powerful conversions in the New Testament: Peter and Paul. In both of their stories, they are compelled to see how their collapse before the crowd's contagious anger made them a part of Jesus' murder. Even passive observers of violence are still participants. While Saul was guilty of overseeing the stoning of Stephen, this entirely unjust murder is taken as identical with Jesus' murder—Jesus asks him, "Saul, why do you persecute *me*?" The injustice of that stoning must have begun to break through to his violent and insane mind; he soon thereafter came to see the light. How appropriate that he summarized his understanding of the Gospel with the words, "Christ crucified." For Peter, the social power of the mob was so strong that he could declare in one moment, "I will never leave you," and in the next deny him. Thus, liturgically joining in with the voice of the mob during the Passion reading is a type of sober penance, leading toward greater humility. We can then begin to see that we are more often subject to the whims of a mimetic crowd than to our own will or conscience.

My parish in Camden, Sacred Heart, has enacted this memorial of Jesus' Passion in a provocative way: we walk the Stations of the Cross around the few blocks of our neighborhood, stopping at each spot where somebody has been murdered; we tell their story, pray, and read a part of the Passion. Sadly, there are too many murders to match to the fourteen stations. And during the last week of that aforementioned harvest time of autumn, when we remember all those who have gone before us, we read aloud the names of all those who have been murdered in Camden during the previous year. With each name, a family member of the murdered comes forward to bear their name, light a candle, and stand in prayer in a place around the church. It is a most horrific combination—each glowing face and candle represents a life extinguished by the nothingness of Satan. The burden of terror is too much to bear as about fifty names each year, along with their ages and causes of death, are read—for example:

> "Jason Bateman, twenty-one, shot to death;
> Ryan Harley, fifty-four, stabbed to death;
> Michelle Reynolds, two months, beaten to death."

The liturgical year ends with this horror, and the next week it begins anew with Advent, as expectant mothers come up to the front with their candles to have their internal wonders blessed.

Even if Christianity exposes our propensity to scapegoat victims, will this result in less scapegoating? The New Testament would seem to suggest it is more complicated than that;

by critiquing the sacrifices, myths, and religion that served as pressure valves for the rivalries of our society, the Gospel places the world in a kind of danger. It is like taking heroin away from an addict—things may get worse before they get better. Or, even more mysteriously, things may get better and worse at the same time.

By Girard's reading, the frightening thought of taking away the "togetherness" of religious or sacred violence accounts for much of the apocalyptic language we get from the New Testament. Apocalyptic imagery envisions that the Gospel, by unveiling things hidden since the foundation of the world, unravels much of what held the world together. Religion, after all, in its obscure etymology, might be translated, "that which binds people together." *Re-ligare* means *re*-binds or *re*-ties something that has been severed. The word root is shared with ligament.[39] If so, religion is barely separable from "culture." They are two sides of the same coin. Whatever is bringing people together, there you have "religion." And if Christ is here "against" culture, it is only because many of our cultures, at their root, unite people through a feverish hatred of the other, the scapegoat, their fear of the outsider. We might understand the Christ story as a sword that cuts the false ties that held things together.[40]

If so, there is a desperate necessity for exalting martyrs in the wake of the Gospel's myth-dissolving force: without being accompanied by a community of compassionate suffering and virtue, the Gospel will only cut and not mend. Simply, the Word of Christ needs to be accompanied by the *Body* of Christ—that community of *positive* mimesis, of a culture bound together by a different kind of "sacrifice," the "anti-sacrifice" of Christ. And so one of the Christian's tasks is not only to proclaim "Christ crucified," that we blindly murdered the Lamb of God, but also that we must remain like lambs in a world of wolves. This strikes me as one reason why the early Church had such a veneration of martyrs, and I think it accounts for the rejuvenated interest in martyrs among many attempted revivals of faith.[41] For martyrs reiterate the problem and solution we see in the gospels: the world is prone to murder the innocent, and we must continually and publically remember the witness of those martyrs to keep exposing the madness—lest we relapse into some naïve optimism or "cover up" their deaths with mythology.

While Girard is generally held in high scholarly esteem, any good theory, even a great one, has its insufficiencies.[42] My very short summary merely beckons readers to read better books about the matter. And it is an attempt to show how, for me, Girard's lens could help me see "the sacrifice of Mass" in a new, virtually anti-sacrificial light, instead of writing it off as some arcane and meaningless ritual. Through Girard's reading of the Passion, I see in the Mass both an unapologetic synthesis of some of humanity's long-held pagan traditions and customs, and something so profoundly critical that it might, in some respects, even be called an anti-religion. In the Mass, we have inherited something that is attempting to walk the fine line of proclaiming something new in the world while at the same time resisting the urge to arrogantly cast off all the previously held traditions.

The Protestant evangelicalism I knew tended to proclaim a *total* rejection of everything having to do with mythology and paganism. Modern Protestant critique of certain sacraments often comes with an air of anti-paganism. To a great extent, the early Church *did* evacuate much of the Greco-Roman ritualistic world, and was renowned for its opposition to pagan sacrifice. But it is worth paying note to how the Church didn't just cast off all "ritual" in general, as if that were even possible. We are inescapably creatures of ritual. We have long-lived customs of eating and drinking with both festivity and gravitas; we have constructed games and play that bring us together; we celebrate the rhythms of repetition, the change of the seasons, and inaugurate the season of harvest. Children too, we might forget, are often insatiably and joyfully ritualistic, wanting, for example, to be read the same book every night for months. And the Church, not because it was egregiously pagan, but because it was human, retained many of these rituals commonly shared with pagans.

But on a deeper level, we must account for one of the most central rituals in human history: sacrifice—animal or human. And, as discussed, this arose to counteract the problems of mimetic rivalry and murder. If we are going to expel from our world the demons of violence and vengeance *and account for the ritualistic and mimetic nature of humanity*, we are going to have to continually engage in healthy and explicit ritual.

In "the sacrifice of Mass" we find that *there is no more need for sacrifice*. The Lamb *was* slain, and we no longer need to get hyped up for the next sacred thing. To illustrate, James Alison contrasts Christian worship with violent sacrifice and scapegoating. He contrasts the Eucharist, what he calls "True Worship," with its emphasis on the *Real Presence* of Christ there, with a Nazi rally:

> In the Nuremberg model, the central apotheosis has to be produced by careful orchestration, a deliberate build up of fascination and mimetic intensity in the worshipping crowd, so that in their eyes the Führer really does acquire an aura and a divinity. In the case of True worship . . . there is no apotheosis to be produced, no whipping up of emotions in order that we glimpse the crucified and risen lamb. Exactly the reverse. Part of the effect of the achievement having already been achieved, is that the crucified and risen Lamb *is just there*. . . . So we can relax, because we know he's just

there. And relaxing is exactly the reverse of a mimetic build up of fascination."[43]

This is describing a core *effect* of transubstantiation—the belief in Christ's Real Presence. Instead of building up an anxious need for sacrifice—our vengeful reprisals that "somebody's got to pay" for the hatred inflaming our hearts—the real, forgiving presence of Christ in "this is my body, given for you" serves to center and calm. In it, we are in the presence of the Divine Victim, who is forgiving us. Again, the eucharistic "host" means "victim."

And since human violence is most conspicuous in its *group* forms—the lynch mob, the stonings, the Nazi rally, the riots—it only makes sense that one attempted solution has arisen, the Mass, which is an attempt to remedy humanity by weekly gathering a potential lynch mob and habitually disarming them as they look upon the One whom they have murdered and who is *constantly loving and forgiving them.* This is one of the best reasons for Christianity to reject mere individualistic applications of faith—of church at home—insisting upon *gathering as a group.*

In many great stories, a scary beast gets defanged, deflated, and disarmed, and the protagonist can then, surprisingly, even become friends with it. A recent illustration of this is in the movie *Howl's Moving Castle*, in which the old, mean, and immensely dangerous witch loses her powers; the hero, once oppressed by her, instead of wreaking vengeance, befriends her and takes her along on the journey. Loving the enemy might also mean appreciating her and even learning from her, perhaps even borrowing some of her customs and culture. This seems to be what Christianity did with pagan sacrifice. It triumphed over it, defanged it, and thereby has no inherent antagonism toward using the word "sacrifice" or any other pagan elements.

Another way to illustrate this comes from a story of a Jesuit missionary in Africa.[44] The missionary was preaching, and some nearby villagers accepted the Gospel. They drew some conclusions from the story and decided to take their homes' small idols to the priest. With a tone of contrition and embarrassment they handed these carvings over to the priest, asking for him to burn them. He said, "Well, why don't you take them home, and allow them to lose their power over you. And when you've done that, then you can bring them back to me." So they did; the idols eventually lost their sacred meaning, the villagers found them as no threat, and then they brought them to the priest. "Shall we burn them now?" they asked. The priest paused, and replied, "Well, now that we look at these things, they are kind of pretty. Nice carving work. In fact, beautiful. Why not keep them around in aesthetic appreciation?" And so they did.

Anticlimactic and boring ending, right? No drama! But that's exactly the point: God holds no fundamental antagonism toward creation—*at all*; there is no big, evil, *Anti-Force*, or *Anti-God*, against which Christians should imagine God as fighting.[45] All creation has *Goodness* as its source; even the bad things are just corrupted good things. Like my Belizean experience of relaxing in the presence of creation, of unpacking my mental bags, the Christian need not feel any anxiety about being on some "side," some "againstness." If the Africans threw their idols into the fire, they would have kept the antagonism alive; the rivalry would remain in their hearts. This is why the orthodox center of Christianity criticized its members for burning down pagan temples, and has rejected iconoclasm—that rowdy habit of running into temples to throw their images, statues, and art upon the fire.[46] These anxious acts, however much they might seem on the surface like Moses casting the golden calf into the fire, misconstrue the Christian revelation about pagan sacrifice. To burn these temples and images down is to participate in the same mimetic cycle of rivalry, scapegoating, and "sacred" violence.

I love the Jesuit's story, since it illustrates how the Church, in its development over the centuries, was able to welcome so many pagan elements into itself. The Faith has no fear, for it is full of affection and love. If Faith "hates the world," it is only that "world" of destruction, murder, and lies—the world of Satan—under which is a creation to be grateful for, to celebrate in. And all parts of this world can be brought in to be refurbished in Love. If this sounds too much like "anything goes," then we are getting closer to the affront the Gospel initially sounded like; its messengers could be caught saying, "Any foods are clean; its what comes out of your mouth that makes you unclean"[47]; or, "everything is permissible, but not everything is beneficial"[48]; or, as for food sacrificed to idols, "We are no worse if we do not eat it, and no better if we do. Be careful however, that the exercise of your freedom does not become a scandal to the weak."[49]

Modern people often dislike the early Christians for failing to be pluralistic or multicultural in their revulsion of pagan idol worship and their contrary insistence that "Jesus is Lord." Perhaps much of this resistance to the Greco-Roman pagan pantheon (and to the violent empires of the world's Caesars) was not due to arrogant hubris or stubborn piety, but, if Girard is right, it was about having seen the violence underneath the temples, myths, robes, priests, and rituals. Having seen this, Christians sometimes looked like atheists.[50] For they weren't adding one more story to the world's myths, but they were unveiling the violence hidden in all of them.

As I close, my reader may be wishing for a more specific dealing with this phrase, "the sacrifice of Mass." In a word, the "sacrifice of Mass" is not about repeating or reenacting Christ's death, as much as *making it present*. The word "remember," said in the Mass, means this.[51] The more I have come to understand this word "sacrifice," the more I have seen that Jesus' death—and the Mass that remembers it—is a "sacrifice" in the way that Jesus is a "lord." These were terms stolen from the language of the day and subverted, or we might say *inverted*. Indeed, virtually *all* of the words basic to Christianity are stolen from the pagan world, and must be understood for the *new meaning* given to them, not with their previous bad reputation.

James Alison points this out by noting that the words "worship" and even the word "god," taken from pagan language and culture, are terms that can only be understood as shady metaphors.[52] The Fourth Lateran Council of the Church, an ecumenical council of Church bishops, held in Rome in 1215, described this by saying, "Between Creator and creature no similitude can be expressed without implying a greater dissimilitude."[53] That is, even when we think we have said something very true about God, it is likely more *untrue* than *true*. So our words like "worship," "sacrifice," "lord," and "god," taken from the violent imagery of mythology, can never be thought to be spoken with the common meaning of that word. They say, "It's *kind of like this*, but even more *totally unlike it*." Christ's death is a sacrifice, but even more entirely "un-sacrificial."

Theologian William Cavanaugh demonstrates the Christian redefining of "sacrifice":

> *Eucharistic sacrifice is the end of the violent sacrifice* on which the religions of the world are based, for its aim is not to create new victims but rather martyrs, witnesses to the end of victimization. Assimilation to Christ's sacrifice is not the continuation of the violence and rivalry needed to sustain a certain conception of society, but the gathering of a new social body in which *the only sacrifice is the mutual self-offering of Christian charity*. Martyrs offer their lives in the knowledge that their refusal to return violence for violence is an identification with Christ's risen body and an anticipation of the heavenly banquet.[54]

Regarding another word associated with violence, it is a scandal to some that Christians use the word "lord" about Jesus—and for some good reasons; just as the word "sacrifice" calls to mind violent transference of sins onto a bloody, slain animal, the title "lord" brings to mind patriarchy and domination. And those who balk at the word "lord" claim, sensibly, that Jesus overturned such oppression with his humility. But the greater Christian tradition has opted not to throw these words out, but to redefine them, even with some bitter irony. Why not make our definition of "lord" the most unlordly, humiliated, and powerless man—a man who was tortured to death? The Christians could get away with this because Christ in his powerful love outdid all the other lords. And why not call the event that unveils the injustice of scapegoating, and signals the end of sacrifices in civilization, the *real* "sacrifice"?

Perhaps the Christian tradition opted to retain, but redefine, these words because they represent certain absolutes in human nature. Even if we refuse to venerate the Lord Caesar, we still need some ultimate role model to set our standards by. Even if we reject having a lord, we still will unconsciously have one. As Bob Dylan insisted, "You gotta serve somebody." Perhaps, because the word has grown out of colloquial use, we might say "lord" just doesn't do anything for us—it signals nothing absolute. Maybe so. I played with calling Jesus one's "president" in my previous book. And that has some particular meaning in our context, especially seeing how quickly our populace recently bowed in deference to the president's wishes to invade Iraq and Afghanistan. For many Christians, their president's command, "Let's roll,"[55] eclipsed their "Lord's" imperative to love their enemies. I welcome reconsiderations of the "Lord" language, but a title for the crucified and risen Christ must retain political tones, and it must symbolize allegiance and affection—otherwise our titles for Jesus will fail to break our subconscious enthrallment with the power of "realistic" governments and authorities. Some have recently tried to replace "lord" with the ostensibly innocuous and generic "god"; but even before the Church could get its hands on this word, "god" carried just as much violent baggage in history.

This problem transitions us to our next chapter—we might find in Christianity a profound revolution, something that, depending on what you mean by the word "religion," is an "*anti-religion*." We might say it is dissolving the boundaries and fake-sacred structures of religion and sacrifice.[56] But how then do we deal with the fact that the Catholic Church *is a structure*, that it has a defined and sacred dogma, it has its rules and regulations, and it most certainly appears to us as a confined religion? If Jesus is as profound as Girard seems to imply, wouldn't his movement dissolve religion? How did Jesus' revelation ever become "organized religion" at all? Shouldn't the Christ-event break open our religious categories enough to do away with "man-made" denominations?

EIGHT:
THE SEARCH FOR NO ACCENT:
OR, THE IMPOSSIBILITY OF NONDENOMINATIONALISM

When I first showed up to Camden and to the Catholic Church, I was about as wide-eyed and "ecumenical" as you can get. With the late-college deconstruction of my ideas of God in full swing, so many pathways felt open to me; I had visited Mennonite, Methodist, Pentecostal, Baptist, Presbyterian, Brethren, and Episcopalian churches. I protested with Quakers, anarchists, and atheists. I sometimes conducted interdenominational ad-hoc communion events as I led evangelical-style worship at retreats and festivals. I took silent retreats at Catholic monasteries. Besides reading Thich Nhat Hahn's *Living Buddha, Living Christ,* and digesting the *Tao te Ching* several times, I formed a relationship with a nearby Zen monastery soon after arriving in Camden. I attended their Zen rituals enough that their Roshi "master" offered me one of their properties to start a joint retreat house.

In light of all this spiritual "openness," one might think it a tragic narrowing that I would "become Catholic," that I would become one thing instead of many. But I do not see it this way.

I don't regret my passion for interreligious engagement *at all*; it is still alive in me. But in this chapter I want to discuss a seriously problematic attitude that was deep within me. You might crudely approximate the problem with the phrase "the arrogance of pretending to have no bias," or, "the closed-mindedness of open-mindedness." Allow me to explain.

Like most people I know (especially those from the Midwest!), I grew up believing I did not have an accent. Everyone else did. The Philadelphians said "water" like "wooter"; Bostonians amused us with their odd, "pahk the cah" talk; Tennesseans said "warsh" instead of "wash"; Californians startled me with their unstartling cool; and Southerners—well, we all know how they talk. But me, I was from the center of the universe, the norm from which everything else deviated. Everything else was exotic.

It takes some big brainwashing to become that small minded. It took me a while to find that I too have an accent, I too have a culture and even an ethnicity. For some Americans, like me, this takes some time to learn. "Mainstream" American culture is, even on a global scale, so pervasive that it makes many Americans believe that the United States sets a kind of standard—cultural, economic, and political. We can be lured into thinking that we live in a "free market," and "free society," one in which there are no rules—at least not any exotic or unfair ones. Many Americans live in the belief that, compared with the rest of the world, their culture is benignly "normal." It sets the standard, and therefore does not have an "accent."

Being neutral, Americans go out to find "ethnic" food, as if American food is somehow without origin or ethnicity. They talk about certain people being very "cultural," as if Americans themselves were detached from history and without cultural inheritance. Having done away with meddling restrictions and traditions grounded in cultural preferences and taboos, Americans believe that they live unencumbered by the hassle of old-fashioned custom and dogma. But is this really true? I would argue that nearly every nugget of the "restriction-free" American culture works to obscure the fact that there are definite intellectual and cultural preferences, taboos, and restrictions that go with being an American, but they are hidden by what I would call a "cult of neutrality."

One quick example of the cult of neutrality, and how it does not necessarily jibe with reality, is the North American Free Trade Agreement. Since it was intended to better trade relations between Canada, the United States, and Mexico, one of the results of NAFTA was that American farmers became free to sell corn in Mexico. Very quickly, Mexico was flooded with cheap foreign corn. But Mexican farmers could not compete against US corn, in large part because the US government has so vastly subsidized the Corn Belt here and the oil used to grow and transport corn. Not "free" to restrict importation, countless small farmers throughout Mexico, who maintained a diversity of several hundred species of corn, soon became obliterated by a cheap mono-crop.[1]

If there was "freedom" here, it was a kind of savage one. It included the freedom to demolish, if one was strong enough, anything like fair competition, and to establish monopoly. The result was countless ruined lives. It was really just a matter of course that an economy not free to restrain this corn-flood with tariffs would result in the disinheritance and displacement of thousands of farmers—many of whom now come to the United States to look for work.[2] We tend not to think about this connection, since words like "freedom" or "no rules" make us coo and sway gently like a rocked baby.

This is but a small example of how the "no rules" philosophy actually means, in practice, immense *restriction* of a fatal kind. True human freedom includes the freedom to restrict and set rules for the good of the community. By obscuring this fact—and insisting that the primary rule is that there should be as few rules as possible—the individual or group capable of destroying the other wins. If someone retorts that this is simply survival of the fittest, I will concur, and say we have degenerated into animals. Survival of the fittest is not competition held in check by any idea of justice; it is simply war.

To use another example, scholar William Cavanaugh notes that when Britain occupied India, the British insisted on calling Hinduism a "religion," which meant that Hindu culture, customs, and traditional laws became relegated to the private realm. Because of this, the occupying British culture could appear "public," secular, and neutral. The fact that British politics, culture, and occupation were deeply influenced by Britain's own tumultuous religious history was not admitted. This allowed the British to push their specific form of politics and culture, while the "religion" of the backward locals could remain in check.[3] A posture of neutrality, which conceals bias, is a boon to the powerful.[4]

Cultures are always maintained not merely by their "freedoms" but by their restrictions, rules, and customs; cultivation is always sustained by the principles of best farming practice; religious groups are always eager to ask the question of what guidelines make for "right worship." To be against rules is to be against the fun of games, since games are made by rules. But in our day, hoping to escape restriction, we find many promoting anti-rules and anti-religion; they have the gall to promote the fun of games while denigrating the rules it takes to make them. We can demean those who are seeking to maintain rules—to save their farms, customs, unions, guilds, cultures, climate, religions, or ecosystems—failing to see how *we* are thereby the ones pressing for the restriction-to-shame-all-restrictions in the first place. Destroying religious taboos, whether or not one thinks it is a good idea, often means constructing a newer, bigger taboo: "Thou shalt not have taboos."

Another way to illustrate how a seeming neutrality can mask a whole set of biases is by noting what passes for an insult these days. We call someone "dogmatic" when we wish to imply that they are too rigid, when it is perhaps closer to the truth that their dogmas collide with ours. We consider being called "opinionated" an insult; but we don't use this word because someone happens to have an opinion—but because they have the wrong one or are pushy about it. We call being "ideological" a sin, not because having ideas is a sin, but because we think our ideas are better than others'. We accuse politicians of getting "political" when what we actually mean is sectarian—not that they had fallen into the heresy of having a political thought. I also hear people speak of "propaganda" as if it were a bad thing, and I wait for the punch line, and it never comes. If I don't like propaganda, it is because it is propagating an idea I don't like, not merely because it attempts to propagate. (The word "agenda," too, is often used like this.) Or, we hear of a group being denounced as "a cult," when it might have been more precise to call it a *bad* cult, for isn't the collective worship of *anything* a "cult?" When we scoff at the manipulation of children by youth pastors in movies like *Jesus Camp*, calling it "indoctrination," it might have been clearer to say that children should be taught better doctrines. All of these instances abuse language with a linguistic sleight-of-hand, distracting the mind by saying a disagreeable idea has a bias, whereas the magician remains unbiased.[5]

I have heard this attempted neutrality parroted countless times in fashionable phrases, each with their own unique twist: "I'm not religious; I'm spiritual," or, "I like Jesus, not the Church," or, "I'm a Christ-follower, not a Christian," or, "I don't interpret the Bible; I just do what it says," or, "I am nondenominational." Many denominations appear to have been constructed under this desire to escape the encrusting of tradition and bias so as to return to "some original purity." Consider some denominational titles: "Disciples of Christ," "Church of Christ," "Church of God"; it seems we've all finally come to an end of all that religious mumbo jumbo and gotten back to basics. Each title seems to be a silver bullet that can destroy the monster of traditionalism! Why hadn't Catholicism, throughout the Dark Ages, ever considered such a clean solution? But some quick research reveals that things aren't so neutral or so plain. No denomination is exempt from building a tradition, even if it is the tradition of attempting to escape tradition.

We can find this search for neutrality popping up centuries ago. Take Johan von Wesel of Erfurt early in the 1500s. "I despise the pope, the Church, and the councils, and I worship *only Christ*."[6] I recently heard someone talking similarly, trying to disguise his brand of Christianity by insisting it wasn't a brand; he called it, "Jesus, *nothing added*." In another case, I was speaking with a fashionable pastor who refuses to categorize the church he started, insisting it is "postdenominational." He contends that this position is more subtle and meaningful than "nondenominational." After asking him three times to explain that distinction I couldn't decipher the difference. I don't wish to go so far as to critique any of the particulars of these denominations (and, seeing as manifold goodness saturates the universe, I can say without reservation there are good things to be found therein); I simply wish to call our minds to this partiality to appear impartial.[7]

At Willow Creek I was proud to distinguish myself from all the other denominations by being "nondenominational."[8] If Catholicism ever momentarily passed through my mind, I would complain, "Why can't they just follow the Bible like I do, instead of embellishing it with traditions and dogmas?" Today this claim appears to me about as ignorant and prideful as saying, "I don't have an accent, but everyone else does." It was a way of ignoring history and a way of ignoring my own traditions and dogmas. I couldn't see, in the evangelicalism in which I immersed myself, that it was *evangelicalism*, a particular interpretation of the Bible, a particular angle with a particular history—a mixture of Reformed Calvinism, American pop culture, and Baptist theology with some other ingredients. Now, when someone tells me they are nondenominational, I know I can fairly guess they mean "Protestant evangelical."[9]

Evangelicals are not the only ones who sometimes operate under the belief that they have no accent. You can't swing a dead cat around our society without hitting someone insisting, "I'm not religious; I'm spiritual." The "spiritual" are too enlightened to participate in dead rituals and believe dogmas just because a tradition told them to. They insist, "Religion is *man-made*." The awkward reality here is that I agree, but I don't think we have many other neutral options—and I happen to fancy numerous things humans have made (homes, for instance). I never hear these spiritualists follow up to clarify what their "spirituality" is made of, since it is even worse than being composed of the centuries of people building upon a tradition. They don't want to admit that their "spirituality" is *self*-made.

But there is a positive conviction in the spiritual person. Usually he or she has identified "religion" as a source of division and conflict, and the logic of escaping such divisiveness goes something like this: all of those rules and dogmas are a recipe for conflict and bullheadedness; rules are a way of galvanizing a false sense of security and identity over and against the other; instead, the "spiritual" person will leave behind the dogmatic and take the gentle. These folks won't be caught dead saying something like, "It is against my religion to ____." For religion, the spiritual person says, leads down the path of judgment, hypocrisy, and ultimately of violence; it is the hobby of Pharisees; dogmatism makes you a ravenous dog; to be religious is to walk down the path that ends in the stoning of a woman in Iran or the drowning of a presumed witch in Salem; the mindless rage in the eyes of those mobs is the full dose of religious ecstasy.

Ultimately, this spiritual person's refusal to adhere to "religion" while remaining spiritual can come from a sensitivity for victims and an unwillingness to take sides in what they see as meaningless feuds. Sometimes, however, it does just the opposite. By not clearly naming its beliefs, the supposedly "neutral" mind can dangerously drift into violence. For to claim to have arrived at "neutrality," to be above the fray of blindness, sounds a lot like accusing our ancestors of murdering the prophets, as discussed last chapter—*they* are guilty of a religious blindness that *we*, in our enlightenment, would never succumb to. *They* are religious, but not I; where they are dogmatic, bound-by-rules, and violent, I shall prove to be a free, gentle lamb. To declare immunity from the forces of scapegoating, an easy claim of superiority over religious ancestors, is yet another form of scapegoating.

One clear example of neutrality's propensity for violence comes to mind in the preparation for the war in Iraq. As things were reaching their boiling point, I tried to convince my fellow, invasion-supporting Christians that we—even as the "good guys"—were all too capable of destroying innocent life, and we ought to consider Jesus' love-of-enemies a great caution. But advocates of the war argued, in return, from what they thought was the neutral center; I was bringing "religion" into politics, whereas they were perfectly unblemished by ideology. I was "politicizing" Christianity; what they were doing with Christianity (if anything) was harmless. Religion must sit in the corner as we run off to war, for religion is too closed-minded and violent.[10]

I am identifying a trap from which it is hard to escape. One thing that has kept me from staying stuck in this sense of anti-religious "neutrality" or "spirituality" is to unearth the deeper and broader meanings of the word "religion"; religion is a daily, cultural activity from which no one is exempt. Religion is as inescapable as having an accent. As mentioned, one of religion's best, however obscure, definitions is *that which brings and binds people together*.[11] All sorts of things bring people together—be it a football game or a liturgy. It can be done through lots of beer, lots of shouting, lots of turkey, or lots of prayer. If professional football or nationalism "bind people together" even more closely than a Mass, should they not be considered "religions" in some sense? Religion is not just dogma; it is culture, it is language, it is customs; it impinges upon economics and politics.[12] This is why those words "cult," "culture," and "cultivation" all work together. The difficulty of using this broader definition is that virtually *everything* can then be considered at some level "religious"—extending its meaning into potential meaninglessness. But, by trying to use the word more accurately, instead of wasting time pretending we've escaped from religions, rules, and dogmas, we could just be more forthright and honest about the ones we hold. Chesterton puts it well:

> There are two kinds of people in the world: the conscious dogmatists and the unconscious dogmatists. I have always found myself that the unconscious dogmatists were by far the most dogmatic.[13]

Even anti-dogmatism is a dogma, just as "free trade" is a restriction.[14] Open-minded people are closed-minded about being closed-minded. White is a color, not a lack of color.

We therefore find ourselves in this difficult paradox that, even if we want to have a constantly open "beginner's mind" (as I wish to), this means that we have roped ourselves into a binding rule, a rule we will have to submit to in our moments of pride and arrogance. That "s" word, *submit*, though it conjures all sorts of mental pictures of slavery, harsh rules, and mindlessness, and though our modern world militates against it, is still something that even the most anti-institutional of people will have to do.

Even anarchist communes still submit to rules—*many*, in fact—even if they are rules in favor of egalitarianism. Coming to see this helped me at least open my mind to consider Catholicism's oft-scorned rules. I might argue with them, but I could no longer simply dismiss them for being rules.

I was once talking with a person who fancies herself an anti-dogmatist. She said, "I wish the Church were not so anti-body, anti-sex, anti-material, anti-this-world. We should have a tradition that is earth-affirming, affirming of the body," and so on. I told her that one of the ways the Church has done that is by denouncing, for centuries, the Manichaeans and Gnostics. (These groups have been renowned for disdaining matter, the body, and sex, preferring a disembodied vision of heaven.) She had not yet seen the paradox that something good might be "closed." It is profoundly open-minded, pro-body, pro-earth, pro-material, pro-sexuality to say, "It is against my religion to be a Gnostic, for they are heretics."[15]

One of the best ways to come to grips with the claim that neutrality is not really neutral is by looking at the biblical tradition—God's sense of fairness is expressed by a *bias for the poor and oppressed*. God "shows no partiality and accepts no bribes. He defends the cause of the fatherless and the widow and loves the foreigner among you, giving them food and clothing."[16] Candidly naming a bias for the weak and oppressed, a bias which you can find echoing through the prophets and the New Testament, strikes me as a safer, more honest form of impartiality.

Throughout the New Testament, we see militancy against the blindness of the rules of the Pharisees—a class of people whom many critics today coarsely associate with Catholic priests. The idea goes something like, "Jesus' movement directs us away from rules to a world of freedom and grace, and a priestly caste gets in the way of this." The Protestantism I experienced used that logic to promote a "justification by *faith*," not works—a claim akin to "spirituality, not religion." But even Paul, whom many Protestants tirelessly use as a mascot, knew that there was still some paradox between being "freed by Christ" and "freed from the Law"—for he also called us "*slaves* to Christ."

Paul's honesty about the nature of Christian freedom has helped me deal with both the idea, "I'm not religious; I'm spiritual," and its corollary, "Shouldn't we all just love each other and call an end to religion and dogmas?" There is a beautiful simplicity to such broadmindedness, but anybody who really wishes to get down to this kind of business will soon ask, "What do you *mean* by love?" For there are countless unhealthy, empty, and destructive ways to express "love." (I, for example, know of many Christians who argue that you can love an enemy and kill them at the same time.) Once someone starts to answer the question of what love is, he or she will need to not only give some values or principles, they will need to give *concrete examples*. They will have to come out of the clouds of universal values and into the real world. This helped me see how Christianity gets great mileage by placing at its center not a mere idea but a *Person—this* specific example of Jesus is where we begin defining Love.

This also helped me see why the Catholic Church bothers defining and celebrating a canon of saints; if Christ interpreted God, we have to keep identifying the best interpretations of his interpretation. Naming saints, people who have interpreted the life of Christ by living in their own unique way, is like being able to sight down the barrel of a long rifle—the longer the rifle is, the more accurate it is; the shorter the barrel, the more dangerous and haphazard. Even if you are nondenominational you eventually have to come to terms with your own biases and selected influences. This is why home-church movements, however much they appealed to me after leaving Willow, look to me now more like a short-barreled shotgun—which perhaps they see as useful in combating Catholic zombies. They attempt to escape slavery to traditions and hierarchies only to construct mini-hierarchies with comparatively little accountability, to repeat the traditions of early-America revival pastors, and to think they have freshly reconstructed the early Church.

In addition, when you refuse to name a canon of saints, the dominant culture will inevitably give you some—they will be printed on your money or billboards, glow from your television, or appear wherever your eye turns. Fashions will guide choices; fads will dominate ethics. In such a case we change our minds as often as we change our hats. Humans, religious or not, are always asking the question, "What kind of person ought I be like?" This is a fundamental force of culture—that of mimicking role models. If you accept no concrete library of role models, of saints, you are prone to collapse into mimicking whatever is current. If we cannot escape mimicry, we must seriously reflect upon just who it is we should mimic.

In the end, I found that the temptation toward a "spiritual, not religious" mindset, pretending to have avoided the biases of religious tradition and quarreling, was a desire for *unmediated experience* with God. I was eager to insist that the Church and its traditions were a secondary reality to my immediate "relationship with Jesus."[17] If this is true, who needs (or wants) a Church, or priests, or sacraments? Let's encounter God directly, without meddling interpreters. Back at Willow I used to imagine the foolishness of Catholics as they would bow to a priest and receive Communion. I had an artist friend who wanted to paint a picture of a Catholic kissing the ring of the pope, while Jesus wept in sadness in the corner. I thought it genius. Though I couldn't put it into words, my pride of nondenominationalism meant I thought I experienced God without tradition's mediation—and certainly without all its props, physical objects, priestly hierarchy, or rituals. Casting off "religious" things like the Church as "man-made," hurdles between me and God, I couldn't see that I was still going to inevitably invent new hurdles, new mediations between God and me—perhaps ones even more burdensome than the ones Peter, the disciples, and the apostles handed down.

The Church as (a Necessary, Mediating) Sacrament

Sacraments, from the perspective of our neutral-seeking culture, may appear as just another set of oppressive rules and restrictions: "How dare we confine the Infinity of God in an object, a ritual, a place!" This objection misses the fact that not all mediations are hurdles to bypass; eyeglasses, for example, are a form of mediation that help and clarify, not restrict. Words can mediate and clarify truth. Rules are a form of mediation that create our games.

Coming to see that mediations are inescapable—and that, in fact, some are quite beneficial—I had to call a cease-fire to my former ridiculing of sacraments, these *"mediations* of God's grace." One of the largest Catholic mediations I've had to wrestle with is the Church itself—for the Church is called "the universal sacrament of salvation."[18] Especially in my college years, I had experimented with some ways to skirt the Church. "I'm not a Christian; I'm a Christ follower," was a subtle way of saying I didn't like the idea of needing a Church and its traditions. I had also tried on the exceptionally fashionable detour around the Church by referencing the "kingdom of God" as some sort of contrary allegiance to God, different from the Church. In my formative evangelical years I had barely a vague notion of why I would use these phrases. I had a foggy idea of Jesus' *real* spiritual movement, and I preferred to call that "the kingdom." Fighting against such a beautiful, inclusive, and universal kingdom were those stupid, small-minded religionists who, always talking about "the Church," are biased with power and hierarchical institutionalism. If asked to be more polite, I might have said that some people prefer lots of bells and whistles, robes and titles, but I, unblemished, prefer just good old spirituality. That was about as intelligent of a reading of "high Church" as I could manage.

But then I found that Jesus' idea of the "kingdom of God" was not so universal. If you asked any first-century Jew, including Jesus, what the kingdom of God meant, he or she would have likely said "Israel," that historical group known through the twelve tribes, which had fallen into disarray. This is why Jesus, in rejuvenating Israel—the kingdom of God—appointed *twelve* disciples.[19] But a difficulty arose over time: the "kingdom of God movement" couldn't simply call themselves "Israel," for much of the Jewish community did not accept Jesus as their Messiah.[20] Nevertheless, Jesus saw his twelve as the fulfillment of Israel, and the Church comes from this. I mention this bit of history because the attempt to move away from the "Church" by invoking the seemingly more universal "kingdom of God" is simply a confusion of language. If anything, "kingdom of God" might appear *small* and limiting, since it so closely implies Israel, and "Church" may appear more open and worldly, since the word (*ekklesia*) came from the most democratic form of public gathering available throughout the Mediterranean.

Given my Protestant background, a most startling way for me to think through the Church has been Mary. She has often been chosen as a symbol of the Church because she carries the Word of God *within* herself; she was the first to worship the Son by making space for him and giving birth to him. She might be seen as a mediator of Jesus in the sense that she is like a mother bear, protecting her cub. This was a necessary outcome of Jesus' being born as a baby, and not as an alien spirit beamed down from Saturn. As the Church sought to make paintings and statues in honor of this great birth, artists ran into a problem: you could not simply depict Jesus lying on the ground, out in the rain. He must be in the arms of the one who birthed him.

> You cannot suspend the new-born child in mid-air;
> indeed you cannot really have a statue of a new-born
> child at all. Similarly, you cannot suspend the idea of
> a new-born child in the void or think of him without
> thinking of his mother. You cannot visit the child with-
> out visiting the mother; you cannot in common human
> life approach the child except through the mother.[21]

Catholic teaching, with a straight face, still calls Christ the "head of the Church," while knowing that someone brought us that gift; that's why Mary is sometimes called the "neck" of the Church.[22] However much we wish to embellish Jesus with notions of "the cosmic Christ" (and I do), Jesus was still an earthy, "mediated" person, birthing a universal movement of grace from a *limited time* and *place*. Thank God his parents handed him over to the world in such good shape; and thank God their parents were shaped in the tradition of Abraham and Sarah. Our parents handed down our lives to us, and we must honor them. Even God has a mother.

And so the Church developed from a finite group. It was not merely a philosophy, but more like a movement—or even a family. To become a Christian did not mean you merely started believing something. It meant that you became a part of the *Body* of Christ through a *physical* ritual—Baptism. It meant that you were part of a growing, international, trans-ethnic body—a "holy nation, a people set apart." In short, you couldn't become a Christian without joining the Church. St. Cyprian put it like this: "You cannot have God for your Father if you have not the Church for your mother."

I was shocked to learn this as I entered into my first serious studies of the Catholic Church—in a graduate ecclesiology course. With all my Protestant instincts in full force, I walked into such a class excited to speculate as an individual, and without reference to history: what do *I* think the Church *should* be?

The syllabus would entirely shatter my hopes; it would ask, what *is* the Church, apart from any of *my* whims or desires. The course would cover the historical growth of the Church from its beginning, examining how and why it developed the way it did, including its leadership structure of bishops, deacons, and priests. How boring and disappointing! But this approach brought to mind perhaps the greatest theological advice I have received thus far, from Dr. Christopher Hall at Eastern University. After I complained to him about the annoyance of Church structures and traditions, he said, "You should take the time to understand something thoroughly before you go about trying to change it."[23]

I had been so arrogant to complain about the hierarchy of the Catholic Church without ever knowing how or why it was made. I knew nothing of its numerous councils, its historical development, its fissure between the East and the West, the reason for its priesthood, or any of its reasons for retaining some rituals and abandoning of others.[24] I critiqued Catholic theology without ever reading Catholic theologians. I had only an adolescent version of Church history—a history that Stanley Hauerwas calls the "New Testament and now"; anything in between the early Church and today is probably just stupid and easily dismissed. In many Protestant circles, and certainly in my own Protestant formation, this view is seen in their always wanting to emulate "the early church," and *only* that. But I never faced the obvious fact that the early Church *did* have leadership structures (however dynamic and evolving). It even had—dare I say it—"hierarchy" or "authority," in the twelve and seven, and the *diakonoi, episkopoi,* the *presbyteroi.*[25]

In short, I had been prepared to denounce and leave behind a long, winding history without knowing any of it. Far from being the more open-minded and patient critic of closed-minded religious tradition, as I fancied myself, my position had actually been one of extreme myopia.[26]

Things became interesting when I studied the Eucharist, learning how it developed, not as a dispensing of sacredness for individuals (as if the Church were a sacrament vending machine), but as a *collective performance* of the unity of the global Church.[27] From the early days, for many Christian gatherings, Eucharist was a physical expression of the unity of the Body of Christ, of people who had physically joined through Baptism. So the Church wasn't meant to just share some belief or philosophical unity, but a physical, enacted, sacramental unity; or, as Paul writes, we share *one bread, one loaf* (1 Cor 10:17). The Eucharist is described with language we normally use for family: "This is my flesh and blood." We say that of our family because we share *physical* connection—DNA, mom, dad, grandma, grandpa. That's why the phrase "Body of Christ" means *both the Church and the Eucharist*. The definition is intentionally blurred together. It is not coincidental that when my Protestant mind had a very low view of Jesus' physical presence in the bread and wine (indeed, I ridiculed transubstantiation), I also had a very low view of the Church's physical global unity.

The more I looked into the Eucharist, the more I saw the *physical* sense of the Church, the "visible Church," expressed in the idea of "apostolic succession"—this is where we get those words in the Nicene creed, "We believe in one, holy, catholic, and *apostolic* Church." All denominations know that the apostles in some way or another served Jesus' movement by spreading the Gospel and so on. But they weren't just servants; they were joints and sinews that connected the Body of Christ. For this reason, a rule started to develop, even around the time in which the gospels were penned, to not enact the Eucharist apart from a bishop's oversight.[28] Church leaders justified this by citing Jesus' granting of leadership to the apostles and doing his ministry with them.

All leaders that came after the apostles needed to be somehow connected to them; often, this connection was made physically through a ritualistic laying on of hands.[29]

My egalitarian critics might think, as I did, this leadership "succession" was a mere grasping for power, the beginning of the fall of the Church, an evil "institutionalizing" of what should have remained a spontaneous, unstructured movement. But I've come to find this unfair. Just as neutrality has a bias, even a movement promoting the most unconditional openness and love must prevent violence and "closedness" from poisoning its flock. What was the Church to do when a Christian gathering popped up down the street, declaring, perhaps, that the "love your enemies" stuff is too much? Or that welcoming Gentiles is too licentious? Wouldn't the apostles find themselves in that paradox of openness? They would be constrained to say, with kindness and gentleness perhaps, that such closed-mindedness is excommunicated!

When describing the apostles, many of the texts in the New Testament put Peter first in the list. And we know of the many passages where Jesus singles out Peter in a special way—as in that famous passage when he hands him the "keys of the kingdom," and when he says, "On this rock (*petra*, Peter's nickname), I will build my Church." Whether Jesus-scholars conclude he actually said this or not, some of the Church used these passages to warrant a certain pattern of leadership. It also created a precedent for a pope, for a bishop among the many bishops who acts as a "vicar of Christ." As Jesus was just one person, so too the Church continues to use one person as a physical sign of its global unity; while there exists a great diversity of parishes, priests, deacons, bishops, and lay people, they all cohere and all point to a center. And while the center, the "head," of the Church is, of course, Jesus, it has been a long-standing tradition, supported by those Peter-passages of the synoptics, to see the diversity of leaders come to a symbolic point in "the successor of Peter," who apparently brought his apostleship to Rome. And that center has the duty to serve to unify the Church as a "bridge builder" (that's what "pontiff" means).

Now, to consider apostolic succession—this passing down leadership authority from the apostles to subsequent bishops—as a peaceful, unbroken chain through the ages is historically unreasonable.[30] Furthermore, the accounts *immediately* after Jesus are less than crystal clear on how Church leadership all came to be.[31] At times there has been confusion and conflict about who had the proper authority to be a bishop or pope. Especially in later centuries, one can't help but despise many of the viciously sinful popes. Dante, after all, threw many of them into hell. There are few sins that have hurt the Body of Christ more than "ecclesial ambition"—that desire to become a shepherd in order to become a boss. But, just because the shepherd's role can be corrupted doesn't mean it can be done away with.

Apostolic succession means a lot. As I said from the start, just as our language always has an accent, so too our truths always come to us through the finite and imperfect conditions of the physical world. It might sound surprising to say that postmodernism's insistence that all truths are mediated led me to the Catholic model of Church—but it is not far from the case. For me, dealing with Jesus means dealing with the Body of Christ, the historical group Jesus handed on to us. For, in turn, this group hands Jesus to us. However perfect I might think Jesus is, an imperfect gang has passed him down to us. The rock the Church is built upon was a shaky foundation. But this is a great advantage:

> He chose for its corner-stone neither the brilliant Paul nor the mystic John, but a shuffler, a snob, a coward— in a word, a man. And upon this rock He has built His Church, and the gates of Hell have not prevailed against it. All the empires and the kingdoms have

failed, because of this inherent and continual weakness, that they were founded by strong men and upon strong men. But this one thing, the historic Christian Church, was founded on a weak man, and for that reason it is indestructible. For no chain is stronger than its weakest link.[32]

I certainly never heard anything about the "visible Church" at Willow Creek; the words still come off as new, awkward, even contentious to me. I would have thought the contrary, that it is obvious that a Church can be a valid Church without connection to a bishop's authority; Willow's board of elders seemed sufficient to me. After all, I thought, Jesus said, "Wherever two or three are gathered in my name, I am there." But in learning of the Church's history, I slowly began to understand why Willow always attached "local" to their use of the word "church"—it was a way of bypassing this history of a *global* body stemming from a *local* source, Jesus. I came to see that talking only about a "local church," disconnected from the global and historical body, is like constructing a building with four walls but no roof— and still insisting upon calling it a house. I suppose, if one changed the definition of a house for the sake of including this poor little square, it would then qualify. But, that's just it: you've changed what it means to be a house. Similarly, the definition of a church, even in the early Church, meant being connected to the leadership of Jesus and his apostles. You couldn't just be a disconnected, nondenominational start-up; you needed to be a part of the Body of Christ, the chain back to Jesus.[33]

This boundedness of the Church was the most scandalous offense to my nondenominational approach. I had never come to see that the Church, from its early years, even if it claimed to be something "universal" (that is, "Catholic"), came from something finite, local, and small. It came, so it seems, from Jesus. This rhymes with the paradox of language described above—even openness takes shape as a form. Even if one were so bold to say something like, "Christianity destroys religion," Christianity is *still* inescapably going to look like a religion. Every attempt at unifying a common humanity will still have shape—for we must ask, *what* unifies it? Will it be a unity built on scapegoating or human sacrifice, as previously discussed? Or will something much more humble bind us all together? It is one thing to critique the *way* the Church took on shape and structure, but it is another to pretend that it could have avoided taking on shape at all.

One enormous reason the Church has bothered with being this bounded body is the Incarnation. If God has come in the flesh, in a concrete, finite, and historical event, and started a *body*, not a philosophy, it was a matter of course that what followed would (or should) be concrete, visible, and united physically over time. The history of the Church is strewn with rejected heresies that denied Jesus' physicality, and this rejection also applies to merely "spiritual" notions of Church.[34] I suppose it only makes sense, then, that the postdenominational pastor I mentioned thinks that Christianity is too Christocentric; I suppose I too would drift, or run, from the Catholic Church if I could no longer tolerate the Incarnation.

Tradition and Scripture

Long before even glancing at the Catholic Church, I read John Dominic Crossan, a biblical scholar who deeply hurt my evangelical feelings; he declared that many of the New Testament passages are early-Church propaganda to support certain leadership structures. He writes:

> Those stories [of Paul's visions], then, are primarily interested not in trance and apparition but in power and authority. . . . I propose that other stories in the gospels, ones from before the execution of Jesus—the

so-called *nature miracles*—serve the same function. They are not about Jesus' physical power over the world but about the apostles' spiritual power over the community.[35]

"No way!" I thought. "The Scriptures don't have an *agenda*!" But this dilemma got *especially* interesting, years later, when I saw the Catholic Church still using those passages in support of "Peter's successor." I initially tried to deal with this by assuming that somewhere in between the lines is the *real* Jesus who, we all know, would never have done something so small-minded as to construct a hierarchy. After all, he was some sort of egalitarian anarchist or something, right? Let's sift out the propaganda and follow the real Jesus.

This is a very rough road to go down. For over a century, some scholars have been splitting the hairs of the gospels to find the real, historical, uninterpreted Jesus, a Jesus not encumbered by tradition. Many seem to think they will find here a "spiritual but not religious" Jesus. It has been quite messy—trying to find which passages were not tainted by the bias and selection of the writer is like trying to discern which words I speak don't have an accent.[36]

But, as Jack Miles puts it, trying to find the Jesus "behind" the text is like trying to look through a stained-glass window to see what is behind it. The point of the stained glass is not to see *through* it, but to *see* it![37] The particular danger in trying to reconstruct the historical Jesus—one free of interpretation—is that we are still *interpreting* the gospels—we trust ourselves to construct a new canon within the canon. Perhaps we think the "real" Jesus only said things against organized authority and we can thus dispose of the hierarchical "Peter-propaganda"; but what if the churches that composed and edited those gospels actually thought the two could fit together in some sort of mystical paradox of leadership? Maybe Jesus actually *did* bestow keys of the kingdom to Peter *and still* had a suspicion of religious authority. It is hard to say. But we do know that whatever gospel verses remain in the Bible, all passed through the Church's filter—perhaps with their own agenda, perhaps with Jesus' agenda.

I have slowly veered from the approach of "finding the Jesus between the lines," coming to terms with the inherently biased version of Jesus in the Bible. I have come to see that the Bible is a Church product—or more particularly, the product of *certain* churches. Perhaps a better word is that the Bible is a "canon"—an edited compilation, a selection of certain books and not others. The Jesus handed down to us is an *interpreted Jesus*. Certain things he said were emphasized, and certain things were edited out; as John declares, "Jesus did many other things as well. If every one of them were written down, I suppose that even the whole world would not have room for the books that would be written."[38] The gospels give us a Jesus interpreted and filtered by several different writers and communities, all of whom served the liturgical and story-telling needs of the Church.[39] And over time the Catholic Church rejected some of these interpretations, and we call those gospels "apocryphal." For better or worse, the communities reading the *Gospel of Thomas,* the *Shepherd of Hermas,* the *Gospel of Bartholomew,* or the *Gospel of Peter* were rejected from the Catholic norm.[40]

To think highly of the Bible is to express some trust in the tradition that selected it; a high view of the Bible implies a high view of the Church.[41] This realization slowly dissolved my held belief in *sola scriptura.* It is not that we *should* believe in "scripture and tradition," as if Catholics like to believe in extra, miscellaneous things. It is that *we cannot* believe in scripture alone; it is simply impossible to believe only in scripture. For scripture *is* a tradition. It is one of the traditions of the Church.[42] The very reason we call scripture inspired is because the Church, over time and in its traditions, told us to. I had it wrong when, at Willow, I would wonder whether Catholicism was justifiable by the Bible. It seemed evident that Catholicism was not in the Bible—and I was somewhat right. But I couldn't see why. For the Bible was *in Catholicism*.

But many of the Evangelical churches I attended always seemed to use the Bible as if it came down only from heaven and not also the pen of humans, confusing "divinely *inspired*" with "divine." For some, the Bible is a constant and never-ending polemic and protest against organized religion, a rock to be thrown against the Church—a hammer to hit on the head of those who gave it to you. Martin Luther once wrote, "The word of God is beyond comparison superior to the church."[43] There is a golden glow of truth to this declaration; but it is easy to forget that what he meant by the "Word of God" was *his interpretation of it*. He wished to remove James and Hebrews since they didn't suit his agenda. *Sola Scriptura*—but *my* version of it please. One can at least appreciate his audacity.[44]

By seeing the inherent connection between the Bible and Church tradition, I am not here arguing for the relative goodness of either. That could be debated elsewhere. I am simply noting how I could no longer easily use the Bible as some sort of pry bar to break up the Church and its traditions. As Stanley Hauerwas has stated, "You can critique the tradition, but only by using the tradition." That the Bible is one of those very traditions leads me toward a more patient and modest posture with the Church, and particularly more capable of engaging with their "non-biblical" traditions and dogmas. Chesterton illustrates this point well:

> To an impartial pagan or skeptical observer, it must always seem the strangest story in the world; that men rushing in to wreck a temple, overturning the altar and driving out the priest, found there certain sacred volumes inscribed "Psalms" or "Gospels"; and (instead of throwing them on the fire with the rest) began to

use them as infallible oracles rebuking all the other arrangements. If the sacred high altar was all wrong, why were the secondary sacred documents necessarily all right? *If the priest had faked his Sacraments, why could he not have faked his Scriptures?*[45]

If I thought the gospels compelled me to distrust Church structures, dogmas, traditions, and hierarchies as somehow "un-Christian," as evangelicalism did, why shouldn't I in turn distrust the gospels, since that very Church edited and passed them down?

And the more I came to see how the New Testament was not neutral but (inescapably) biased, the more the Catholic position appealed to me. It appeared more durable for the coming onslaught of historical-critical scholarship, which will continue to demolish, if it has not already, any sense of the scriptures having no particular agenda. The evangelicalism I know will have few resources to live through this critical shakedown; for evangelicalism was *founded* upon the claim to have bucked tradition and bias, opting instead for "the Bible," as if the two were separable. A storm in Belize brought my worldview down to earth; it made possible for me to see the Incarnation coming in actual flesh and the miracle of matter. But another storm has struck me, and it brought my understanding of the Church and the Bible down to earth as well—making them more visible, more solid, more human. The challenge is whether, like the Incarnation, we can also see the divine in the human.

Conclusion upon Tradition, and Its Constructive Works

Coming to see tradition as inescapably woven into the way we think, so much so that even the Bible turned out to be a tradition, my little soul entered into a state of shock. Is there no solid, objective foundation to think from? In the words of Gerald Schlabach, I was seeing, "there is really no place outside of some tradition from which to judge the adequacy of traditions."[46] If this chapter sits between Friday and Sunday, within that dark "Holy Saturday," it is about feeling a fearful absence of any perfect, ready-made answers. Without some kind of golden ticket like, "The Bible is our sole foundation!" it can feel like we are left without something comforting to fall back on, without some obvious trump card whenever we want a definitive answer. Even the claim, "Jesus is our sole foundation," is still challenged—for we must ask, *whose version* of Jesus?

This felt about as frightening as jumping from my Belizean boat, in the middle of the night, into a dark abyss of ocean. But, as I did with my night snorkeling, I tried to turn this fear around. I began to see the wild, even with its dangers, as an adventure— that *any* form of Christianity, even nondenominational or "spiritual" ones, risks trusting in the tradition which handed it down.[47]

The Catholic Church's pattern of "scripture and tradition"[48] offered me a way past the dead ends of neutrality and *sola scriptura*. This alternative, as I see it, looks something more like democracy—that is, a process that receives and builds up truth over time, like the build-up of topsoil. Or, like science, the Catholic long-view of truth involves the trial and error of centuries, the observations and conclusions of many people throughout the progress of time, as they gather the best (hopefully not the worst) of cultures on their pilgrimage to the "heavenly city." The Church is a "pilgrim Church." Becoming Catholic for me has not merely meant arriving as much as journeying—a process of becoming a participating member of an "open narrative," a Church unfinished.[49]

Catholic tradition, as a type of "gathering in" the best of the old and new over the centuries, is therefore not just a mere democracy of those living, but it includes what Chesterton calls the "democracy of the dead." It is a body through time. Even if the Church can edit and compile its canon, it cannot just make stuff up out of thin air. It started by being constrained by Jesus' commands and apostles. And ever since it has had to engage that dreadful difficulty of listening to the Spirit, listening to what was passed down, and listening to our current context. "The Tradition is really a centuries-long, authoritatively guided, but still-continuing conversation, not a pure datum that might be reducible to a hefty single catechism."[50]

But anyone who has tolerated living in anything akin to a democracy—whether among three hundred million people or three—knows that things never feel as democratic as it says on the tin. For every group, no matter how egalitarian, will still need some structure. In this regard the Catholic Church calls itself a "hierarchical communion"—not because it loves that hated word "hierarchy," but, for all the reasons discussed in this chapter, it is impossible to be a purely neutral "communion."[51] Decisions, structure, authority, and engaging things that appear objectionable, be they cover-up bishops or befuddling dogma, are never easy to navigate. And to that difficulty I now turn.

NINE:
ON BEING PART OF A TERRIBLE ORGANIZATION:
OR, HOW TO TREAT THE CHURCH LIKE A (DYSFUNCTIONAL) FAMILY

The church, like Peter, is both a stumbling block and a cornerstone. It is the latter only when it is consciously contrite for being, and having been, the former.[1]

I began attending Catholic Mass, not only as the war in Iraq was beginning, but also as the heinous pedophile scandal was reaching the world's ears. As people set about interpreting these tragic events, one obvious complaint has emerged: it is time to abandon this institution that is failing us. Given the atrocious nature of child abuse, the tone of many of these criticisms sounded similar to George W. Bush's stark dichotomy proclaimed in the wake of the 9/11 terror attacks: "You are either with us or against us"—either ditch the Church or be considered complicit in the molesting of children. In this case, to bow to a priest or even walk into a bishop-sanctioned location is a betrayal of the innocence of children. The wounds are deep enough for many to revile even the sight of a priest, seeing their robes as visible reminders of a cover-up. If our last chapter covered the problems we must face with the Church mediating truth, this priest scandal makes the problem even more concrete—might it be the most progressive mark of our day to despise even the sight of a priest, to do away with all of these "corrupt hierarchies"? Put another way, if my claim of the last chapter was that tradition is inescapable, we might still wonder here, shouldn't we at least do away with *this* particular Catholic tradition?

I certainly had to ask myself whether this horrific evidence for the corruption of the Catholic Church was reason enough to write it off completely. I had to ask whether staying was culpability in pedophilia, or at least quiet acceptance. To work it through, I followed two trains of thought. The first is quite simple, and something that every Catholic (and critic of Catholicism) should know: the Catholic Church is not merely made up of its bishops, priests, and deacons, but it is *all* of its baptized members.[2] Our grievances are with a *part* of the Church, in the abuses in the priesthood and its oversight; and while this is an important part of the Church, it is only a *part* of it.[3] Beyond that, this extremely important grievance is with *part* of *a part of* the Church—that is, with the leaders who either molested children or covered it up. The great majority of Church leaders did nothing of the sort. This is not a linguistic sleight-of-hand, for it clarifies the critique from a vague condemnation of the whole to a portion of it. For what could it mean to critique a billion-member body, without crudely and unjustly overgeneralizing?

In my second accounting of the problem, I examined how the scandal was playing out in public discourse. One of the greater curiosities was how some of those (rightly) blowing the whistle on the cover-ups were calling for not only a stern disciplining of the perpetrators, and, of course, an appropriate public justice, but full-blown excommunication. Cast them out! I agreed that grave discipline was called for. But here is the awkward part: a severe response implies hope that the Church might become *more* hierarchical—or at least use the one it has more firmly. For all of the valid complaints about the hierarchy of the Catholic Church, in this scandal we were not essentially complaining about a hierarchy—but the lack of a good one. Having a hierarchy is partly what makes the abuse crisis *a scandal* for the Catholic Church. How could there ever be such a thing as a widespread "Baptist cover-up," since it has virtually no hierarchy to cover anything up? The other institutions or groups which are home to abusers do not maintain much of an organizational structure compared to the Catholic hierarchy, and therefore they have much less authority to critique.

Grievously, all sectors of civilization display some rate of child abuse (perhaps disqualifying them from being "civilized"), some certainly more than others, averaging for men, appallingly, around 10 to 20 percent (as known offenders).[4] The rate among priests is around 4 percent.[5] So why do we despise an organization whose priests show lower than half (or even a fifth) the average rate of abuse? The answer is simple: their tradition claims to know better, and they can do better. I agree with this. But I found it odd that the especially vitriolic voices who hoped this scandal would serve as a fatal dynamiting in the Church's demolition are actually hoping the Church will be *more* churchy—to adhere *more* to its teachings and scriptures (where any abuse of children is regarded with violent hatred by Jesus),[6] and *more* effectively use its hierarchy to discipline wrongdoers. Even the champions of "inclusivity" were calling for millstones around the necks of pedophiles. As with my last chapter, we find that even "openness" is a dogma; even the liberally open-minded denounce many things—and some things even violently and appropriately. Thus, it seems to me many critics of the Church are offering an unreflective defense of the Church's authority. While immediate reactions might lead many to simply leave the Church whole hog, at a deeper level we might be asking ourselves if this is throwing out the baby with the bathwater.

I have begun to question my habit of throwing around vague, categorical rejections of hierarchy, since we might at any minute call on that very authority to discipline the wrongdoer. Similarly, while it has become fashionable to loathe the Church's harsh language about the pervasiveness of evil and sin in the world—its bleak rhetoric about "original sin"[7]—these detractors reignite that language the moment after they are done deriding it. Likewise, it is easy to forget that all of these objections about women not being able to join the priesthood, whatever your position on the matter (I have tended to share a sympathy), are attempts not at destroying a priestly hierarchy, but *increasing* its membership!

Lastly, when I heard critics saying that the current scandal is cause for abandoning the Catholic Church, I found it very significant that these acts became roped in with a broad bundle of the general evilness of the Church throughout history. The critique expanded from something specific to an overall condemnation. In assigning and compiling blame for the evils of the past, be it through Crusades or Inquisitions, I found critics tended to stand back, point across the whole time line, and call the Church one unified den of thieves.[8] *But,* when faced with the Church's accomplishments, like the biblical canon or its catalog of saints, those same critics insisted that the Church is a disparate spattering of disunity which cannot be considered unified throughout time; the Bible, even if compiled and ratified by the Catholic/Orthodox Church, is a vaguely generic "Christian" document, constructed as a donation for future Presbyterians and Baptists, or whomever, to use as they see fit. In this view, the evils belong solely to the Catholic Church, but its goods are everyone's. We can completely condemn Catholicism for its inquisitors, but we cannot exalt it for its saints. The Catholic Church is too disparate to praise as one thing, but plenty singular to condemn. We have no problem drawing a straight line of responsibility from the Catholic Church today to the Crusades; but for some reason we won't draw the same connection to responsibility for the preservation of Western culture following the collapse of the Roman Empire. This contradiction seems to me like the scapegoating process rearing its head again, but on the level of tradition—*I* would never have been an inquisitor; *I* would never have been so small-minded as those crusading ancestors; and so *I* stand above, against, and separate from them.

Hanging in There

I have gotten some mileage out of that provocative claim, "The Church is a whore, but she is our mother."[9] While she—in both her leaders and her common members—often dirties the bathwater, she is also the one who championed water sanitation and told us how to wash up. The Church indeed has a track record of stoning some prophets; but it has also illuminated to our minds this harsh trend, and is aiming to fix it. We've all heard the old and easily misused proverb to hate the sin, love the sinner. In applying this to the Church, I'm not only suggesting to love it but to hate its sins. I'm coming to see a more profound reality: that the Church's tradition is the very thing that told us what sins *are*. This has helped me forgive the Church for her evils—for the Church taught me forgiveness and how to identify evil. (And, we are all prone to forget, that forgiveness does not mean approval. Exactly the opposite is the case: forgiveness implies the act *is wrong*.)

In such a situation I can see how "honor thy father and mother" can be helpfully applied to the Church and the traditions that have come before us. Given that the Church always fell short of its own ideals, very early in its history it had to clarify that *its sacraments are meaningful apart from the quality of the priest dispensing them*—that we must not let the priest taint our perception of his priestly role.[10] (In the military, they might say, "You salute the *rank*, not the person.") This was what the "Donatist" debate was largely about. Back in the fourth century, the excessively pious Donatists looked down upon any clergy who had forsaken Christianity under torture during Diocletian's persecution (AD 303–05). Donatists thought they should either not be allowed back into the Church or, at least, their sacraments should not be considered valid. Persons baptized by such lapsed priests insisted on being baptized again. They wanted a saint's Church, not a sinner's Church. But the Catholic Church, despite Donatism's popularity, rejected this position.

A critic might think the Church was only giving excuses with this declaration—now the Church could live more comfortably as hypocrites. Certainly the Donatists had a legitimate fear that welcoming lapsed priests back in might make a slippery slope into a sinful and compromising Church. But to reject Donatist piety is also a profound statement about how to relate to the failing institutions around us; when you see the supposed defenders of goodness fail at being good, this doesn't mean we leave them behind. To leave them is partly a failure of grace and mercy; but it is also a failure to see that you cannot improve something if you abandon it. Failing to recognize this has led to numerous divisions in the Church, since hopes for a more pious priest, a community with less warts and better people, lead people to think they can find a better church around the corner at any moment.

Having joined the Catholic Church in the midst of its scandal, eight years ago, I am under no false pretenses about the current quality of its members and leaders. But I am convinced that anything true the Church's critics have said is drawing upon the Church's own tradition and teaching, which I am quite clear on. Besides its denunciation of pedophilia, it is a tradition in defense of the widow, the orphan, the defenseless, that also denounces the extortionist, the murderer, the abuser, the liar, and (even more loudly than its critics) the usurer. But even more importantly, the Church's tradition has also acknowledged that these sins are in all of us to some extent, cautioning us to mingle our justice with mercy and grace.

One of humanity's perennial problems is that of the neighbor's grass being greener. A foundational tenet of the Protestant mind is that we can start over and construct a better church than the current one. I certainly felt this. But I've also come to see how this vibrant but misguided urge doesn't just come from imagining better alternatives, but from our *own* development, from within.

I'll take my own house as an analogy. I moved in seven years ago. It had been abandoned for a while. When my wife and I first walked in, she cried, feeling it too disgusting and sad to be livable. There was a big hole in the ceiling underneath the upstairs bathroom, the walls were disgusting, and the kitchen stunk with cockroaches. I didn't feel like crying, though, since I had been learning some construction skills over the years. I could see through the decay into a remodeled beatific vision. So, we risked it and moved in.

But there was a problem that came with my solution. I remodeled rooms, learning more and more along the way. I found better ways to demolish, plumb, wire circuits, mud and tape drywall, and install trim as I slowly renewed the house. Every room is a watermark in my evolution of skills—the earlier being poorer than the later, more skillfully done rooms. I sometimes feel doomed to live in a museum of trial and error; as I walk to the kitchen I see errors I now know better about—sanding divots in hardwood refinishing, bad corner beads on drywall. And these marks of my own development *make me want to start fresh, buy up a house next door, and do it all over again.* Until I find the time to fix them, I am constrained to live amid the mistakes.

This seems to me to be how life in the Church works, being part of a body through time. Much of my Protestant formation had this good and bad element to it. So much of the rigor and excitement that gushed from the pulpit and into the average person often made me into a more energetic Christian, causing me to renovate my life. (And to be sure, I am deeply grateful for the inspiration those church leaders passed on to me.) Their growth is real, their hearts are sincere, and their convictions are often searing with passion. But such progressive spiritual growth can make your neighboring pew or church look populated by sloths, or the pastors and priests look like hypocrites. Surely, we think, it's time to start looking for better surroundings. I see numerous Christians taking hold of the Gospel, or some isolated parts of it, in this way, and it makes them want to leave and start a better church, one that has more of this, less of that.[11]

The way through this problem is by learning a difficult skill: the ability to reform *with continuity*, the ability to repair without resentment, to live patiently amid a construction zone. Theologian Gerald Schlabach outlined this skill in his book *Unlearning Protestantism*. In it, he did not try to make Protestants turn Catholic; his aim was more modest. He hoped to bring before the reader's eyes a dying skill that our unstable world needs more than ever: stability. As a world of illiteracy would need a group cultivating proficiency in language studies, so our world of fragmentation, divorce, war, and increasing Church-splits needs a demonstration plot in stability. We need to see ways to renew crusty traditions without reinventing the wheel—or worse, without always separating ourselves from the very group we hope to improve. In short, Schlabach aims to find ways for people to "hang in there."

He points to the Second Vatican Council as one great place to see this skill in action. In the decrees of this long gathering of bishops from around the world, he sees a spirit of progress without resentment, of reforming something without deforming it. The council faced the challenging mixture of appreciating the modern world without mirroring its fashions or repeating its mistakes. Its thousands of attendees all had to work, over a period of *years*, in a democratic tension with each other, voting and debating, revising documents and statements that would come to shape Church policy for the coming decades. This process was further complicated by the difficult necessity to honestly and democratically work within their tradition—tradition, again, being "the democracy of the dead," by Chesterton's definition. Historian John W. O'Malley, S.J., declared of this council, "I know of no other such assembly in history that undertook such a bold reshaping of the institution it represented, and did it with more fairness, serenity, and courage."[12]

While I certainly share sympathies with folks who criticize the Church for being insufficiently democratic, I also urge us to imagine another group composed of about one billion people, like China. Can you imagine China holding a multiyear conference with thousands of representatives, inviting hundreds of outside "observers" to comment and criticize, and then attempting to shape its future policies? It's no easy task. "At least sometimes when Rome seems intransigent, this is not so much because it is being Roman as because it is being global, and in its unitive ministry it must represent the consensus of the global church."[13]

Denominations and Divisions

Almost all the churches I have visited, spanning many denominations, have critiqued the prevalence of "consumer Christianity," "buffet Christianity," and "church shopping." In an age of gluttony, I often hear, we have carried this sin of consumerism into the Church. I tend to agree. But some suspicious listener might wonder if this rhetoric against consumer Christianity solely serves the pastor's desire for stable tithers. After all, stable church members who aren't arbitrary consumers make for steady budgets. But whether or not this complaint against church consumerism is there just to keep seats warm, I think we can all still admit that churches will struggle to retain membership in such an unstable, mobile culture of consumer Christianity.

Historian-theologian Dr. Eugene McCarraher has said something that can apply not just to economics, but to the Church: "Talking about consumerism is a way of not talking about capitalism."[14] We are prone to talk about symptoms, not the heart of disease itself. When we condemn "consumer Christianity" we are failing to talk about the root problem, about what caused this attitude. Discussing the shopping around for denominations is a way of not talking about the real history and divisions of the Church. If we are going to talk about shopping around for churches, we are going to have to talk about why we have come to see different denominations as similar "products" sitting on the shelf for our choice and preference—as if Baptists are bran flakes and Catholics are corn flakes.

Full-bodied consumerism pays no mind to the history of a product; it does not matter whether it says, "In Business Since 1897," or, "Just Started Yesterday!" Who cares? "Maybe they are *better* if the company just started!" we exclaim. It rarely crosses our minds to ask, "Where and how was this product made, and was it made under just conditions?" No, the consumer simply tends to bark, "Does this work for me, and is the price right?"[15]

Similarly, in the church-shopping mindset of today, the history of a denomination is becoming utterly obscured and irrelevant. A church is just one among many products that can, at any moment, lose one's support and patronage if something better comes along. Our companies abandoned all our factories for Southeast Asia and their slave-cost labor, and we can vacate any cathedral for a shinier denomination down the street.

In my journey from Protestant evangelicalism into the Catholic Church, I've come to see that, to truly escape the lure of consumer Christianity, we must stop seeing denominations as brands, or as "diversity in the marketplace." Historically speaking, denominations are not diversity; they are *divisions*. Each division is the sign of an instance in which reform was aborted —perhaps by the stubbornness of both sides—for separation. I lament these divisions in light of the New Testament's command that the Church is to be *one*, a unified whole.

It pains me to consider how some denominational schisms were formed on matters of justice. Some denominations were created, for example, over the issue of slavery, like the southern Baptists splitting from the northern Baptists. And yet, even though the Southern Baptist Convention officially declared remorse over racism in 1995, those denominational dividing lines exist to this day.

But besides splits over justice issues, obviously many splits have been over theology. One key example of a theological breaking point for Protestantism was over "salvation by works." I mimetically parroted this critique. But, once I was forced into proximity with Sacred Heart, I became tired of lodging general complaints, and I looked at the *Catechism of the Catholic Church*. I found that Catholics resolved the issue quite plainly: they agreed in "justification by grace through faith" but acknowledged with the epistle of James that, "faith without works is dead." There were some further details to name, and I don't want to paper over the difficulties of the debate, but in the end they cited their scriptures and reasons, and that was the end of it. The Protestant protest was no longer obvious enough to warrant a division. (In fact, Catholics and the Lutheran World Federation have come to an agreement that this issue is no longer a matter of difference.[16])

In another case, many Protestants have taken the idea of "the priesthood of all believers"[17] as an obvious reason to split with a Church that has priests. But upon bothering to study the Catholic position, I found they wholeheartedly declare that all baptized form a "common priesthood," but for reasons that stem from very early Church tradition, from (supposedly) Jesus' words in the gospels, and from other scriptures, they see it is not so simple as abolishing a ministerial priesthood.[18] When this problem turned from obvious to subtle, my criticism didn't disappear, but turned from aggressive to patient.

But another difficulty with priests remains—women and ordination to the Catholic ministerial priesthood. Entire books on both sides are intelligently written on this, and I hesitate to only briefly mention a topic that is a deal breaker for many. Speaking for myself, I was particularly scandalized by the absence of women priests, since Willow Creek had numerous women taking center stage. But, then again, I realized Willow didn't have *priests*, for they had also done away with the altar. So it wasn't that at Willow "I believed in women priests," because I didn't even believe in *priests*. So, I was forced to slow down my critical posture and listen in on the history of the debate, to learn what priests *are*.[19] The position from the Magisterium is that Christ instituted men for the twelve apostles, and it is therefore "not possible" to ordain women into the bishop's or priest's role.[20] At the same time, they maintain women are part of the "common priesthood" and play numerous other roles in the Church. Many are not compelled by these traditional arguments, and I must say I do not feel wholly at peace with the tradition either. But it is a tension over which I am not yet willing to leave, and I highly encourage critical observers to respectfully learn about the historic symbolism of priests and the history of the debate.[21] Some feel they have mastered the nuance of the debate and are ready to ordain women (or as a woman, be ordained) and thereby are excommunicated. I don't feel I am in such a position of mastery.

Especially as I started attending Mass at Sacred Heart, I began to wonder about this habit of splitting from a church over matters of theology. It was no longer so obvious and easy as quoting the Bible to counter or overturn tradition—and then walk out with a posture of clear triumph. As stated in the last chapter, the Bible is a selection of the tradition. One of the more helpful ways to interpret these disputes and divisions, for me, came from Chesterton's pen. He puts it well enough to warrant a longer quotation:

> [A]ll the other revolts against the Church, before the Revolution and especially since the Reformation, had told the same strange story. Every great heretic had always exhibited three remarkable characteristics in combination. First, he picked out some mystical idea from the Church's bundle or balance of mystical ideas. Second, he used that one mystical idea against all the other mystical ideas. Third (and most singular), he seems generally to have had no notion that his own favorite mystical idea was a mystical idea, at least in the sense of a mysterious or dubious or dogmatic idea. With a queer uncanny innocence, he seems always to have taken this one thing for granted. He assumed it to be unassailable, even when he was using it to assail all sorts of similar things . . . The Calvinists took the Catholic idea of the absolute knowledge and power of God; and treated it as a rocky irreducible truism so solid

that anything could be built on it, however crushing or cruel. They were so confident in their logic, and its one first principle of predestination, that they tortured the intellect and imagination with dreadful deductions about God, that seemed to turn Him into a demon . . . . They had assumed the Divine foreknowledge as so fixed, that it must, if necessary, fulfill itself by destroying the Divine mercy. . . . Then came Wesley and the reaction against Calvinism; and Evangelicals seized on the very Catholic idea that mankind has a sense of sin; and they wandered about offering everybody release from his mysterious burden of sin.[22]

This account of divisions in the Church will not satisfy all. But it certainly stung me, as I had long used my Protestant evangelicalism in just the isolated, rash, and misguided way he explained. Chesterton here helped me look at the proliferation of denominations, amid a Church called to unity, and understand why groups keep breaking apart—and it is partly due to rashly overemphasizing one forgotten part of the tradition against the other parts, tearing down a fence without being clear on why it was put there.

One cheap way forward would be to say that we should forget the whole schism thing by just going to the church across the street, thinking all schisms are created equal. But few Christians, when pressed, could adopt this. Even back at Willow, though they spent little time trash-talking other denominations (since that might have drawn unwanted attention to their place among them), they certainly drew a strong line of critique against Jehovah's Witnesses and Mormonism. Even nondenominationalists still think some denominations are off.

For those not yet warming up to mending denominational divisions and re-converging with those from whom they split, a modest recommendation is to research one's own denomination's history of division—to understand why Methodists broke from the Anglicans, Quakers from the Calvinists, the Anglicans or the Mennonites from the Catholics, and, one of the oldest divisions, the East from the West.[23] Perhaps the deepest studies in Church separation look at how Christianity, first a Jewish movement, became separate from Judaism—possibly the source of all other divisions.[24] A slew of efforts to reunite is peppered throughout these histories of division, many of which we are commonly unaware of. For example, your average Catholic, Lutheran, and Orthodox may have no clue that in recent years their leaders have been forging ecumenical bonds.

Many readers will rightly ask if I am suggesting that there is never a time to leave. Am I not outlining some marriage-like vow of commitment to the Church? In a way, I *am* promoting the marriage analogy; and I admit that in marriage there may be some rare, but appropriate instances for separation—like irreconcilable adultery or abuse. But, exceptions ought to be treated as exceptions, not the norm. This is especially important to point out in an age when there is an over 50 percent divorce rate and denominations splitting left and right.

But critics might press further: how could the Galileos of the world innovate in the stifling traditionalism of the Church, apart from breaking off? Don't we *need* to walk away for the sake of progress? Does not deference to tradition and authority destroy an individual's ability to act on conscience, to stand for what is right against the inquisitor? In thinking this through, I've attempted to refuse choosing between tradition and progress. For it seems that, while tradition may at times hinder progress, it is also what *enables* it. Galileo himself was an innovator within a tradition; he too had to learn from the traditions of physics in his day in order improve them. He offered a remix of the world, a remix that would again be remixed after continued research and thought. Chesterton tried to put his finger on the modern dualism between tradition and progress:

Among the more ignorant of the enlightened there was indeed a convention of saying that priests had obstructed progress in all ages; and a politician once told me in a debate that I was resisting modern reforms exactly as some ancient priest probably resisted the discovery of wheels. I pointed out, in reply, that it was far more likely that the ancient priest made the discovery of the wheels. It is overwhelmingly probable that the ancient priest had a great deal to do with the discovery of the art of writing. It is obvious enough in the fact that the very word hieroglyphic is akin to the word hierarchy.[25]

Perhaps he also had in mind that an Augustinian priest, Gregor Mendel, a person who saw no contradiction between scientific innovation and his religious tradition, invented modern genetic studies. A stream of other religious scientific thinkers comes to mind as well: Georges Lemaître, Pierre Teilhard de Chardin, Francis Collins, Kenneth Miller, John Polkinghorne.[26] I see no good reason to set up tradition in diametric opposition to progress.[27] Joining the Catholic tradition for me has not meant becoming a curmudgeonly traditionalist or a flagrant libertine. And, importantly, it doesn't even mean becoming more "into ritual."[28] I see it as a way of drawing out the best of the old and new, holding them together, so that real and stable progress can be made.

One of the more popular Chesterton quotations states it succinctly, implying his attempt to avoid the worst in both camps: "The business of Progressives is to go on making mistakes. The business of the Conservatives is to prevent the mistakes from being corrected."[29] This skill of stability, of change with continuity, is not just necessary in the Church, but in the entire world. It is a fundamental principle of sanity, of innovation, of coherence. Gerald Schlabach puts it this way:

To learn to dissent while respecting authority, to act on personal conscience while recognizing the claims of tradition, to seek change that is not merely a reactive "deconstruction" but a complex *aggiornamento* or updating[30]—these are capacities that change agents and indeed entire cultures need in order to relate respectfully to other cultures. No global civil society or multicultural polity will be just if its basis is the subtle violence that corrosive individualism inflicts when it trivializes the ancient wisdom embodied in communal traditions.[31]

This summarizes one of the better reasons why I chose, after a long time away, to complete my initiation and be confirmed in the Catholic Church: I cannot improve it by abandoning it. And I continue to appreciate it because, among other reasons, I am surrounded by a long, multi-century tradition of people building, innovating, and progressing amid and despite all the pitfalls along the way. Unlike the unhappy appeals to "return to the early Church" while despising the current one, I now feel the Church to be more like a farm, with the potential of building better seedbeds and patterns each year—or like an orchestra that, with practice, can continue to play the song better and better each year. Sure, the fields are strewn with thistles, and the violinists screech worse than a kid in their first lesson; but this is all the more reason to put our hand to the plow or begin music training, and not to walk out in frustration.

When I first moved into Camden and started attending Sacred Heart, it was also my habit to attend a Brethren in Christ gathering on Sunday nights (a denomination born of a schism with other Anabaptists over baptismal immersion). I helped lead worship there; the services were more in the evangelical style I was used to at Willow, and young persons like me attractively populated the gathering. But Cassie and I found it hard to attend two gatherings on a Sunday, since our piety only went so far. Given that I was largely a "church consumer" at the time, I had no deep reasons to choose between the two except that Sacred Heart was across the street and we wanted to worship where we lived. And so we sat down to meet with the Brethren pastor. We told him that it was a difficult tension to be a part of two faith communities and that we weren't sure what to do with it. His response was intriguing: "Well, it's obvious to me that God's next thing in the world is not going to come through the Catholic Church. I think you should covenant here."

I couldn't determine where he managed to find such lucid, privileged, inside information on the future of God's plans. I began to wonder if his conviction was mirrored in his denomination; they were a break-off of a break-off—each rifting with its initial community over some sense of what "God's next thing" is, each getting smaller and smaller with each successive schism, each emphasizing one idea that had fallen out of balance. Looking back on that conversation, if I had to hazard a guess about the future on mere historical grounds, I might have said that in two hundred years the Brethren will be dead and the Catholic Church, in whatever shape, will remain, for it has so far weathered the rise and fall of empires and epochs. (Due partly to its being in charge of some of these empires, lamentably.) But, to be more precise in my guess, I might have rather wagered that, in whatever era the Catholic Church is buried, the Brethren will also be dead. (God rest us both.) I might also guess that in such a world we will probably have substituted eating the Body and Blood of Christ for eating each other, as in the great apocalypses. That is certainly a guess, and I don't wish for the Brethren tradition to die, but it is an educated guess. Years later, as I read Chesterton, this quotation mingled with my memory of that conversation with the pastor, and I applied it to the Church: "A man who is perpetually thinking of whether this race or that race is strong, of whether this cause or that cause is promising, is the man who will never believe in anything long enough to make it succeed."[32]

But all that is beside the point, for at the time I supposed he was correct. And yet, I still chose to stay part of this so-called "dying institution" (though I conjecture now that it is not). For, judging from people like Dorothy Day, I thought I could still attempt to live "prophetically," not in creating a new church, but in enlivening the old one. And, I wondered, so what *if* the Catholic Church was on its deathbed? Might it not be some act of love to care for the geriatrics, even on their way out?[33] Who says you must only participate in "the next big thing"? That—it took me years to see this—is an overhyped grasp for survival, to which I think Merton speaks well: "The last thing in the world that should concern a Christian or the Church is *survival* in a temporal and worldly sense: to be concerned with this is an implicit denial of the Victory of Christ and of the Resurrection."[34]

In the history of the Church as I see it, a better alternative to denominations and divisions has been the formation of religious orders. That is, if you think the Church is not aggressive enough in its asceticism, jubilant poverty, or commitment to the poor, you start the Franciscans or the Vincentians; if you think the Church is not intellectually robust enough, you start the Dominicans; if you think the Church is not sufficiently missionary, you start the Jesuits. In short, if you think the Church is in need, you start helping it in your own unique way. You don't leave it. After all, it is the sick who need a doctor. This is partly why Chesterton felt that the real reformers were not Calvin and Luther but Thomas Aquinas and Francis of Assisi—and, for that era, we might add people like John of the Cross and Teresa of Avila.[35] They all saw a need for change, but they did so in an attempted continuity with the current order in the Church. Even when they encountered serious tensions with the status quo, and had to swim upstream against their critics, they aimed to inspire the Church and its institutions from within—even if their space of renewal was at times as small as their souls within, like John of the Cross locked in a tower. Each in their own different way, all the saints, at least the ones I can call to mind, displayed a revolutionary subordination toward the profligate, noninnovative, and drooping Church;[36] they never regarded their spiritual innovations as reason enough to leave it. For, if they were emphasizing some mystical idea that had fallen from the Catholic balance, they wanted to retrieve it for the sake of the whole Body of Christ. Certainly, not every saint started a new religious order, but the Church's category of religious orders may be one of the best social factors to have kept it united, *and* diverse and progressing, for so many centuries. These orders made a space for new growth that wasn't also a new chasm of division.

Take Francis of Assisi, for example. Contrary to those who see him as some kind of rabble-rouser, Francis ceaselessly tried to harmonize his movement with the papacy and the Church hierarchy. And, while he was moved to go barefoot, he removed his *own* shoes, not somebody else's. This is why he gave his dad's clothes back to him, even if it left him naked. But Francis would be in the dustbin of Church history if he had proceeded to claw clothes off his father and knock the pope's hat off. But take the Reformer John Calvin by contrast. For all his admirable intellectual passion, I see his social program as a sort of negative reversal of Francis's; he too shared a conviction for asceticism, but he felt that his entire city, Geneva, needed to become as ascetic as his dream, and he turned it into a "glass city" of surveillance and forced monasticism. He aimed to make monasticism a norm for everyone, even if they weren't ready for it.[37]

So, in these smaller religious orders there is a wonderful witness for healthy reform: when you become convicted of some great truth, you don't leverage it against the entire Church, but use it as a beacon of inspiration for a smaller group, a proving ground. And if this group needs to die over time, it will; but its moment of inspiration, in upholding some forgotten ideal, will not make the entire Church populace turn and bow in obedience to them alone.[38]

I've interpreted these questions about how to reform the Church from the perspective of my own small, "neo-monastic" community in Camden. Granted, we are one of the least rigorous communities in this loose multi-denominational network—we meet only a few times a week, share some of our resources, do not take lifelong monastic vows—but we still embody a way of life in Camden that hopefully challenges our current cultural milieu. But when we started, my Protestant impulses were in full force, like Calvin, seeing my renewed piety as a new universal conviction for the Church at large. When people would visit our sprouting community in Camden, I would loathe hearing things like, "Well, that way of life is good for you guys, but I'm going to keep living the American dream out in the suburbs." (That's at least how it sounded to me!) These pats on the back felt condescending, and worse, too relativistic; how can it be right for us, but not for you? Instead I wanted to prophetically draw them into my own specific, new dream of a different way of doing Christianity.

But I now see that my conviction had dangerously divisive and unloving undertones. My complaints about upper-class Christians saying "Well, that's nice for you, not me," were a way of avoiding a serious truth: my tiny community of reformers is not the center of truth in Christianity. Quite a conclusion, I know. It's not that there is any problem with cultivating progressive convictions; it's just that they don't make us separate from and better than the universal Church. We can quarrel with the

Church; but it must remain a lover's quarrel. Just as we shouldn't play the Bible off against tradition, we should also not universalize our convictions to break up the Church. Rather, it seems more loving and compassionate that our convictions should inspire us to remove the log from our own eye, set roots of stability and fidelity amid the community we know, refurbish the Church there as best we can, and thereby inspire—if we do at all—from the bottom up. With Francis as perhaps the most popular and widespread invigorator of Christianity since Jesus, it is helpful to remember how he honored the Church as his mother, never using his convictions as a badge of superiority or a warrant for leaving behind the uninspired masses.

It is here that I find a bonus for Church unity: after a long week of spending all my energy to take a log out of my eye and forming a fresh pattern of my own Christian discipleship within my own little cluster, by Sunday I have less of a need to make every last nook and cranny of Mass suit all my personal needs and tastes. Sunday is no longer merely about "feeding my spiritual needs or I'm outta here." Church, for me, is now more about gathering around the Body of Christ, the Eucharist, with all sorts of people and leaders that may or may not suit my fancy and enacting the traditional rituals that may or may not suit my fancy. Such a gathering may, at times, be as begrudging as some people's dreaded family reunions; but I am no longer the center around which others must revolve. Something Greater draws us together.

In thinking all this through, I've come to see that my love for Camden mirrors my love for the Church. Both entities have their dreadful shortcomings. Both may, at times, appear to have hopelessly more darkness than light in them. But I moved into Camden seeing its overwhelming evils clearly—as clearly as I saw the pedophilia scandal. Despite this, I attempt to abide in Camden, oftentimes without any light at the end of this city's tunnel. But, as the saying goes, it's better to light one candle than to curse the darkness. There is a kind of love that serves, and a kind that wants to be served. So, I might do well to take Chesterton's quotation about that dreaded neighborhood of Pimlico in England—which I applied to Camden—and apply it to the Church:

> It is not enough for people to disapprove of the Church: in that case they will merely cut their throats or create another one. Nor, certainly, is it enough for someone to approve of the Church: for then it will remain as it is, which would be awful. The only way out of it seems to be for somebody to *love* the Church: to love it with a transcendental tie and without any earthly reason. If there arose someone who loved the Church, then it would rise into ivory towers and golden pinnacles; the Church would attire herself as a woman does when she is loved. . . . If people loved the Church as mothers love children, arbitrarily, because it is *theirs*, in a year or two it might be fairer than Florence. . . . People did not love Rome because she was great. She was great because they had loved her.[39]

Now, my reader might say this is exactly the problem: that people *did* love the Church, but in some mutated and excessive manner—that it *did* create its ivory towers and golden pinnacles, and in so doing we encrusted over the poor and humble Savior. I turn to that question in my next chapter.

TEN: ART AND APOCALYPSE

I knew I had hit a turning point with Catholicism when I visited St. Peter's basilica in Rome for the second time. Each time I have been privileged enough to visit this immense site, touched by the hand of Michelangelo and countless craftsmen, I have been delighted to take the long, winding, and narrowing stairs up through the dome, past the Latin, six-foot-tall letters inscribed around the base of the dome,[1] to its peak, overlooking the Eternal City.

The first time I was in Rome I was full throttle in the midst of my Protestant piety. I knew the place's historical significance, and I could appreciate it as an architectural accomplishment, but my overarching sentiment was negative, since any positive impressions were eclipsed by the sinfulness of its opulence. I could perhaps appreciate some beauty, but ultimately this was a place to be derided, a place where people's sins, through indulgences in the late medieval era, paid for an exquisite monument to decadence—much like many of our televangelists seem today to prey upon the troubles and ailments of lonely and searching people.

Besides calling to mind Martin Luther's critiques on that matter, I also remembered Jesus' disdain for the Temple. He was walking around the Temple, and his disciples were impressed by

the grandeur—to which Jesus replied with an aggressive proclamation about how it will all crumble, mingling thoughts of
his own death with the future destruction of the Temple (AD
70). I thought, "Professional religionists exploiting widows and
covering it up with fake glory—there is nothing to adore here;
move along."

But for my second visit, with my wife Cassie, I found myself
in a new posture. I had grown in admiration of great architecture, and had become a confirmed Catholic. At the time, though,
I had barely internalized its meaning. I still retained a lingering
distrust of this place as I walked through—a distrust that has
still not entirely left me. But something was different this time.
Somehow I had a heart of appreciation, even a love for the place.
It may have been partly my growing carpentry skills; I marveled
at how any craftsman could ever make anything like St. Peter's
dome, or how a twenty-eight-year-old could carve the Pieta.
And as I walked about, examining the ornate statues, impos-
sibly carved into long, flowing shrouds of marble and images of
saints, raising my eyes to the sculpted angels, some high-flung
sixty feet in the air, I came to a side entrance of the basilica. And
before I could realize what was going on, people quickly started
gathering around the entrance, the door was opened, and a
briskly walking procession of men in robes came from it. And,
I couldn't believe myself, I was struck not only with a moment
of respect for them, I even wanted to bow to them! In fact, I
momentarily thought to myself that, I might even kneel were
the pope among this chain. "Blasphemy!" I thought. My residual
Protestant impulses bubbled up from the lower recesses of my
mind's recycling bin. "Never! You are from Willow Creek; you
are a Protestant evangelical at heart. And what of the poor? You
can't go about smothering your affection for Jesus with all these
additives: opulent statues, high-vaulted ceilings, superstitious
holy-water fonts, processions in robes, frescoes on Sistine ceilings,

golden chalices, embellished spires, intricate gargoyles, swinging censures of incense."

I needed to find a way to work through the problem that St. Peter's could simultaneously make me want to vomit and genuflect. It is a problem of ascetics and aesthetics, of simplicity and beauty. Christians like the Quakers and Shakers have struck their own balance; their minimalism and simplicity *is* their beauty—marked by durability and light touches of flare (like a dovetailed joint or a subtly curved piece of wood). But the Catholic tradition, obviously, is a world of difference. They treat the Impoverished God with golden embellishments, the crucified criminal with gifts of ornate marble and domes, the one born in a cave with a spire in the sky, the one who fasted in the desert with feast days of wine and bread, the one who had no place to lay his head with rich displays of flowers and candles. How can they take themselves seriously with these discrepancies, these tensions between their ascetic Lord and their aesthetic art projects?

The story of *Schindler's List* further illustrates the problem. A German leader and businessman, Oskar Schindler, undergoes a spiritual conversion during the Nazi-led genocide. He finds that his exploitation of factory workers plays into the murderous spirit taking over his country, and so he begins to find ways to save Jews from the horrors of the SS. In a wrenching final scene, we find Schindler realizing how much more he could have done with all his possessions. He looks at a watch, a ring, a car, and comments on how each one of them could be sold for the sake of saving just a few more people from the gas chambers. I wholeheartedly embrace his conviction, lament, and anguish, knowing full well from the street-people I regularly see in Camden, that at any time my money could go to a more beneficent place than I had in mind. And while I don't have the proximity of labor camps to daily consider, it is a fearful thought, one that never ceases to haunt me; for bloody oppression continues on in different forms in our day.

But, one might wonder whether somebody might have made a sequel to this movie, portraying Schindler ten years later. How could he (and we) ever manage to live with the tension between having something while others have nothing? Wouldn't we picture Schindler going insane if he took his conviction to its logical end? *Everything*, really, everything we have and use can be used for another needy person's benefit. I might imagine Schindler struggling to eat a sandwich, realizing that a few calories of it could be parsed off to share; or putting on a pair of pants, quickly seeing that he could cut half of them off and sell the shards of cloth for the sake of a few more pennies for the poor; or, if he had already given up his house for the benefit of others, he could find his way to sleep under a highway overpass, only to find that resting his head upon a pillow picked from the garbage is too luxurious, and proceed to pawn the pillow and give a few more cents away. Someone suffering from this complex might be transported back to Jesus making wine at Cana, begin siphoning off Jesus' miracle wine into jugs, bring it to a liquor store to pawn it, bring the money back to the wedding, and start giving the money to the poor beggars outside. After all, shouldn't the story of Lazarus, the beggar at the gate, "scare the hell out of us" for failing to give all we have to the poor?

In our own day, when the pains of genocide, conflict, and famine seem as strong as ever, we still feel a struggle with simplicity and abrogation. Mother Teresa, for example, was well-known for her deformed feet, caused by taking the worst shoes in a pile of donations. As a sort of St. Francis and St. Clare reiteration, she was also known to step out of banquets to go search for the needy. With a mind to the needy and the examples before us, how can we enjoy *anything* of redeemable monetary worth with our eyes wide open in our context? And how might we ever take Vatican opulence as acceptable, or even barely tolerable? Wouldn't we just hope that they would sell off the entire Vatican City, give the money to the poor, and consider that a good start?

A cheap shortcut here is to note that the Catholic Church's service to the poor nearly counterbalances this critique, since this Church serves more poor people in the world than any other organization (containing, as well, countless subsidiary religious orders and lay people). That would imply that their serving the poor atones for their "sin" of being indulgent on other things. But that won't work, since they don't really think it sinful to create and enjoy our aforementioned list of embellishments. Another shortcut would be to hold, as many Christians unconsciously do, that Jesus (or the early Christians) took the end of the world far too seriously, got it wrong, and so the Church needs to get over Jesus' idealism and let the problems of poverty and injustice work themselves out. In that case, we can dismiss any urgency for justice with a misquotation: "The poor will always be with us." In short, we can wave off the urgent concerns of "living simply so that others may simply live," and carry on.

Not taking these shortcuts, we're left with an apparent contradiction between Jesus' poverty and the Church's wealth. To be forthright, I am not fully at peace with any explanation, but I don't find the problem reason enough for me to revoke my membership. Perhaps one way to look at the problem is through the story of Jesus having dinner with Mary and (the raised) Lazarus.[2] In John 12:3 Mary pours an expensive perfume, worth a *year's wages* (unbelievable!), on Jesus' feet. It is so opulent a gesture that Judas blurts out that it would be better sold and given to the poor. Now, we can, of course, say that Judas wasn't sincerely defending sacrificial charity, and that his mind was already showing signs of mammon-possession. After all, the text reads, "He said this not because he loved the poor, but because he was a thief; as the purse keeper he helped himself to the money." But in the end, many of us are prone to think that Judas was nevertheless right—if only he would really sell it and give the money away instead of using it. Some might argue the point further, quoting from another gospel Jesus' command, "Sell your possessions and give to the poor."[3]

But Judas's spirituality, besides being insincere, misses an immense point: real things (like perfume) have a purpose, but money in itself is a useless abstraction. He would only learn this too late with his few silver coins. Mary *was* giving to the poor, just not in the form of money; she was giving to a poor guy named Jesus. Being poor, he had no place of his own to eat dinner that night, and she gifted him with a beautiful though bitter anointing in anticipation of his burial. You shouldn't rub money on Jesus (or anybody for that matter, I would advise), but you can rub perfume on him. One of the delightful goals of perfume, besides selling it, is to use it. After Jesus accepts her luxurious gift, he says they can care for the poor anytime, since they are always around—but Jesus won't be. Far from casting off concern for the poor because of their ubiquity, Jesus is quoting the Torah, which says, "There should be no poor among you, and yet because the poor are always with you, you must always have your hand open to them."[4]

Mark, in his version of this story, adds that this "wasteful" outpouring *is essential to the proclamation of the Gospel.*[5] It might seem like too great a gap between expensive perfume and the building of a cathedral, but it is one starting place to make some connections between the Vatican's opulence and Jesus' seeming asceticism. We see here that Jesus will have none of what has come to be known as "the Protestant work ethic," that unrelenting drive of frugality and industry, that crude separation between the enjoyment of human culture and matters of "God's will."[6] Jesus refused to melt down a thing—like his burial anointing—to its monetary cost, even though it had a cost. Though money buys your funeral, there is no use in selling it.

We might imagine Jesus with the Protestant work ethic, calling to mind Jesus' reputation as a drunken party animal.[7] Do we imagine him spending time with drunkards, wondering in the back of his mind whether he could better spend their drinking money elsewhere? I might also imagine Mary and Joseph asking Melchior, Balthazar, and Casper for gift receipts—so that they could cash in their gold, frankincense, and myrrh, and give the money to the poor. We might also imagine Jesus turning water into wine to sell it at a street kiosk. (The whole thought experiment becomes more absurd when we ask whether anyone asked him to turn dirt into cash.) If we remove some of the absurd modern propensities to associate things with money, Jesus might appear less and less like a dreary ascetic. He may even emerge as a person whose love is big enough to appreciate beauty, the lavish ritual at a wedding, and a multiday, wine-drenched celebration while *also* caring for the poor. And again, it is not that his charity atones for these indulgences, but that *both* are essential to a big and bold enjoyment of the world. For it is possible for ascetics to make an idol out of money too.

At some point, we must acknowledge that, in many matters of life and death—and the ritual solemnizing of them—we ought not defile them by focusing on their price tag, even if they have one. At Sacred Heart, one of the most indulgent and embellished rituals of the year (besides our Passover Seder) is a procession at the end of Holy Thursday Mass, representing the end of the Passover meal, just before Good Friday. Every year I am deeply drawn in by its beauty. It is a very solemn (and long) Mass that shares much of the tragic and reverent tones of Mary's anointing with perfume. Some of the consecrated hosts are saved and brought down to a breathtaking display in the church basement; there, unending vases of flowers, candles, and incense are brought in by the processing parishioners (all singing, "You satisfy the hungry heart, with gift of finest wheat. Come give to us, oh Saving Lord, the Bread of life to eat."). As we enter the room, we all create a luxuriously flower-filled space to place the Eucharist, the Body of Christ. After the Eucharist is placed amid this cornucopia, we sit in silence as incense clouds the room and candles flicker. The sight is surreal, heavenly. We then sing ancient songs that feel too powerful to describe in mere writing, and I cry each time we sing them. After it all, we all sit in an extended period of silence, adoring the Bread of Presence. It all rhymes with Mary's perfume bottle; it is unapologetically honoring, with lavish flora and candles, the Body of Christ on his way to death.

I have felt this adoration to be an especially important lesson for us today, when so much of our beauty and art seems to be judged by its mere marketability and its monetary worth. Chesterton, if you will tolerate him again, puts the modern problem with art and money this way:

> I should say the first effect of the triumph of the capital-ist (if we allow him to triumph) will be that that line of demarcation [between art and advertising] will entirely disappear. There will be no art that might not just as well be advertisement. I do not necessarily mean that there will be no good art; much of it might be, much of it already is, very good art. You may put it, if you please, in the form that there has been a vast improve-ment in advertisements. . . . But the improvement of advertisements is the degradation of artists. It is their degradation for this clear and vital reason: that the artist will work, not only to please the rich, but only to increase their riches; which is a considerable step lower.[8]

His distinction calls to mind how much of the Renaissance-era art was indeed contracted out by and for rich people, like for the homes of merchant families. And much of it was commissioned for ornate public projects, like pilgrimage sites and cathedrals. But whether we call that era lamentable or glorious, it cannot be an improvement that in our day art is now growing more in its service for advertisements to make the rich richer, than in private or public enjoyment, worship, or homage to saints. Wendell Berry echoes this lament for our day:

> If we look at the great artistic traditions, as it is necessary to do, we will see that they have never been divorced either from religion or from economy. . . . The arts, traditionally, belong to the neighborhood. They are the means by which the neighborhood lives, works, remembers, worships, and enjoys itself.[9]

In a culture that tends to commodify and individualize art, it is easy to miss the fact that much of the Catholic artistic embellishments were often constructed by, and for, the community. They are not merely visions of grandeur built to glorify powerful dictators.

At exquisitely constructed cathedrals like Chartres or Cologne, or in painfully beautiful installations like the Loretto chapel's staircase in Santa Fe, New Mexico, I can only imagine the affection that craftsmen, pilgrims, roaming masons, and volunteers poured in.[10] Similarly, my Irish parish priest, Fr. Michael Doyle, spoke of how the Irish (both back on the island and as American immigrants) worked through their poverty. Even though individual families didn't have much, they could all together share something great in their space of worship. And so they focused their energy and funds toward a beautiful collective space for worship in which to revere the divine. The problem between loving the poor and aesthetic embellishment takes on a new shape when you realize that the poor, too, want to create and see artistic accomplishment.

I too, though not poor, have felt great satisfaction worshipping in spaces where my pottery or woodwork is on display. And I imagine the same has gone for the countless waves of craftsmen who sculpted, and then worshipped in, their community's cathedrals. In our own society, with its increasing worship of managers and their glory shining above the laboring class, I wonder if some of the complaints about immaculate aesthetics stem from our growing alienation from the pleasure of highly skilled, manual trades.

Speaking for myself, living in a desperately poor city, which often cannot even afford a snow plow or a replacement light bulb, I don't want St. Peter's dismantled, sold, and the proceeds sent over to us in small payments. I don't want the Pieta sold off to an aristocrat in order to pave my streets and restore our homes; I don't want Michelangelo's Moses sculpture chipped off Julius II's tomb and sold to a museum; I don't want Bernini's sculpted Solomonic columns melted down for the sake of our city's deficits, and—this is harder to say—even to feed our poor. I don't picture those accomplishments of art as preferably deconstructible, just as I don't see Mary's bottle of perfume as deconstructible.

Besides seeing the asceticism problem through the bottle of perfume story, another limited way to resolve this tension between ascetics and aesthetics might be to approve of beauty *rooted in justice*. For beauty turns ugly with unjust ingredients. It might be easier to appreciate a cathedral *if it is not built on the backs of the poor*, to crown a statue of Mary (if you can tolerate that) with a rich wreath of flowers *if they are grown sustainably and justly*, not imported from overseas or anointed with the sweat of immigrant labor. This would seem to provide a way forward in our (seemingly) increasingly green culture. I would find it an elevated beauty if our eucharistic bread and wine were sustainably grown and harvested (and many churches are doing this—my parish hand-bakes ours), or if our church buildings were adorned with solar panels (as the Vatican's are). But something here doesn't fully satisfy, since green consumerism doesn't necessarily sanctify the consumerism. I think an enormously important way past these problems is in our ability to appreciate things we have inherited, *even from imperfect and sometimes unjust sources*. Virtually all the saints of the canon who have come before us had limitations, blind spots, and maybe even injustices. Paul appears to have not spoken out as directly as moderns would hope about issues of slavery and women's rights. Augustine, for all his contributions to philosophy and literature, at times, appears to not quite hold to the ethics of twenty-first-century progressivism (like in feeling that Original Sin is transmitted by concupiscence). Or, Joan of Arc appears not to have considered the enlightened path of Martin Luther King's nonviolence.

But to avoid the error of scapegoating our ancestors, we are challenged to not judge accomplishments of the past by the standards of today. Instead, we do best to learn from their mistakes but also to receive and appreciate their contributions. No one, ultimately, hands down perfect and unblemished gifts. Even Jesus handed us something as imperfect as Peter. So, in the matters of cathedrals and expensive Vatican art, it is a great stain upon some of them that they may have come from less than admirable sources—be they the sale of indulgences or exploitative labor. But I have found it an important act of forbearance to see the bad in what we have received and learn from it (hopefully any new buildings and art we produce will be made in a more enlightened and just fashion), while *also* allowing myself to appreciate the good for what it is. In short, I am attempting again to not throw the baby out with the bathwater, to not condemn something on the whole for its offenses in part. This way, I can walk into St. Peter's and appreciate it while not whitewashing over its disgusting funding through simony. Isn't that what we must do with *everybody*, even ourselves? Can we not praise Martin Luther King Jr. for his accomplishments, but still critique his questionable relations with women in a way that does not eclipse or cancel his memory? Perhaps this is one of the psychological beauties that comes from believing that we are all part of an enormous Communion of Saints, a cloud of witnesses including even the dead. When we gather at Mass, all times and people are mystically re-gathered as simultaneous sinners and saints. We are compelled to treat ancestors with the same grace with which we hope future generations will treat us.

The tension between asceticism and aesthetics becomes three-dimensional when we bring in the question of eschatology and how we relate to the future. I see the problem in how the Catholic Church maintains some tension between their seemingly apocalyptic Jesus and their cultivation of long-term projects of opulent beauty. Jesus appears very ready for an end of the world in much of the Gospels—his celibacy seems to speak of an urgency with no time for playing house and rearing children; his itinerant, homeless mission seems to symbolize a sacrificial abandonment of society's comforts for the sake of an imminent spiritual revolution. And yet, the Church has cathedrals that took hundreds of years to build, liturgies that back away from impromptu, charismatic zeal into planned annual rhythms, and (most generally but importantly), time spent on things besides the creation of a more just and equitable world. Didn't Jesus eagerly spend all his time on love and justice before the apocalypse would arrive? And here we are wasting time cleaning pews, carving gargoyles, folding altar cloths, adorning shrines, polishing chalices, and dusting stained glass.

Let's draw out one place where the Christian mind is tempted to find some solace in natural beauty, in opposition to costly human art:

> Consider the lilies of the field: they do not toil or spin, and even Solomon in all his splendor was not as well dressed as these. Now if God so clothes the grass of the field, which today is, and tomorrow is thrown into the fire, will he not more clothe you?[11]

This little jab at Solomon rhymes with Jesus' apparent disdain for the Temple. But however much Jesus might redirect the mind to natural beauty, he does not deny that Solomon had *some* splendor, however inferior to a flower's elegance. The coming fire Jesus imagines does not bar us from the human urge to build things, and build them beautifully. The fires of apocalypse might consume all our architecture, but that's no reason not to build them. We might even consider it a playful element of our architecture to anticipate apocalypse, as, to me, Gaudi's Sagrada Familia cathedral in Spain appears to do (particularly with its Nativity façade)—it almost looks as if a great apocalyptic fire is melting the cathedral to the ground, with all the creatures familiar and exotic present for the catastrophe.[12] It is a way of building that can foresee the end of the building—though it takes centuries to build and will hopefully last for thousands more. My son, on his best days, can construct a delicate spire of blocks and magically execute a paradox: he can step back to smile and enjoy it, all the while taking it lightly enough to knock it down the next instant.

An oddity of our day is that many now no longer take religious apocalyptic imagery literally (street preachers seem to have stripped the enterprise of its respectability), but we still eat up apocalyptic art and movies like crazy. Long after the books of Daniel and Revelation blasted the world with images that subverted the empires, we still have a bounty of earth-shaking movies: *Armageddon, Battle: LA, I Am Legend, War of the Worlds, District 9, Cloverfield, 28 Days Later, The Day After Tomorrow, Mad Max, 2012, The Book of Eli,* the *Terminator* movies, *Children of Men,* just to name a few. Whether or not you liked any of these, something I take from them is their urging the mind to imagine a world stripped entirely of its current order. What we take for granted—the daily, stable structures, our food and sanitation systems, government order, art, museums, and public concerts, and even the mellow luxury of going for a walk in the evening—are wiped away in flash.

I must confess that I have grown particularly fond of the apocalyptic genre precisely because of my living in Camden, virtually a pseudo-apocalyptic setting. My place has already fallen apart. I don't need to describe Camden more than I already have, but I might have my reader imagine a city in which sometimes entire blocks are abandoned and have been stripped by metal scrappers; and even new homes attempting to be built are often ransacked for their goods after just a day or two of construction. The city is virtually bankrupt, and police are left in a state of triage, unable to even remotely respond to all calls. And, sadly, sometimes people strung out on crack and cocaine look like zombies. It is counterproductive to think too much about this, but it bears a striking resemblance to the popular apocalyptic scenes in our film and literature.

A deep apocalypse, for me, is the exquisitely painful book and movie *The Road,* written by Cormac McCarthy. The story begins after a global catastrophe. Civilization has collapsed, and even the ecological landscape has withered, preventing agriculture or hunting. There is no need for zombies in this horrific vision, since humans serve as the mindless murderers—roving gangs of cannibals can be found at any turn. The protagonist, whose wife has killed herself in a fear of being eaten alive, travels on foot through the country with his young son, attempting to reach the coastline. To what end, he doesn't know; but the ocean must bring *some*thing. With numerous scenes of escaping cannibals by the skin of their teeth, with virtually *everything* gone, the story pushes the limits of hope—if there is a God here, he or she can only be cursed, it seems. In the process of fighting off murderers and scrounging for scraps of food, the father and son must guard the hope that someday, maybe several generations from now, the small germ of civilization ("the fire" they carry) might grow.[13]

A most basic luxury of humanity—telling a story—even seems lost in *The Road*'s apocalypse. The father, sitting around a fire with his son, as they, emaciated, eat what might be their last morsels of food, gropes to tell his son something true, something beautiful, something inspiring, and he can barely draw anything from the dried up well of culture and religion. It has all been lost.[14] He can hardly offer him immaculate sagas of overcoming evil, miraculous myths of intervention, biographies of great heroes, inspiring orations of philosophy, no complex compositions of music, no lengthy citations of poetry, no dance parties let alone complex ballroom orchestrations. He can only hope that someday his distant descendants might be able to start reconstructing those things. For the moment, they can barely construct a lean-to or a place to avoid being eaten alive. And yet the father, amidst his hopelessness, declares, "*Where you've nothing else construct ceremonies out of the air and breathe upon them.*"[15]

A profound part of *The Road*, as I saw it, played out in the father's mental breakdown—as if he shouldn't be having one every few hours. The father and son had come across a once-grand, abandoned house that had in it a rare artifact: a piano. (This is, with creative license, embellished beyond the text in the movie.) Pianos would normally be cut up and thrown on a fire, to make a spit on which to grill and eat the flesh of, perhaps, a child. In the face of a desperate and gruesome world, a piano looks like a luxurious tool from the heavens. Who can imagine leisurely stroking the keys to a classical tune when there are raging cannibals outside? In the postapocalypse, amenities—let alone basilicas—are light years away. A piano represents embellishment, culture, the arts, the luxuries of civilization. And as the father sits before the piano, partly remembering his dead wife, partly lamenting the loss of the world, he weeps bitterly. Something in this scene spoke to me of a primal human need: it is my most banal point for coming to appreciate the opulence of Catholic worship: humans want and need to create beautiful things.

Imagining an apocalypse can help us do a few things. Most radically, it can critique oppressive authorities and current reigning governments. Daniel's apocalypse is known for this, since it speaks in the context of the Jewish enslavement to foreign rule. Daniel pictures the powers of the world together as a statue that will someday crumble, breaking because of their unstable foundation. Mary's *Magnificat*, too, borders on the apocalyptic, since she imagines a world where God has torn the mighty down from their thrones and aided the poor. Similarly, many have read John's Revelation as a politically subversive account of God versus Rome, of Christ versus Caesar, questioning the unquestionable empire.[16] This prophetic imagination makes possible a new world, since it destroys our unreflective comfort in the current one. I, and many of my anarchist friends, exalt in this language. We have identified our current world order as a violent and exploitative system, not nearly as shiny and beneficent in reality as it appears in the brochure. Apocalyptic imagery, then, is a way of claiming the emperor has no clothes, unveiling the ignored truth before our eyes.

But besides subverting the powers of the world, apocalypse can also be used in a different way, and this is the crux of my point here: apocalypse leads toward immense appreciation of the world, toward a more robust and creative engagement with it. It leads us to give thanks—that is, to "eucharist." It leads us to look forward to the redemption of all things human, of all the creations of our culture. In exploring McCarthy's destroyed world in *The Road*, we are left desperately caring for those fragile beauties, ceremonies, sagas, pianos, and food that we normally take for granted. Without this thankful counterbalance, apocalyptic imagination can become just a veiled form of resentment, of the weak loathing the strong, of merely hating civilization and waiting for heaven. Just as things get ugly when the Bible is torn from its balance with tradition (chapter 8), and as schisms fester from using our ideals of the Church against the Church (chapter 9), so too the apocalyptic imagery becomes dreadful when used in a one-dimensional fashion, as nothing more than hating the world.

It seems to me that the Church, in retaining both a staunch concern for the poor *and* very ornate aesthetics, is attempting the immensely difficult task of both loving and hating the world at the same time. Chesterton speaks of this balance:

> For our Titanic purposes of faith and revolution, what we need is not the cold acceptance of the world as a compromise, but some way in which we can heartily hate and heartily love it. We do not want joy and anger to neutralize each other and produce a surly contentment; we want a fiercer delight and a fiercer discontent. We have to feel the universe at once as an ogre's castle, to be stormed, and yet as our own cottage, to which we can return at evening. . . . Can he hate it enough to change it, and yet love it enough to think it worth changing? Can he look up at its colossal good without once feeling acquiescence? Can he look up at its

> colossal evil without once feeling despair? Can he, in
> short, be at once not only a pessimist and an optimist,
> but a fanatical pessimist and a fanatical optimist? Is he
> enough of a pagan to die for the world, and enough of
> a Christian to die to it?[17]

I see here a way to come full circle on the question of asceticism and aesthetics. I don't just want charitable giving to the poor to cancel out our pleasures or luxuriant liturgies. It's not that we need our apocalypse to be "balanced" with an appreciation for civilization; no, civilization indeed is corrupt and terrible and in need of all sorts of upheavals, changes, and revolutions. Likewise, we don't just need appreciation of the Church to cancel out its insufficiency; no, the Church is profoundly insufficient. The challenge is to combine both an extraordinary appreciation of human creativity, beauty, art, and embellishment, while also orienting one's mind, with apocalyptic eagerness, toward remedying our world's decay and assisting the poor among us.

It would be too much to claim that any singular grouping in the Church has perfectly combined these. But it would be closer to the truth to say that some have done it better than others. With much history and tradition standing behind me, I suggest that the stereotypical image of a monk—walking barefoot, clothed in one of his few possessions, constrained by the vows of poverty, chastity, and obedience—passing through a gloriously adorned chapel of stone, arches, and gargoyles on the way to his duties of service, is one helpful guiding vision. Or, I often imagine St. Francis rebuilding a small yet beautiful stone chapel, the Porziuncola, by begging for stones. Even while renouncing his possessions and serving the poor, he still was driven by a desire to reconstruct a sacred and beautiful place of worship. These are images, for me at least, that won't go away—even if they are romantic and fanciful. They speak of a person who not only serves the poor, but is poor. And at the same time, he serves in a community and worships within a grandeur that overshadows both the monk and the beggar. As such, he is not poor. I think this mythic image of the monk won't die, even in the modern world, because in him we have some vision of "owning as if it was not theirs to keep," of "using things of this world as if not engrossed in them,"[18] and of being happy with little or plenty.[19] Chesterton saw this great combination of simplicity and beauty in St. Thomas Becket, as contrasted with the modern capitalist: "Becket wore a hair shirt under his gold and crimson . . . for Becket got the benefit of the hair shirt [an old custom for penance and renunciation] while the people in the street got the benefit of the crimson and gold. It is at least better than the manner of the modern millionaire, who has the black and the drab outwardly for others, and the gold next his heart."[20]

My first Easter, and all subsequent ones, after entering the Catholic Church have opened up an appreciation for the Resurrection that I had never previously imagined. I have entered into the suffering of the Passion week in such a way that I virtually feel like *I was there*. Walking the Stations of the Cross through the streets, recounting the torturous horrors our neighborhood has seen and the suffering of Christ, has rooted me in a very bleak and dramatic view of the world. Not only do we recount our world's immense suffering, but we walk amid abandoned factories and imploding homes, seeing the scars on our landscape, air, and soil. We walk in prayer past drug dealers, some of whom may have participated in shootings around town. They awkwardly stare. At times, I have stared back. The hope and desire for a new world is elevated into anguish in this dolorous walk on Good Friday.

But, on Sunday morning, at 4:30 a.m., our parish gathers in bleak darkness in the sanctuary. A dark, dim glow from streetlights barely passes through the stained glass—enough to help one make out the edges of a pew. Then we hear a voice boom from the darkness, reading from the book of Genesis: "In the beginning . . ." Starting in darkness and chaos, a feeling not foreign to me in Camden, we read, "God created." All the cosmos is a movement from chaos to order, of swimming upstream against death, the abyss of darkness. The entire creation story is read, emphasizing that our world is good, even though it doesn't seem like it. In Camden it is not easy to feel that the world is, underneath it all, a good thing. We need a reminder of hope more than ever. Maybe this is why the poor and marginalized are often renowned as great champions of hope in our tattered world, upholding patience amid suffering.

At the end of the garden story comes the end of the utopian vision—we are cast out of Eden. We can no longer return to the ideal, since the flaming sword blocks passage.[21] And so the parish rises silently in the darkness, and leaves the sanctuary. We are to go out into "the tomb"—for now, the old cellar of this 1886 building. This time it is pitch black, with not even a hand in front of the face visible. And, after all have seated, in continuity with ancient traditions in the Church, the Genesis narrative jumps to the Exodus out of Egypt, the great celebration of release from slavery. We read the story of God unshackling the poor from bondage, telling them they need not fight, but that "God will fight for you." After Pharaoh's army is drowned we sing in the darkness, "Come sing to our God, who has triumphed gloriously!"

And, as if to leave our minds to ponder the implied spiritual connections, the reading jumps to the women in search of the tomb on Easter morning—from Garden to Tomb to Exodus to Resurrection. It is like a time machine, dramatically tying together the meaning of events over centuries of history, bringing chills to my spine in a way that only the most magnificent art, vistas, movies, and stories can do. As the women look for the tomb, a voice breaks in from the darkness, jolting a turn in the story line: "You are looking for Jesus. But he is not here; he is risen." A shofar (ram's horn) is blown, tearing through the dark, tying the Resurrection with the great Jewish Jubilee wherein debts were to be cancelled and slaves released. Then, a match is lit, the first light seen in over an hour of pitch black, and our priest starts a fire upon an altar. From this fire, our seemingly druidic priest, who holds his hands up above the fire as if to bless it in some kind of pagan appreciation, lights several candles from it. He walks around the fire to four women—the first evangelists and progenitors of the Church—and gives them each a candle. "Go, spread the good news: Christ is risen." Each of these women walks through the darkness out to us seated, saying, as they reach their candle toward us, "Christ is risen." We all light a candle from theirs—a symbol of how the Good News is spread from person to person—and in moments, the darkness is filled with the warm, orange glow of fire. The priest exclaims, "Christ is risen!" and we all lift our candles in the air, saying, "Indeed he is risen"—and this is repeated two more times in honor of the Trinity.

After the candle-lifting, two beloved opera singers, who have blessed our parish with their voices, roll out a scroll about ten feet in length and, with its ornate writing (akin to the Book of Kells) illuminated by their candles, they begin to sing from it.

> Rejoice, heavenly powers! Sing, choirs of angels! Exult, all creation around God's throne! Jesus Christ, our King, is risen! Rejoice, O earth, in shining splendor, radiant in the brightness of your King! Christ has conquered! Glory fills you! Darkness vanishes for ever! Rejoice, O Mother Church! Exult in glory! The risen Savior shines upon you! Let this place resound

with joy, echoing the mighty song of all God's people!
. . . For Christ has ransomed us with his blood, and
paid for us the price of Adam's sin to our eternal
Father! This is our Passover feast, when Christ, the
true Lamb, is slain, whose blood consecrates the
homes of all believers. This is the night when first
you saved our fathers: you freed the people of Israel
from their slavery and led them dry-shod through the
sea. . . . This is the night when Jesus Christ broke the
chains of death and rose triumphant from the grave.
. . . O happy fault, O necessary sin of Adam, which
gained for us so great a Redeemer! Most blessed of
all nights, chosen by God to see Christ rising from the
dead! Of this night scripture says: "The night will be
as clear as day: it will become my light, my joy." The
power of this holy night dispels all evil, washes guilt
away, restores lost innocence, brings mourners joy; it
casts out hatred, brings us peace, and humbles earthly
pride. Night truly blessed when heaven is wedded
to earth and man is reconciled with God! Therefore,
heavenly Father, in the joy of this night, receive our
evening sacrifice of praise, your Church's solemn
offering. Accept this Easter candle, a flame divided
but undimmed, a pillar of fire that glows to the honor
of God. . . . Let it mingle with the lights of heaven and
continue bravely burning to dispel the darkness of this
night! May the Morning Star which never sets find
this flame still burning: Christ, that Morning Star, who
came back from the dead, and shed his peaceful light
on all mankind, your Son, who lives and reigns for
ever and ever. Amen.

With that long scroll now strewn on the ground and candles lifted high, we proceed to baptize a catechumen who has
been preparing, through biblical study with a church-appointed

teacher, to join this mysterious resurrection cult. We start the Baptism by renouncing "Satan, and all his works, and all his empty promises," and we do so by turning to look *outside* the gathered throng of candles into the darkness.

We then turn to the front, where the fire of resurrection was first lit, and, with its remains now only in ashes, in its place stands a multitude holding up candles. In response to the priest's question, "Do you believe in . . ." naming all the major points of the Apostles' Creed, we respond, "I do believe," raising our candles at each proclamation. The baptismal candidate is told that this is the faith we together profess and the communal faith into which he or she is joining.

The priest then proceeds to "bless" the water, speaking to it in appreciation for all it has done. The really startling part here is how it is actually true—molecules of this water indeed *were* present at the Baptism of Jesus by John the Baptist; if you can fancy Jesus actually walking on water, it follows that he walked on *these* molecules—not ones from another fairy tale world; Moses did part *these* waters; and, tracing back to the beginning of all things, indeed these very particles have been present since the genesis of the universe. Again, *this* world, and these drops of water before your eyes, are touched by the divine—not, as my mind once pictured, another ideal world. The liturgy is doing what it is meant to do: not give me a sacred fairy tale to hope for, as if to give me an opiate to deal with a dreary universe, but give me *new eyes to see this world as immense, glorious, and mysterious as it is.* While the culmination of the universe may still seem far off, its direction and goal has been sighted in the Resurrection.

This revelation of cosmic significance is soon brought to the highest form of celebration that I've experienced, eliciting the deepest movements of the soul by proclaiming that the "wedding feast of the Lamb has been prepared" and we are all welcomed to celebrate. I do not exaggerate in saying it is an event on par with witnessing the birth of my son. And this is not because my son's birth wasn't of the most profound nature for me, but because this dramatic worship of life's triumph is the well from which I draw meaning *in* my son's birth—it is the backdrop which gives all the rest its meaning. All present ring bells, with their candles lifted high, and sing "Alleluia" in glorious fashion. The bell tower joins our little bells as we emerge from the cellar-tomb and slowly process, behind a leader lifting a crucifix of the murdered-God high, through the fragile and murder-ridden streets. Fellow friends and parishioners are revealed to be not mere mortals, but greeters in a great eschatological procession, lining the streets swinging incense censures, singing, ushering us along the path into the cosmic banquet over which the tortured victim presides as the loving, forgiving host. The sun has just risen, and the sky feels cool and freshly awakened for the new day of creation—the *eighth* day, extending beyond Genesis' seventh day into a new era. (That's why baptismal fonts are eight sided.) It is a celebration of the utterly uncelebrated—what we, up until the last few thousand years of this long, weary history of our world, have avoided celebrating. Christianity actually is news; and it actually is good.

We turn a corner in the procession, following the lofted crucifix, and I look to the back of the procession. Our priest Michael, at the back of our enchanted parade, swinging a censure of incense, swiftly turns around in about face, as if he had dropped something. He shuffles with his white robes to the place where a young woman had been shot a few months prior—he had tended to her while the ambulance arrived—and died a few hours later. A few remnants of a weathered memorial, ribbons and teddy bears, hang from a street sign. He stops there, all alone as the procession carried on, and swings incense at the memorial with a blessing of prayer and affection for this slain lamb.

From the streets, we approach our old, stone church, from which come pealing bells and amplified sounds of the organ and cantor inside. (Sleeping neighbors are constrained to tolerate, if just once a year, this loud celebration.) When we reach the interior, with incense rising high up to the frescoes of ancient scenes, we continue to ring bells and circle the church, elevating our hallelujahs even louder than before and raising our candles, with the organ belting between macabre minor chords and triumphant major chords—as if to mirror the paradox of celebrating the triumph of a forgiving resurrection over murder and death. After processing throughout the interior of the church, we gather in the pews to face the front, and all raise their candles high for the climactic hallelujahs. Then the singing and organ cease, and the priest proclaims, "Christ is risen!" and in reply we say, "Indeed, he is risen!"—again, three times, lofting our candles in each declaration. "Welcome to the wedding feast of the Lamb. The Lamb that is slain has triumphed." It is a liturgy that seems to have found a crack in the base of heaven, and, just for a moment, it has squeezed down into our time-and-space continuum. We break open our weary views of this world with a universe-bursting apocalypse—all for the sake of seeing with new eyes what is before us. Just like our proclamation about the Incarnation, heaven and earth have become one for a short glimpse of time, to open our eyes to the impossible.

Even to believers my account may appear fanciful. For others, it may sound like nothing more than a silly ritualistic opiate to ward off the fright of facing the dark abyss of stars above. I might have thought so a decade ago. But, for me, it is now real, and only by experiencing it did it become real to me. Words and theology are only words; but participating in this liturgy brought things into physical reality and practice. Even pictures wouldn't suffice to convey a liturgy of the Easter mysteries. A parishioner darted about the paschal procession, attempting to capture some photos. I actually believed that her camera might burst from the excessive reality squeezed into this eschatological morning. At least, I was sure, the lens would crack from the gravity. Never before had I wept in desperate hope for, and celebration of, the transfiguration of our universe, in a divine culmination of life. This was my ceremony, and I breathed upon it.

CONCLUSION

Just as joining the Catholic Church, for me, is not so much a destination as an *open process*, writing this book has changed me. Perhaps most importantly it helped me see more clearly how my engagement with Catholicism is mirrored in my engagement with Camden, and vice versa. In these pages, I have pondered how to engage with the hopelessness of our world and, at times, of the Catholic Church. And I have ventured to say that, for me, I found reasons to engage with hope—not because circumstances warrant hope, but because there is no enduring way forward except with a sort of "fanatical pessimism and fanatical optimism" combined. Prompted by an unrelenting evangelical fervor—for which I am truly grateful—to dive into a broken world, I risked living in Camden. And with a similar reckless abandon, I opened myself up to all the challenges and questions of the Catholic Church. I especially hope that these stories invite my readers to their own journeys, to stretching themselves.

And, as for my reflections on the Mass and how it relates to murder and violence, I hope they will encourage both Protestant and Catholic readers toward deeper reflection on what the "sacrifice of Mass" uniquely offers our bloody era. And I hope that in interpreting the Mass through Girard I've opened up some fresh ways of seeing the gospel's intriguing relationship to paganism, rituals, dying-and-rising-gods, and atheism. Perhaps, too, my reflections on the impossibility of being nondenominational offer some way beyond the contradictory fashions of "Forget the Church, Follow Jesus." If those thoughts implied to my reader that Christianity is somehow "stuck" with dealing with tradition, they are right; and perhaps my "hanging in there" with a dysfunctional family has highlighted one way to enact an urgently needed patience. Ultimately, however, I've found that patient engagement with tradition doesn't make us "stuck" with a static faith, but enables the most intelligent forms of progress and critical engagement. And I hope that my reflections upon art, asceticism, and the apocalyptic imagination will spur readers to retain their prophetic defense of the poor and denunciation of the exploits of the rich (globally speaking, I the author and you the reader ought to be considered among them), but find some creative, joyful, and hopeful way forward. My hope is that the path forward will minimize dreary resentment of embellishment, allowing for new, just, and substantial contributions to religious art and ritual. From the perspective of a city which has all but lost these celebrations of life and God, I can only beckon readers to again step into the imagination of the father in *The Road*, who had lost everything, except his innocent, hungry, and vulnerable son: "When you've nothing else, construct ceremonies out of the air and breathe upon them." Beauty is non-optional to me now.

Lastly, let's say a fair-minded person, or even a briskly insane one, said that I love the Catholic Church only because I've found such an appealing parish—that I love it because the liturgy (its tone, pace, symbolism, and order) is finely tuned there, the architecture and ceiling frescoes haven't been touched by the always-dated, ugly, avant-garde hand of modernism, and, more curiously, the setting of urban devastation makes the celebration of the Resurrection all the more profound. I would have to concede that they are partly right. It isn't fair—Sacred Heart is one of the more amazing churches I've been to, aesthetically and socially, and I'm lucky enough to live under its wings, just across the street. I would imagine it *much* more difficult for anyone to work through the challenges of the Catholic Church without visiting a parish as alluring as mine. While many folks find Sunday mornings to be like eating sand, my experience is often more like fine wine and aged cheese.

But the criticism that I love the global Catholic Church only for these local features (which I could lose any day with a sanctuary fire or the reassignment of a pastor), is a specious argument; it's almost like telling someone, "You like that ballet only because of the eloquent dancing," or, "You like that band merely because their music is enjoyable." One could imagine that conversation proceeding awkwardly.

While Sacred Heart indeed has a well-tuned liturgy and amiable community, I don't hesitate to say there are many things *I dislike* about Sacred Heart—and, much more, the global Catholic Church—and that my dislikes sometimes weigh on me heavily. For example, like at any organization, at Sacred Heart there are hurdles to truly feeling a part of things, whether in leadership or friendships; and being used to the well-prepared and exegetically insightful sermons at Willow Creek, it has taken some time to appreciate the homilies at Sacred Heart; I have sometimes felt that Mass was like a penance of boredom to chastise my over-hyped evangelicalism. Especially at the beginning, I often referred to myself as in evangelical-hype-detox. For all the meaning I tried to find in attending Sacred Heart, I still had to challenge myself to go there. I had to step outside my comfort zone, to be vulnerable to something I initially opposed.

I readily admit that somebody could just as well experience something beautiful in leaving Catholicism and being moved by Protestantism. That, after all, is exactly what my family did when I was young. I know from experience that wherever Christians build into and love their local gathering—whatever its denominational affiliation—it will likely become all the more lovable. But as discussed in these latter chapters, there are reasons (very good reasons, I think) not to treat denominations like brands of cereal, choosing simply what satisfies us. In this regard, my book might be seen as an experiment in finding Chesterton's difference between *liking* something and *loving* something.

Sacred Heart is simply breathing upon ceremonies that are globally available in the Catholic Church—and local parishes can choose to breathe upon them as well. It is Sacred Heart's beautiful execution of this shared, rough, liturgical structure that drew me in at first. But after seeing the bones inside the Body of Christ (its teachings on unity, its corpus of philosophy and history, its stability, its [I know, disputed] claim to apostolic succession, its meaningful play between scripture and tradition, its catalog of saints), I more deeply affirmed a global commitment to the Church, stemming from my local experience. It is my hope that I have enough faith in God to abide in this body, wherever my life leads, even when the Church appears to droop, or even —God help us—when we've lost our civilization, crying, "My God, my God, why have you forsaken us?" Whatever floods may come in the coming centuries, we must ask, will it be an ark worth boarding?

AFTERWORD

I am generally allergic to apologetic theology, in both senses of the term. Apologetics, in the form of breathless tales of conversion, usually leave me cold, especially if the author claims to have finally found certainty in the Catholic Church as a bulwark against the chaos of the age. People who are seeking certainty above all else should be followers of Vladimir Putin, or maybe Simon Cowell, not Jesus. Following a crucified God should not give you a sense that you have a firm place to stand; it should leave you wondering what hit you. At the same time, people who are apologetic about being Catholic—that is, who apologize for being Catholic, as in the lay homilist who introduced himself as a "recovering Catholic"—also miss the mark. I can find plenty in the Church to complain about, but it is hard to sustain a faith life on negativity alone.

Chris Haw has written a wonderful account of his own journey to Catholicism that avoids both triumphalism and negativity. Haw has joined the Church and lived in it with his eyes wide open, without being wide-eyed. He gives a compelling account of how it is possible to live a beautiful life in the Catholic Church, and how the Church makes that life possible. This is the one book I would put in the hands of anyone who wonders why they should join the Catholic Church or why they should not leave it.

What gives Haw's account credibility is that Haw has lived. He has been around the block a few times. It takes courage and openness to the uncomfortable and awesome messiness of life to go around the particular block in Camden that Haw has called home for a number of years now. He has earned his judgments on God and human beings and the material world where the two meet. He is not trying to construct a vision of the Church that will keep him safe. In the Church instead he has found a way to make sense of and celebrate the grace of a God that became incarnate in an ugly and gorgeous and dangerous world.

Haw's personal account of his own searching for authenticity in an unjust world makes for compelling reading. Many readers will relate to the stories of youthful zeal, of struggling to make intentional community, of a middle-class white guy negotiating inner-city life. But I confess that, as a theologian, my favorite part of the book is the second part, where Haw steps back to contemplate and explain his thoughts on the Church in which he has found himself. It turns out that Haw is an excellent theologian. He has, to my mind, all the right instincts when it comes to reflecting on God and faith and the Church. He begins by turning his attention to the concrete rituals and things with which a Catholic deals: kissing the crucifix on Good Friday, making the sign of the cross, approaching the altar for the Eucharist, and much more. There he finds the Catholic emphasis on encountering God in the material world. Sacramental life is not an occasional ritual but a whole way of living in the world that allows for no fundamental antagonism between God and God's good creation.

Haw's comments on denominationalism and the Church are also rich. In a capitalist society we tend to treat faith life as another item subject to consumption. We want to avoid commitment, shunning "organized religion," and flitting from one spirituality to another in the hopes that our needs will be met. The idea that we can step back into such a neutral position is illusory. In our aversion to formation, we are deeply formed in the habits of avoiding habits, of which the virtues are a type. Haw shows how being "open-minded" is one of the primary prejudices of our age; we want to make up our own minds even when they are not worth making up. Haw makes good use of the idea that the

Church is more like a family than a group of Facebook friends; the Eucharist makes us "flesh and blood" to each other. Perhaps this is why Catholics complain so much about the Church rather than just leave. You don't secede from your family; you complain about them. You're stuck with them, so you try to love them, even when they drive you crazy. And they probably feel the same way about you.

Hierarchy, dogma, tradition—words that have all the sex appeal of "orthopedic shoes"—Haw explains how they have come to make sense to him. Perhaps in a world where "freedom" is what we kill for—you gotta fight for your right to party, as the song goes—the practice of obedience is what it takes to be a rebel. Haw's obedience is a radical obedience. He does not attempt to whitewash the manifold sins of the Church, both of its leaders and its laity. We must remain perpetually dissatisfied with the Church. As Dorothy Day reminds us, the Church is the cross on which Christ is crucified, but you can't have Christ without his Cross. At the same time, Day constantly called the Church Christ's Body, where, as Paul says, the weak and the strong members suffer and rejoice together. When the Church is deficient, Haw indicates, we must do what we do habitually for our troubled friends and family members: love them into being better.

I have experienced this book as a gift. This book has renewed my tired old faith that I live in a tired old Church. Converts often make the best Catholics—Thomas Merton, Walker Percy, Dorothy Day, Marshall McLuhan, G. K. Chesterton, and Alasdair MacIntyre are just a few that come to mind. If this is true, then Catholics owe a debt to others, often Protestants. Chris Haw would probably not have been a good Catholic without Willow Creek, not just because he found out what he was missing there, but because he found there the urgency for the Gospel that was missing from the Catholic Church he knew as a young child, and from many other Catholic churches, sad to say. Perhaps Willow Creek is a gift to the Catholic Church, and perhaps the Catholic Church can be a gift to Willow Creek too.

This book, then, is in part about why the Catholic communion is good, but it is not about why the Protestant communions are bad. This book is blissfully free from polemics, which we don't need. Haw's book is a gift to a Church too often divided by "conservatives" who demand submission and "liberals" who demand freedom. Chris Haw has, through his witness and his words, opened up a broader vision of a truly Catholic life beautifully lived.

William T. Cavanaugh, PhD

NOTES

Introduction

1. This video can be seen at www.youtube.com/watch?v=1IAhDGYlpqY.

2. A popular presentation of this idea can be found in Phyllis Tickle's *The Great Emergence* (Grand Rapids, MI: Baker, 2008).

3. This lesson can be seen in the Hebrew language and practice of memory: "Ancient Israel, unlike modern Western people, did not look to the future. It always imagined the future as *behind it*. It had the future at its back. The Hebrew word for future is 'behind' (*ahar*). The past, on the other hand, is 'before' (*qedem*). The Israelites would not have said 'Auschwitz is behind us,' but 'it is before us, it lies before our eyes.'" Gerhard Lohfink, *Does God Need the Church?: Toward a Theology of the People of God* (Collegeville, MN: Liturgical Press, 1999), 105.

Chapter One: From Mass to Megachurch

1. Dietrich Bonhoeffer, *Life Together* (New York: Harper Collins, 1954), 33.

2. It would take me several years to find that anyone could spar with such an erudite Oxford don and show that his logic was not the final word. Lewis was stopped in his tracks in a debate with Catholic linguistic philosopher Elizabeth Anscombe. She apparently dismantled Lewis's defense of God and miracles. And while she thought not too much of the exchange, Lewis was forever changed; he thereafter never wrote another theological nonfiction book and stuck to fiction, children's stories, and devotional literature. See G.E.M. Anscombe, *Metaphysics and the Philosophy of Mind* (Oxford: Bail Blackwood, 1981).

3. The Economic Policy Institute's State of Working America, "Ratio of Average CEO Total Direct Compensation to Average Worker Compensation, from 1965–2009." See also Mercer/Hay Group Study (2010).

4. Though the numbers are disputed by different sources, as of 2011, the Department of Defense reported 611 total foreign bases, and 4,825 total bases: "Base Structure Report: Fiscal Year 2011 Baseline (A Summary of DoD's Real Property Inventory)."

5. This school, located in Fort Benning, Georgia, was known as the US Army School of the Americas (or "of Assassins," to its critics) and because of criticism changed its name to Western Hemisphere Institute for Security Cooperation. People of faith and critical goodwill gather there annually in protest and civil disobedience, in hopes of its eventual dissolution or reform.

6. *The Hauerwas Reader*, eds. John Berkman and Michael G. Cartwright (Durham, NC: Duke University Press, 2001), 30.

Chapter Two: From Class to Streets

1. Joint Session of Congress, September 20, 2001.

2. See Philip Zimbardo, *The Lucifer Effect: Understanding How Good People Become Evil* (New York: Random House, 2008).

3. James Aho, *This Thing of Darkness: A Sociology of the Enemy* (Seattle, WA: University of Washington Press, 1994), 12.

4. Matthew 10:16.

Chapter Three: From Streets to Jungle

1. For some examples, see US General Accounting Office, Report to Congressional Requesters, "Marine Pollution: Progress Made to Reduce Pollution by Cruise Ships, But Important Issues Remain," GAO/RCED-00-48, February 2000.

2. 1 Thessalonians 4:17.

3. Steven Bouma-Prediger, *For the Beauty of the Earth* (Grand Rapids, MI: Baker, 2010), 69. The rapture doctrine, which in my evangelical world I had identified as elemental to Christianity, was actually constructed around the seventeenth century.

4. 2 Peter 3:10.

5. Bouma-Prediger, *For the Beauty of the Earth*, 68. Note how the different translations of the last part of 2 Peter 3:10 imply a potentially enormous difference. Some point toward a dissolution of matter and physicality, but others to a refining of matter: "shall be burned up" (NASB, KJV, DBT, DRB, ASV, AKJV, WBT, ERV, WEB, YLT, NJB); "will be laid bare" (NIV); "will be found to deserve judgment" (NLT); "will be exposed" (ESV); "will be utterly burned up" (Weymouth New Testament); "will be disclosed" (NRSV); "will be found out" (NAB). An even more exciting translation is the *Aramaic Bible in Plain English*, "The Earth and the works that are in it *will be discovered*." (Emphasis mine.)

6. Bouma-Prediger, *For the Beauty of the Earth*, 70. Cf. Thomas Finger, "Evangelicals, Eschatology, and the Environment," Scholars Circle monograph, 2 (Evangelical Environmental Network, 1998), 5.

7. Genesis 28:16.

8. *Soma pneumatikon* (1 Corinthians 15:44). Matthew 24:31, 35, 40–43. John 20f.

9. Wendell Berry, "Christianity and the Survival of Creation," in *Sex, Economy, Freedom and Community* (New York: Pantheon Books, 1993), 99ff.

10. David Kirkpatrick, "The Evangelical Crackup," the *New York Times*, October 28, 2007.

11. Address to the Diplomatic Corps accredited to the Holy See, January, 13 2003.

Chapter Four: From Jungle to War

1. For a solid interpretation of Romans 13, see John Howard Yoder's *The Politics of Jesus* (Grand Rapids, MI: Wm. B. Eerdmans, 1994).

2. Isaiah 2:4; 11:6.

3. Wendell Berry, "A Citizen's Response to the National Security Strategy of the USA," oriononline.org.

4. Wendell Berry, *Sex, Economy, Freedom and Community*, 85ff.

5. Ron Sider, Mennonite World Conference, Strasbourg, France, 1984.

6. Unattributed source of Catholic Worker oral tradition—apparently from a poster in a hall in Washington, DC where Dorothy Day once spoke.

7. Wendell Berry, "The Failure of War," in *Citizenship Papers* (Berkeley, CA: Counterpoint, 2004), 25.

8. Thomas Merton, *Conjectures of a Guilty Bystander* (New York: Doubleday, 1966), 81.

9. Eugene McCarraher, "This Book Is Not Good," review of *God Is Not Great*, by Christopher Hitchens, *Commonweal* (June 15, 2007), http://commonwealmagazine.org/book-not-good-0, accessed March 26, 2012.

10. Dallas Willard, *The Divine Conspiracy* (San Francisco: HarperOne, 1998).

Chapter Five: From War to Concrete Jungle

1. Published memorandum from Frank Matula to Michael Klein, Section Chief, New Jersey Bureau of Technical Services, "Stack Test Report for Camden County Energy Recovery Associates—Camden," (PI No. 51614; BOP No. 100003; TST No. 100003), December 28, 2011.

2. Jonathan Kozol found Camden worth documenting in his book *Savage Inequalities* (New York: Crown Publishers, 1991). See also Howard Gilette's *Camden After the Fall* (Philadelphia, PA: University of Pennsylvania Press, 2006) for more history on the city.

3. An excellent documentary on these events is *The Camden 28*, directed by Anthony Giacchino, aired by PBS's "Point of View" series. Also, a book of numerous letters from Msgr. Michael Doyle is titled, *It's a Terrible Day, Thanks Be to God* (Camden, NJ: The Heart of Camden Inc., 2003).

4. Matthew 25:40.

5. Henri Nouwen, *The Wounded Healer* (New York: Doubleday, 1972), 41.

6. Alan Lindsay Mackay, "Archimedes ca 287–212 BC," in *A Dictionary of Scientific Quotations*. (London: Taylor and Francis, 1991), 11. The actual quote is, "Give me a place to stand, and I shall move the earth with a lever." Quoted by Pappus of Alexandria.

7. Wendell Berry, "Manifesto: The Mad Farmers Liberation Front," *Reclaiming Politics* (IC #30) Fall/Winter, 1991, 62.

8. G. K. Chesterton, *Orthodoxy* (San Francisco: Ignatius Press, 1995 [orig. 1908]), 72.

Part Two: Contemplation (with Some Action)

1. John A. T. Robinson, *Honest to God* (Louisville, KY: Westminster John Knox Press, 2003 [orig. 1963]).

2. Robinson, *Honest to God*, 29ff.

3. Herbert McCabe writes, "If the question of God were a neat and simple question to be answered in terms of familiar concepts, then whatever we are talking

about, it is not God. A God who is in this sense comprehensible would not be worth worshipping, or even talking about (except for the purpose of destroying him)." McCabe summarizes Wittgenstein, saying, "Not *how* the world is, but *that* it is, is the mystery." *God Matters* (New York: Continuum, 1987), 5.

Eugene McCarraher puts this problem fairly succinctly, "As Aquinas and many others have patiently explained, God is not an entity and thus is not ensnared in any serial account of causality. Not a thing himself, God is rather the condition of there being anything at all. Thus, 'creation' is not a gargantuan act of handicraft but rather the condition of there being something rather than nothing. Creation didn't happen long ago; it's right now, and forever. (This is why 'creationism' is bad science—*because* it's bad theology.)" "This Book Is Not Good."

4. Swarms of interpretations surround this name; "I am *that* I am" is better at describing self-existence than the Popeye-like "I am what I am"—for anybody could say the latter. "I will be what I will be" is another interpretation of this mysterious name. Thanks to Dr. Godzieba at Villanova University for the insight.

5. Cited from Chesterton's "notebook" by his biographer, Maisie Ward, in *Gilbert Keith Chesterton: A Biography* (Sheed and Ward, 2005 [orig. 1943]), 56.

6. Paraphrase of G. K. Chesterton, *The Everlasting Man* (San Francisco: Ignatius Press, 1993 [orig. 1925]), 170.

7. Ludwig Wittgenstein, *Tractatus Logico-Philosophicus* (London: Routledge, 2001 [orig. 1921]), 3, 89.

8. Acts 17:28.

9. I use the term "invent" here with inspiration from Professor Terrence Tilley of Fordham University. His book *Inventing Catholic Tradition* (Maryknoll, NY: Orbis, 2000) draws out the dual meaning of this word. Some inventions, like nuclear fusion, are in fact revelations and harnessings of something found in the world; other inventions, like money, are entirely human constructs.

Chapter Six: Murder and the Mass

1. My astute readers should note that Good Friday worship in the Catholic Church isn't officially a "Mass" in its own right, in that its Eucharist has been consecrated the night before on Holy Thursday. Catholic worship on the Evening of Holy Thursday, the afternoon of Good Friday, and the Easter Vigil make up one complete liturgy known as the *Triduum.*

2. Years after this, as the casualties piled up, a study was released, estimating the innocent dead in the wake of the US invasion of Iraq to be over 600,000. Gilbert Burnham, Riyadh Lafta, Shannon Doocy, Les Roberts, "Mortality after 2003 Invasion of Iraq: A Cross-Sectional Cluster Sample Survey," *Lancet* 368, Issue 9545 (21 October 2006): 1421–28.

3. Nicholas Wolterstorff, *Lament for a Son* (Grand Rapids, MI: Wm. B. Eerdmans, 1987), 81.

4. The revised missal states it as "willingly entered into his passion."

5. Chesterton, *Orthodoxy*, 145.

6. Jams Alison, "God's Self-Substitution and Sacrificial Inversion," in *Stricken by God?* eds. Brad Jersak and Michael Hardin (Grand Rapids, MI: Wm. B. Eerdmans, 2007), 175.

7. "We preach Christ crucified . . ." (1 Cor 1:23). "The cross of Christ" (Gal 6:12) also appears to serve, at least in this epistle, as Paul's summary of the Gospel. Consider also the centrality of the cross in the song of Philippians 2.

I must acknowledge here Rita Nakashima-Brock and Rebecca Ann Parker for their impressive work in *Saving Paradise: How Christianity Traded Love of This World for Crucifixion and Empire* (Boston, MA: Beacon Books, 2008). By examining the history of art, they found that the Cross as a form of devotional art comes much later in Church history, interlaced with an unhealthy appraisal of suffering, obscuring the more primordial Christian vision of *paradise.* "The authors of the Passion narratives constructed an innovative strategy to resist public torture and execution. They created a literature of disclosure and wove the killing of Jesus into the fabric of a long history of violence against those who spoke for justice. . . . The purpose of such writing is assuredly not to valorize victims, to praise their suffering as redemptive, to reveal 'true love' as submission and self-sacrifice, or to say that God requires the passive acceptance of violence. . . .We disagree with these theological perspectives because they contravene assumptions of power by the oppressed and suggest that life can be saved by passivity. Not so" (51ff, 437). Space and scope prohibit me from outlining how my reflections here and in the next chapter harmonize and, at times, might stand in tension with their perspective.

8. Luke 11:47; Matthew 23:29.

9. A comical aside regarding optimistic idealism: I heard a hilarious story while writing this book that a courthouse somewhere had experimented with the artsy installation of glass stairs. Now women prone to wearing skirts started finding this troublesome, as another flight of stairs was under the glass. One defender of the stairs proclaimed, "If we could all just be mature, responsible adults about this, we can just move on." A judge responded quite wryly about his optimism: "Sir, if we all just acted like mature, responsible adults, we wouldn't have needed to build this courthouse."

10. Bonhoeffer spoke of this as "cheap grace": "Cheap grace is the preaching of forgiveness without requiring repentance. Baptism without church discipline. Communion without confession. Cheap grace is grace without discipleship, grace without the cross, grace without Jesus Christ." Dietrich Bonhoeffer, *The Cost of Discipleship* (New York: Touchstone, 1995), 44.

11. John H. Yoder, *The Politics of Jesus*, 51.

12. The apocalyptic imagery in Revelation, where the final triumph of the Lamb is envisioned, is not what one normally imagines. Books like the *Left Behind* series often entice readers into thinking that some immense violent struggle is somehow envisioned or even prescribed by Revelation's wild visions—or worse, that we have to anxiously prepare our hearts and minds to engage in such violence. To the contrary, Revelation's images of triumphing over the "forces of evil" are about the Word of Truth—that is, Christ's tongue, speech—immediately wiping away forces of death and destruction. There is no vision of a *Lord of the Rings*-style epic battle;

Armageddon is immediately resolved by the Truth; there is not even a drip of sweat or effort. And though his tongue indeed wipes out anything in opposition, represented by blood washing out like a river, the real center and epitome of "blood" language in Revelation is the "the Lamb that was slain." In that haunting image of Christ "riding in on a horse, with his robe dipped in blood," that is not the blood of his enemies, but his *own*. (And if this reading of John's intention is not convincing, we might simply ask what Revelation *meant* for its early readers—early Christians were renowned for their nonviolence and martyrdoms.) See Eberhard Arnold, *The Early Christians in their Own Words* (Rifton, NY: Plough, 2011).

13. A continued theme from the *Saving Paradise* endnote above: feminist interpreters rightly raise caution here, as such language is easily, and has been, a tool for the oppression of women, encouraging passive submission. I suppose a crude line of demarcation here is whether to view such abuses as *essential* to the cross-centric Gospel (and thus it should all be thrown out) or to view such abuses as corruptions of an otherwise laudable veneration of the victim.

14. John 14:27.

15. William Cavanaugh, *Torture and Eucharist* (Malden, MA: Blackwell Publishing, 1998), 229.

16. Ibid., 231–32. He also writes here: "Unlike ordinary food, the body does not become assimilated into our bodies, but vice versa. Thus Augustine reports in his *Confessions* that he heard a voice from on high say to him, 'I am the food of the fully grown; grow and you will feed on me. And you will not change me into you, like the food your flesh eats, but you will be changed into me'" (Ibid., 231ff.).

17. Thanks to Logan Laituri for pointing out to me that this word, "liturgy," for Greeks, was mostly used to describe cleaning the sewage from the streets.

Chapter Seven: Pagan Christianity

1. G. K. Chesterton, "The Thing: Why I Am a Catholic," in *Collected Works vol 3* (San Francisco: Ignatius Press, 1990), 237.

2. Matthew is the winged man or angel; Mark is a winged lion; Luke is a winged ox or bull; John is an eagle.

3. Luke 20:38; Mark 12:26–27.

4. In recent years, however, I understand Willow Creek has attempted some experimentation in ritual.

5. Andrea Cohen-Kiener, et al., *Claiming Earth as Common Ground: The Ecological Crisis through the Lens of Faith* (Woodstock, VT: Skylight Paths, 2009), 107. She continues with many examples from our neighborhood gardens: "We plant potatoes in the garden on St. Patrick's Day. We fire the bread oven that we made from natural materials and cook these potatoes when they are harvested on June 16 for Blooms Day . . . On March 25, nine months before Christmas, on the Feast of the Annunciation of the Virgin Mary, the day of Angel Gabriel's visitation announcing her pregnancy, we plant the marigolds for our garden, waiting in expectation for the glory they will bring for the Feast of the Assumption of Mary in August . . ." (107ff.).

6. Chesterton, *Orthodoxy*, 152.

7. G. K. Chesterton, *Heretics* (Norwood, MA: Plimpton Press, 1905), 156.

8. One such popular work, by Frank Viola and George Barna, is *Pagan Christianity* (Carol Stream, IL: Barna Books [Tyndale], 2002). It considers this blend of paganism and Christianity not a good but a *betrayal* of some "pure" faith. By contrast, I found Chesterton provocative in describing how much of our goods in Western Civilization, indeed, come from paganism and Christianity combined. Paganism handed us down its festivals and rituals preserved in Christianity, along with its "sad and reasonable" virtues like justice, temperance, and fortitude. Christianity added to these the "gay, mystical, unreasonable, and exuberant" virtues of faith, hope, and love. But, "Everything else in the modern world is of Christian origin, even everything that seems most anti-Christian. The French Revolution is of Christian origin. The newspaper is of Christian origin. The anarchists are of Christian origin. Physical science is of Christian origin. The attack on Christianity is of Christian origin. There is one thing, and one thing only, in existence at the present day which can in any sense accurately be said to be of pagan origin, and that is Christianity" (*Heretics*, 157).

9. Dionysus, also known as Bacchus, was one of the more popular of the Mediterranean gods. Numerous stories proliferated about him; in them, he was killed by the Titans. They consumed his flesh, and he rose again via his heart being grafted into Zeus's thigh. Among other things, Dionysus was the god of the wine and grape harvest.

10. *The Girard Reader*, ed. James G. Williams (Chestnut Ridge, NY: Crossroads, 1996): "There is no sacrificial religion without a drama at the center, and the more closely you observe it, the more you discover that the features common to the *martyrdom* of Dionysus and Jesus are also common to an immeasurable number of other cults not only in Greek or Indo-European religions but in the entire world. This remarkable similarity is one important reason why the later Nietzsche can resort to a single symbol, Dionysus, for countless mythological cults" (248). Also, "[Nietzsche] singled out the biblical and the Christian not because Jesus' martyrdom is different but because it is not. It has to be the same for the martyrdom of Jesus to be an explicit allusion to the genesis of all pagan religions and a silent but definitive condemnation of pagan order, of all human order really" (250).

11. René Girard, "Dionysus Versus the Crucified." *Modern Language Notes*, Vol. 99, No. 4, French Issue (Sep, 1984), 816–835, Johns Hopkins University Press, 821–822. See also fragment 1052 in "The Two Types: Dionysus and the Crucified," from Frederick Nietzsche, *The Will to Power*, ed. Walter Kaufman (New York: Vintage Books, 1968): "It is *not* a difference in regard to their martyrdom—it is a difference in the meaning of it. Life itself, its eternal fruitfulness and recurrence, creates torment, destruction, the will to annihilation. In the other case, suffering—the 'Crucified as the innocent one'—counts as an objection to this life, as a formula for its condemnation" (537).

See also, René Girard, *I See Satan Fall Like Lightning* (Maryknoll, NY: Orbis, 2001), 170ff.

See also, Peter Wick, "Jesus gegen Dionysos? Ein Beitrag zur Kontextualisierung des Johannesevangeliums," *Biblica* 85, no. 2 (2004): 179–98. Given that Dionysus is the god of wine, and that he was widely worshipped in Syria and Palestine at the time, it fascinates me to consider how the Cana event (and perhaps elements of the eucharistic stories and the entire gospel of John) might be considered a sort of comparative polemic for first- and second-century readers, exalting Jesus above Dionysus. See also Hengel, Martin Henel, *Studies in Early Christology* (New York: T & T Clark, 1998), 330ff.

12. That and a rivalry with a contemporary Richard Wagner. See René Girard, "Superman in the Underground: Strategies of Madness—Nietzsche, Wagner, and Dostoevsky, MLN," *Comparative Literature* 91, No. 6 (December 1976), 1161–85.

13. *The Girard Reader*, 256. Nietzsche, *Gay Science*, aphorism 125. See also Nietzsche, *The Will to Power*, fragment 1052.

14. Gil Bailie, *Violence Unveiled* (New York: Crossroads, 1996), 116.

15. Exodus 20:17, my rendition. See also Girard, *I See Satan Fall Like Lightning*, 7.

16. James 4:1.

17. Girard, *I See Satan Fall Like Lightning*, xi. "Scandal" can also mean "trap" or "snare."

18. You may recall this was the assertion of Reverend Jerry Fallwell and Pat Robertson.

19. Many myths use natural disasters to symbolize a social crisis (a drought, a plague, a storm); and it is "solved" through some expulsion—consider Jonah's self-expulsion calming the storm as one example. Another historic example is a "miracle" performed by Appolinarius of Tyana in the third century: a community is suffering a "plague," and a "prophet" comes to town, and after he compels the community to stone a beggar, the town is "healed." Girard, *I See Satan Fall Like Lightning*, 49ff.

20. Consider also Joseph's brothers casting him into the well, Cain killing Abel, Jonah being cast off the boat to quell the storm. Isaiah (53:1ff) recounts a community converging on a victim. Numerous Psalms also recount a sense of being irrationally converged upon by enemies; Girard, in fact, regards the book of Psalms as "the first sustained outcries in world literature of the single victim who is persecuted by enemies" (*I See Satan Fall Like Lightning*, xviii).

21. Chris Hedges's *War Is a Force That Gives Us Meaning* (New York: Anchor, 2003), is another good source to explore this meaning-making power of collective violence.

22. For an articulation of Tezcatlipoca's story, for example, see Bailie, *Violence Unveiled*, 100ff.

23. Being demonized and then divinized is also called "double transference." "Now if the victim could cause all their troubles and yet also produce such peace and prosperity, he or she must be a different sort of being, a higher, more powerful sort. This is the birth of the gods" (Girard, *I See Satan Fall Like Lightning*, xvi).

24. Mark 6:14–16.

25. My claim here is an extension of how Chesterton regards the social meaning of "original sin": "Theosophists for instance will preach an obviously attractive idea like reincarnation; but if we wait for its logical results, they are spiritual super-ciliousness and the cruelty of caste. For if a man is a beggar by his own pre-natal sins, people will tend to despise the beggar. But Christianity preaches an obviously unattractive idea, such as original sin; but when we wait for its results, they are

pathos and brotherhood, and a thunder of laughter and pity; for only with original sin we can at once pity the beggar and distrust the king." Chesterton, *Orthodoxy*, 164.

26. "Why do certain cultures bury their victims under heaps of stones that they often shape into a pyramid form? We can explain this custom as a by-product of ritual stonings" (Girard, *I See Satan Fall Like Lightning*, 91). Also, Bailie, *Violence Unveiled*, 231.

27. Girard, *I See Satan Fall Like Lightning*, 51. Also, Bailie, *Violence Unveiled*, 86.

28. More specifically, the *diablos*, which means "scatters," is followed by the *satan*, whose accusation "gathers" a community (Bailie, *Violence Unveiled*, 206). "'[A]nd if Satan casts out Satan, he is divided against himself; so how can his kingdom stand?' Jesus does not answer, but the answer is obvious. If it is divided against itself, the kingdom of Satan will not stand." René Girard, *The Scapegoat* (Baltimore, MD: Johns Hopkins University Press, 1986), 185.

29. "Homer Simpson versus the eighteenth amendment," *The Simpsons*, Episode 171, (Original air date, March 16, 1997).

30. John 8:44.

31. Consider, for example, how Peter lauded Jesus' excellence, wanting his triumphant version of a Messiah, disdaining the thought of his suffering. Jesus thus identifies Peter as "Satan." This also gives some perspective to the film adaptation of Nikos Kazantzakis's *The Last Temptation of Christ* (New York: Touchstone 1998 [orig. 1953]; film directed by Martin Scorsese, Universal Pictures, 1988). There, Jesus angrily declares to his disciples, "I'm inviting you to a war. . . . The devil is outside us, in the world all around us. Pick up an axe and cut the devil's throat. We'll fight him wherever he is. In the sick, the rich, even in the Temple." This "war on Satan" means, *in effect*, going out to the marginalized to heal them, defending and mending those cast out, bringing scapegoats back into the community.

32. Matthew 13:35; Psalm 78. Cf. *The Girard Reader*, 163.

33. Bailie, 33. With this reading of mythology as "covering up," hiding, sanctifying violence, the gospel's myth-fighting truth is the remembering of a dissident minority: "Initially, Jesus' disciples almost surrender to the mimetic power of the many, but on the third day, thanks to the Resurrection they secede from the deluded mob and proclaim the innocence of their lord. In mythology no dissenting voice is ever heard." Girard, *The Scapegoat*, 2.

34. Chesterton, *Everlasting Man*, 175.

35. This, of course, depends on how one defines "mythology" and "god."

36. The choice between two paths, of insurrection and Jesus' creative nonviolence, is underlined by "Barabbas," whose name roughly means "Son of God" or "Born of the Father." The text seems to imply we are offered a choice between two "Sons of God"—which do you choose?

37. Matthew 23:29–33.

38. Bailie, *Violence Unveiled*, 240. We might call this an ancient cycle began in Adam's scapegoating Eve: "*She* made me do it."

39. William T. Cavanaugh, *The Myth of Religious Violence* (New York: Oxford University Press, 2009), 62.

40. "Do not think I have come to bring peace on earth; I did not come to bring peace, but a sword. . . . And he who does not take his cross and follow me is not worthy of me (Mt 10:34ff).

41. *The Martyr's Mirror*, by Thielman J. von Braght (first published in 1660), virtually a second Bible to many Anabaptists, serves as a sort of echo chamber around the Cross by telling hundreds of victim-martyr stories following Jesus' crucifixion.

42. Just a few of Girard's critics are Hans Urs von Balthasar (in *Theo Drama*, vol 4, "The Action" (San Francisco: Ignatius, 1994), 298ff.), Hans Boersma (in *Violence, Hospitality, and the Cross* (Grand Rapids, MI: Baker Academic, 2004), 133–151) and John Milbank (in *Theology and Social Theory* (Oxford, UK: Blackwell, 1990, 319f). For example, von Balthasar writes: "Girard's synthesis is a closed system, since it wants to be 'purely scientific,' jettisoning all 'moribund metaphysics.' All philosophy is secularized religion, and religion owes its existence to the covert scapegoat mechanism. There is therefore no such thing as a 'natural' concept of God. . . . For Girard, religion is the invention of Satan." (308ff.). Oddly, Girard intrigues me for precisely this reason, and I think it is an exciting entry point for many secular and "post-secular" thinkers.

Likewise, I see much need for further explanation of Levitical sacrifice. Jack Miles's *Christ: a Crisis in the Life of God* (Vintage, 2002), though somewhat sympathetic with Girard, stands in disagreement precisely on Girard's "anti-sacrificial" reading. Instead, he regards Christ's death more like God sacrificing himself out of repentance for failed promises to Israel. The general Girardian reading of sacrifice appears to be that the Jewish prophets continually pushed Israel away from sacrifice (starting with human sacrifice in the binding of Isaac story), ultimately aiming for its dissolution. James Alison has helped unpack a Girardian reading of Levitical sacrifice in "God's Self-Substitution and Sacrificial Inversion," in *Stricken by God?*

43. James Alison, "Worship in a Violent World," (www.jamesalison.co.uk/texts/eng13.html, accessed Mar 12, 2012), also in *Undergoing God* (New York: Continuum, 2006).

44. This story was verbally shared with me by James Alison, as he heard it from the Jesuit priest himself.

45. This is a notion Christianity has continually denounced as "Manichaeism."

46. Some might invoke Jesus' cleansing of the Temple as some kind of iconoclastic proof text, but Christians have always needed to be cautious with that incident. It is not a condemnation of religious art or human creativity, just as it is not a support for whipping people or animals. Some say it was a denunciation of money changing where Gentiles were supposed to be allowed to pray; hence the wailing "This is a house of prayer for all peoples!" Others see it as a categorical rejection of sacrifice, as does Gehard Lohfink, *Does God Need the Church?*, 187. "Jesus' action in the Temple was intended to put an end to the entire business of sacrifice."

47. Matthew 15:11.

48. 1 Corinthians 10:23.

49. 1 Corinthians 8:8–9.

50. Robert Louis Wilken, *The Christians as the Romans Saw Them* (New Haven, CT: Yale University Press, 1994), 176.

51. "[T]his presence has come to be understood not merely as a psychological remembering of the sacrifice of Christ (against a spiritualizing reductionism), but also not as repeating or re-enacting of the unique and unrepeatable historical sacrifice of Christ (against naïve realism), but as a making present, a re-presentation (*Vergegenwartigung*) of the perfect, once-and-for-all (as the Epistle of Hebrews emphasized) sacrifice of Christ." Robert Daly, "Sacrifice Unveiled or Sacrifice Revisited: Trinitarian and Liturgical Perspectives." *Theological Studies* 64 (2003): 24–42. The *Catechism of the Catholic Church* states, "The redemptive sacrifice of Christ is unique, accomplished once for all; yet it is made present in the eucharistic sacrifice of the Church. The same is true of the one priesthood of Christ; it is made present through the ministerial priesthood without diminishing the uniqueness of Christ's priesthood: 'Only Christ is the true priest, the others being only his ministers.'" (*CCC* 1545).

52. Alison, "Worship in a Violent World."

53. The *maior dissimilitude* proclamation is outlined in Canon 2 of the council.

54. Cavanaugh, *Torture and Eucharist*, 232 (emphasis added). See also Robert Daly, "Sacrifice Unveiled or Sacrifice Revisited," 28, 38. See also Edward Kilmartin, S.J., *The Eucharist in the West: History and Theology*, ed. Robert Daly, S.J. (Collegeville MN: Liturgical Press, 1998), 381–83. Kilmartin writes: "Authentic sacrifice can never be something that someone does to someone else. At its core, sacrifice is *self*-offering—in the Father, and in the Son, and in us."

55. George W. Bush, 2002 Presidential State of the Union Address.

56. Robert Daly, S.J. "Is Christianity Sacrificial or Antisacrificial?" *Religion* 27 (1997): 231–43. Here, the prime challenge is defining what exactly we mean by the word "sacrifice" in its varieties of meanings. See also Robert Daly, "The Power of Sacrifice in Ancient Judaism and Christianity," *Journal of Ritual Studies* 4/2 (1990): 181–98; Robert Daly, "Sacrifice: The Way to Enter the Paschal Mystery," *America 188, no. 16 (May 12, 2003)* 14–17.

Chapter Eight: The Search for No Accent

1. Wendell Berry was the first to bring this to my attention in his work *Sex, Economy, Freedom, and Community*, ch. 3, "GATT a Bad Big Idea." On another note, much can be said of the significant difference in dietary health and ecological diversity between these two situations.

See also William Cavanaugh, "The Unfreedom of the Free Market," from *Wealth, Poverty, and Human Destiny* ed. Doug Brandow and David Schindler (Wilmington, DE: ISI Books, 2003), 103–128.

2. One summary of three studies (Yúnez-Naude 2002; Yúnez-Naude and Becerrias 2003; and Puyana and Romero 2004) suggests that NAFTA is *not* to blame for depressing incomes for Mexican farmers. See Norbert Fiess and Daniel Lederman, "Mexican Corn: The Effects of NAFTA," World Bank Group Trade Note 18 (11/24/2004). They nevertheless admit, "If US subsidies and protection in corn—in the form of price supports, ethanol programs, and high fructose corn syrup subsidies—were to be

phased out, Mexican farmers would likely benefit, and some of the pressure on Mexico's own budgetary outlays would be relieved."

3. Cavanaugh writes: "[. . .] Hinduism originally included all that it meant to be Indian, including what modern Westerners divided into religion, politics, economics, and so on. But if Hinduism is what it means to be Indian, then by identifying and isolating a religion called Hinduism, the British were able to marginalize what it means to be Indian. Under British colonization, to be British was to be public; to be Indian was to be private" (*The Myth of Religious Violence*, 91).

It is fascinating to learn that there has been a movement of Indians who refuse to call Hinduism a "religion," given the tiny meaning we usually allow that word. "The proponents of Hindutva refuse to call Hinduism a religion precisely because they want to emphasize that Hinduism is more than mere internalized beliefs. It is social, political, economic, and familial in nature." Cohen, "Why Study Indian Buddhism?" in *Invention of Religion: Rethinking Belief in Politics and History*, ed. Petersen and Walhof ([Piscataway, NJ: Rutgers University Press, 2002),], 27. See also Cavanaugh, *The Myth of Religious Violence*, 92.

4. The late Howard Zinn, aware of how history is told and controlled by the victors, long argued that you cannot be neutral on a moving train. Howard Zinn, *You Cannot Be Neutral on a Moving Train* (Boston, MA: Beacon Press, 1995).

5. A very important political point here is how commonly language is abused regarding the terrorists of September 11. I often hear, "Their politics and religion were too closely aligned." Every intelligent Muslim I have heard on the matter has declared the exact opposite: the terrorists' politics *eclipsed* their religion and ate it up. If they had brought their "religion into the politics," it would have meant that essential Muslim tenets—compassion, tolerance, peaceableness—would have guided their politics. We should rather say, "The terrorists were *not religious enough!*" The same would go of critiques of George W. Bush's often-cited "bringing religion into politics"; it might be more accurate to say that his politics weren't *religious enough*, given the love of enemies commanded in his Christian faith or the Just War tradition.

6. William Manchester, *A World Lit Only by Fire* (New York: Back Bay Books, 1993), 150 (emphasis added).

7. Many of my reflections here are indebted to thinkers like William Cavanaugh, Stanley Hauerwas, and Alasdair MacIntyre. The latter's work *Whose Justice? Whose Rationality?* (Notre Dame, IN: University of Notre Dame Press, 1998) probes this chapter's questions more professionally and insightfully than my more cursory walk-through.

8. After leaving Willow Creek, I imagined myself starting some church plant that every week engaged a *different* tradition—one week would be Quaker silent week, another would be energetic praise and worship, another would be liturgical. I think there are a few decent reasons this idea failed to get off the ground! After experiencing the cycles of Mass for a while, I have found at our church a pretty fair attempt at this diversity, while maintaining some coherent continuity; while the Mass keeps a familiar structure throughout the year, some seasons are very somber, like Lent, while others are grand and refuse even kneeling, like Eastertide!

9. Lieven Boeve puts it well. "There is no Christian faith or Christian community outside the framework of the Christian tradition." Or, "Every tradition is inseparably *embedded in a specific historical context.*" Or, "Even today, we are incapable of occupying a disengaged, independent observer's perspective. The fact that we are part of history makes such a position impossible." (Lieven Boeve, *Interrupting Tradition: An Essay on Christian Faith in a Postmodern Context,*) 20, 22, 34.

10. "It is a great irony of our day that we hear so much of how 'religion poisons everything' from atheists like Sam Harris and the late Christopher Hitchens. Meanwhile, they have been among the most ardent supporters of recent American wars. While defaming the myopic poison of religion, they urge us to bomb the religiously stubborn into enlightenment" (Cavanaugh, *The Myth of Religious Violence,* 13, 217–218). It is likewise easy to forget that an atheist regime could kill more people in one night and in one city (like Stalin's Great Purge, Leningrad, 1934) than in four hundred years of the Inquisition in the whole of Latin America (Merton, *Conjectures of a Guilty Bystander,* 99).

11. Specifically *re-ligare* means "*re*-binds or *re*-ties something that has been severed." Cavanaugh, *Myth of Religious Violence,* 62.

12. And it is for this reason we might raise our eyebrows when we hear of "cultural religion"—isn't *all* religion cultural, somehow?

13. G. K. Chesterton, *Generally Speaking* (1928), 23.

14. Similarly, freedom is not the same thing as responsibility, just as free trade is not the same as fair trade.

15. Now, to counter my inflated rhetoric here, a nuance is in order: "Research in the history of theology has shown that many Gnostic ideas exercised a significant influence on the development of orthodox Catholic dogmatic teaching while the Gnostic movement as such was condemned as heretical." Boeve, *Interrupting Tradition: An Essay on Christian Faith in a Postmodern Context,* 105.

16. Deuteronomy 10:17–18. Consider, likewise, the paradox of this sentence: "Glory and honor and peace for everyone who does good: first for the Jew, then for the Gentile, for God shows no favoritism" (Rom 2:11).

17. This inseparable connection, between faith and living amidst the community which declares it, is precisely where Stanley Hauerwas has inspired me the most.

18. See *Catechism of the Catholic Church,* 774–76.

19. Lohfink, *Does God Need the Church?,* 161. The verb for "appointed" (*epoiesen*) means "he made" or "he appointed" and implied a genuine, public, official institution, like officeholders, judges, or priests.

20. "What Jesus does is therefore not *immediately* directed to the Church, but to the eschatological Israel. We can only speak of 'church' at a time when it is clear, after Easter, that the greater part of Israel will not come to believe. However, to the extent that the post-Easter *ekklesia*—even though incomplete because the synagogue is absent—*is* the eschatological Israel, one can and must say that Jesus laid the foundation for the Church in all his actions. What Jesus founded, when he appointed the Twelve, was not the Church but the eschatological people of God." (Lohfink, 163).

21. Chesterton, *Everlasting Man,* 171.

22. St. Pius X, Encyclical, *Ad diem illum AAS* 36 (February 2, 1904), 453–54. See also St. Bernardine of Siena, *Quadrag. De Evangelio aeterno, Sermo X*, a. 3. c. 3. Also, Leo XIII wrote, "Nothing at all of that very great treasury of all grace which the Lord brought us—for 'grace and truth came through Jesus Christ' [Jn 1:17]—nothing is imparted to us except through Mary, since God so wills, so that just as no one can come to the Father except through the Son, so in general, no one can come to Christ except through His Mother." Encyclical, *Octobri mense adventante ASS* 24 (September 22, 1891), 196.

23. On this matter, John F. Kennedy apparently penned the phrase, "Before you try to tear down a fence, you should know why it was put there," and he was likely paraphrasing a passage from Chesterton ("The Thing: Why I Am a Catholic," from *Collected Works vol 3*), 157. Chesterton also writes there, "Nobody has any business to destroy a social institution until he has really seen it as an historical institution" (157).

24. "Religious authority has often, doubtless, been oppressive or unreasonable; just as every legal system (and especially our present one) has been callous and full of a cruel apathy. It is rational to attack the police; nay, it is glorious. But the modern critics of religious authority are like men who should attack the police without ever having heard of burglars. For there is a great and possible peril to the human mind: a peril as practical as burglary. Against it religious authority was reared, rightly or wrongly, as a barrier. And against it something certainly must be reared as a barrier, if our race is to avoid ruin. That peril is that the human intellect is free to destroy itself." Chesterton, *Orthodoxy*, 38.

25. For a helpful exploration of the early Church's oblique, though nonetheless real, structures and roles, see Raymond E. Brown, S.S., "Episkope and Episkopos: The New Testament Evidence," *Theological Studies* 41 (1980): 322–338. For some New Testament instances of Church roles (e.g., bishops, deacons, priests—however different from modern connotations), see Philippians 1:1; 1 Peter 5:1–5; Acts 11:30, 14:23, 20:17, 28; Titus 1:5, 7–11; 1 Timothy 3:1–7; 1 Corinthians 12:28; 1 Corinthians 7:17.

26. It has been regarded, in certain circles, as very progressive and open-minded to cite a Native American tradition that we ought to think several generations in the future and several in the past. I wonder whether some might consider applying this to our *own* Christian religious tradition. To do so would be to admit that any version of progress will inherently involve blending progressivism with some conservativism. The two must work together.

27. One good place to see where individualistic notions of the Eucharist are condemned is in 1 Corinthians 11:20–22, where people were not "discerning the Body" as they ate the Lord's supper—with the rich ignoring the hunger of the poor. See William T. Cavanaugh, "The World in a Wafer," in "A Geography of the Eucharist as Resistance to Globalization," *Modern Theology*, 15:2, April 1999, (181–196).

28. St. Ignatius of Antioch (died circa AD 98–115) wrote, "Thus, as the Lord did nothing without the Father (being united with him), either by himself or by means of his Apostles, so you must do nothing without the bishop and the presbyters." *To the Magnesians*, vi–vii. "Likewise let all men respect the deacons as they reverence Jesus Christ, just as they must respect the bishop as the counterpart of the Father, and the presbyters as the council of God and the college of Apostles; without those

no church is recognized" (*To the Trallians*, ii–iii). "Let no one do anything that pertains to the church apart from the bishop. Let that be considered a valid Eucharist which is under the bishop or one whom he has delegated. Wherever the bishop shall appear, there let the people be; just as wherever Christ Jesus may be, there is the catholic Church. It is not permitted to baptize or hold a love-feast independently of the bishop." *To the Smyrneans*, viii.

29. In an intriguing tradition, we find that for some ordinations of those who had faced persecution, they might be exempt from this gesture, as hands had already been "laid" upon them. "But a confessor, if he was in chains for the name of the Lord, shall not have hands laid on him for the diaconate or the presbyterate, for he has the honor of the presbyterate by his confession." Hippolytus, "On Confessors" in *Apostolic Tradition* Dix 10. See Geoffrey J. Cuming, *Hippolytus: A Text for Students* (Bramcote, Nottingham: Grove Books Limited, 1991), 14.

30. Diarmaid MacCulloch's recent book *Christianity: The First Three Thousand Years* (New York: Viking Adult, 2010) is just one work among many that demonstrates how inconsistent and tumultuous this chain of popes and bishops has been.

31. Raymond Brown writes with a bit more nuance, "[T]he manner and exercise of supervision varied greatly in the different places and different periods within the first century or NT era. Only at the end of the century and under various pressures was a more uniform structure of church office developing. The death of the great leaders of the early period in the '60s left a vacuum; doctrinal divisions became sharper; and there was a greater separation from Judaism and its structures. By the '80s–'90s the presbyter-bishop model was becoming widespread, and with the adjustment supplied by the emergence of the single bishop that model was to dominate in the second century until it became exclusive in the ancient churches. Many of us see the work of the Holy Spirit in this whole process, but even those who do must recognize that the author of *1 Clement* is giving overly simplified history when he states (*1 Clem* 42) that the apostles (seemingly the Twelve) who came from Christ appointed their first converts to be bishops and deacons in local churches." Brown, "Episkope and Episkopos," 338.

32. Chesterton, *Heretics*, 67.

33. Here are a few passages that later Church leaders used to this end: "Therefore we will refute those who hold unauthorized assemblies—either because of false self-importance, or pride, or blindness and perversity—by pointing to the tradition of the greatest and oldest church, a church known to all men, which was founded and established at Rome by the most renowned Apostles Peter and Paul. This tradition the church has from the Apostles, and this faith has been proclaimed to all men, and has come down to our own day through the succession of bishops. For this church, that is, the faithful everywhere, must needs agree with the church of Rome; for in her the apostolic tradition has ever been preserved by the faithful from all parts of the world" (Irenaeus, circa 189–90).

St. Cyprian (died 258) wrote in his *Letters*, "'[T]hou art the Son of the living God.' There speaks Peter, upon whom the Church had been built, teaching in the name of the Church and showing that, although the stubborn and proud multitude of those unwilling to obey withdraw, yet the Church does not withdraw from Christ, and the people united to their bishop and the flock clinging to their shepherd are the Church. Whence you ought to know that the bishop is in the Church and the Church is in the bishop and, if there is anyone who is not with the bishop, he is not in the Church. And, in vain, they flatter themselves who creep up not having peace with the priests of God and they believe they are in communion secretly with certain ones when the Church is one, Catholic, is not divided nor rent, but is certainly united and joined, in turn, by the solder of the bishops adhering to one another."

See also Acts 1:15; 2:1, 44, 47 for an emphasis on the notion of the assembly gathering in *one* place, that the unity of the *ekklesia* is demonstrated by not splitting into different assemblies. See also 1 Clement 34:7; Barnabas 4:10; Ignatius *Eph.* 5:3; Ignatius *Magn.* 7:1; Ignatius *Phld.* 6:2, 10.1; Justin *Apol.* 1,67.3. Lohfink, *Does God Need the Church?*, 221.

34. "The early Church's theological disputes about the real bodiliness of the Risen One reflected in this text also touch on the bodiliness of the Church. It is visible, palpable, tangible. . . . Because the Church is sacrament of salvation it must be as physical as its sacraments." Lohfink, *Does God Need the Church?*, 207.

35. John Dominic Crossan, *Jesus: A Revolutionary Biography* (San Francisco: HarperOne, 1995), 169ff.

36. And it is difficult to find the purpose of the search: if he did *actually* say, "Sell your possessions," who among us (or these scholars) is *more* ready to do it?

37. Jack Miles, *Christ: A Crisis in the Life of God* (New York: Knopf, 2002), 265ff.

38. John 21:12. Luke also tells us that there were many *other* accounts that had been drawn up about Jesus (Lk 1:1).

39. This does not have to mean that the gospels have no historical grounding and that they are *only* representative of Church traditions. Biblical scholar Richard Bauckham, among others, argues in *Jesus and the Eyewitnesses* (Grand Rapids, MI: Wm. B. Eerdman's, 2006) that the gospels are historically grounded and in one sense "biographical."

40. The Gospel of John represents, by most scholarly standards, a different kind of Church "community" that chose not to emphasize the Eucharist at the Last Supper—that public space where apostles and bishops played a special role. Some see in this the "Johannine community's" preference for a hierarchy-busting foot washing. Dr. Paul Danove of Villanova posits that it is possible that the "Johannine community"—perhaps because it kept from such an organizational structure—eventually died out or was absorbed into the synoptic communities.

41. My point here does not exclude that the Scriptures may contain things that the tradition does not yet understand. At issue here is the postmodern question of whether texts "auto-deconstruct"—whether certain texts have such powerful messages within that they continue to be revealed, critiquing perhaps the very people who wield those texts.

42. Boeve writes, "What lay at the foundation of the decision to recognize the four gospels as canonical was the insight that it was impossible to grasp the truth about Jesus Christ unmediated, and that this truth could only be evoked via a plurality of images and narratives. . . . Radcliffe also describes the canon as a symbolization

of the church that, in its plurality of traditions, felt itself one in Christ: 'the canon was the symbol of the incessant dialogue between the churches, one and many, united in a faith that surpasses every separate theological perspective.'" *Interrupting Tradition*, 141.

43. Martin Luther, "Pagan Servitude of the Church."

44. Willow Creek's official position on the Bible and tradition states it well, "The sole basis of our faith is the Bible." "Heart of Willow 2010," "What We Believe," willowcreek.org.

45. G. K. Chesterton, "Is Humanism a Religion?" in *Conversion and the Catholic Church*, in *Collected Writings*, 152. Emphasis added. He also states the problem well in *All is Grist* (1931, www.gkc.org.uk/gkc/books/GKC_All_is_Grist.html, accessed March 16, 2012): "The fundamentalists are funny enough, and the funniest thing about them is their name. For, whatever else the fundamentalist is, he is not fundamental. He is content with the bare letter of Scripture—the translation of a translation, coming down to him by the tradition of a tradition—without venturing to ask for its original authority."

46. Gerald Schlabach, *Unlearning Protestantism* (Grand Rapids, MI: Brazos, 2010), 203.

47. One author who helped me broach the difficulties of "nonfoundationalism" was Dale Martin, *Sex and the Single Savior* (Louisville, KY: John Knox Press, 2006).

48. I don't see the Wesleyan quadrilateral (scripture, reason, experience, tradition) as any sort of definitive betterment to these two, since reason and experience would be brought under Catholicism's "tradition" category. And, more importantly, the Wesleyan model still ends up with scripture as a sole source of truth, and the other three simply act as a lens to interpret it.

49. Lieven Boeve described this "open narrative" in his *Interrupting Tradition* and Bernard Prusak in his *Church Unfinished: Ecclesiology Through the Centuries* (Mahwah, NJ: Paulist Press, 2004).

50. Schlabach, *Unlearning Protestantism*, 137.

51. "The universal church and the individual church are mutually inclusive. They dwell within one another mutually. That is why it is part of the essential structure of the church to have two focuses, like the two focuses of an ellipse: *iure divino*, it is both papal and Episcopal. Neither of the two poles can be traced back to the other. This unity in tension is the foundation of the union in communion. The communion which is both Episcopal and papal is the essential organic expression of the essential structure of the church, its unity in catholicity, and its catholicity in unity." Walter Kasper, *Theology and Church* (Chestnut Ridge, NY: Crossroad Publishing, 1989), 160.

Chapter Nine: On Being Part of a Terrible Organization

1. Bailie, *Violence Unveiled*, 275.

2. The Second Vatican Council (in session from to 1963 to 1965) was adamant in this claim. See especially *Lumen Gentium*.

3. Catholic theologian Karl Rahner writes, "In the light of the church's nature church-people are not merely recipients of what is done by the institutional Church

but are themselves the Church." "Structural Change in the Church of the Future," *Theological Investigations*, vol. XX, 115–32 (128–9), 123.

4. Ernie Allen, president of the National Center for Missing and Exploited Children, counts the American rate to be around one in ten. Margaret Leland Smith of the John Jay College of Criminal Justice counts it at around one in five. (Pat Wingert, "Mean Men," *Newsweek*, April 7, 2010, www.thedailybeast.com/news week/2010/04/07/mean-men.html, accessed March 29, 2012.)

5. Pat Wingert, "Mean Men"; See also Rev. James Martin, S.J., "It's Not About Celibacy: Blaming the Wrong Thing for the Sexual Abuse Crisis," *Huffington Post*, April 10, 2010, www.huffingtonpost.com/rev-james-martin-sj/its-not-about-celibacy-bl_b_533037.html, accessed March 29, 2012.

Dr. Thomas Plante, in an essay "A Perspective on Clergy Sexual Abuse" (www.psywww.com/psyrelig/plante.html, accessed March 29, 2012), writes that the rate among Catholic priests "is consistent with male clergy from other religious traditions and is significantly lower than the general adult male population which may double these numbers." See also, Thomas Plante, *Sins Against the Innocents: Sexual Abuse by Priests and the Role of the Catholic Church* (Westport, CT: Praeger, 2004).

See also Thomas Plante, "The Sexual Abuse Crisis in the Roman Catholic Church: What Psychologists and Counselors Should Know," *Pastoral Psychology* 52, No. 5 (May 2004).

6. Mark 9:42 and Matthew 18:6.

7. I love Merton's correction of the seeming bleakness of this doctrine: "Note of course that the doctrine of original sin, properly understood, is *optimistic*. It does not teach that man is by nature evil, but that evil in him is unnatural, a disorder, a sin. If evil, lying, and hatred were natural to man, all men would be perfectly at home, perfectly happy in evil. Perhaps a few seem to find contentment in an unnatural state of falsity, hatred, and greed. They are not happy. Or if they are, they are unnatural." Merton, *Conjectures of a Guilty Bystander*, 85ff.). Chesterton humorously regards the doctrine of original sin as the doctrine of the equality of all people. *Heretics*, 167.

8. While I entirely reject the aims and methods of the Inquisition it has surprised me that, *at the time*, the Inquisition courts were generally regarded as the most humane, fair, and merciful courts. We have reports of individuals blaspheming in civil courts so they would be transferred to ecclesiastical courts where sentences were more fair and just (Library of Iberian Resources Online, Charles Lea, *A History of the Inquisition of Spain*, Vol 4, Book 8: Spheres of Action, Chapter 15: Blasphemy). And with some scholarship finding that torture in ecclesial proceedings was rarer than the public proceedings, regulated at no more than fifteen minutes, and forbidding permanent harm or drawing blood, one might wonder about the exact scale of improvements made between then and, say, modern Abu Gharib or Guantanamo Bay (cf. Edward M. Peters, *Inquisition* [University of California Press, 1989], 111–112, 65). Also, Stephen Haliczer, *Inquisition and Society in the Kingdom of Valencia, 1478–1834* (University of California Press, 1990), 79.

Also, James Alison notes that "the first written records we have in European history of people standing out against, and questioning Witch trials came not from enlightened sceptics but from people whose religious understanding led them to

be highly sceptical of the craziness of the systems of goodness which were leading people to the pyre. Of the first four voices, two (1549 and 1612) were Spanish
Inquisitors who understood perfectly well that their job was to introduce the boring
secularism of due process into areas which would otherwise have tended to exciting lynch deaths. These Inquisitors would have been considered 'not sufficiently
religious.'" "Sacrifice, Law, and Catholic Faith: Is Secularity Really the Enemy?"
The Tablet, Lecture, 2006.

I point this out, again, not in *defense* of these inquisitorial acts, but to show how
the modern condemnation of (who I wish to call) "religious ancestors" is not just
arrogant, but it also distorts our understanding of history.

9. This quotation is often attributed to St. Augustine, but it seems we have no
origin for it. In fact, it appears Dorothy Day, a Catholic anarchist, was known to have
quipped about the Church, "she's a whore, but she's my mother."

10. This is what is meant when they say a sacrament works *ex opere operato*, "from
the work done"—meaning that it is valid in its own right, apart from the priest's
spiritual quality.

11. Max Weber observed something similar in his assessment of capitalism's
growth and Protestantism. In his commentary on Calvinism, he writes: "This con-
sciousness of divine grace of the elect and holy was accompanied by an attitude
toward the sin of one's neighbor, not of sympathetic understanding based on con-
sciousness of one's own weakness, but of hatred and contempt for him as an enemy
of God bearing the signs of eternal damnation. This sort of feeling was capable of
such intensity that it sometimes resulted in the formation of sects. . . . [T]he Donatist
idea of the Church appeared, as in the case of the Calvinistic Baptists." Max Weber,
The Protestant Ethic and the Spirit of Capitalism (New York: Routledge, 2000, [orig.
1930]), 122.

12. Schlabach, *Unlearning Protestantism*, 119. John W. O'Malley, S.J., "Develop-
ments, Reforms, and Two Great Reformations: Toward a Historical Assessment of
Vatican II," *Theological Studies* 44, no. 3 (1983): 399.

13. Schlabach, *Unlearning Protestantism*, 146.

14. Eugene McCarraher, "The Enchantments of Mammon," in *Modern Theology*
21 (July 2005): 438.

15. Boeve writes: "The narrative of the market embraces such relativism in order
to impose its own logic on culture. Where choices are arbitrary, where identity
becomes entirely relative, where orientation is no longer to be found, the logic of
the market functions supreme. The narrative of marketisation has every interest in
stimulating pluralisation (including relativism and the loss of orientation). Every
day the media inundates the individual with overwhelming messages, cultural
fragments and incentives, a torrent with which no one is in a position to cope. In
this sense, the market and its all-important 'primacy of arbitrariness' becomes the
unquestioned and virtually irreproachable background of life and thought." *Interrupting Tradition*, 76.

16. In their "Joint Declaration on the Doctrine of Justification," the Catholic Church
and the Lutheran World Federation came to an agreement on the "justification by
grace through faith," and released it in 1999. Through fifty sessions of dialogue

between these groups, held over a period of forty years, they resolved that they no longer share basic disagreement on the question of grace, works, and justification. This is quite an enormous matter, given that this was an essential tenet of division in the Protestant Reformation. The World Methodist Council also agrees to the joint declaration.

17. 1 Peter 2:9.

18. *Catechism of the Catholic Church*, 1546–7.

19. A decent dialogue between opposing views is by Sara Butler and Robert J. Egan: "Women and the Priesthood?" *Commonweal* (July 18, 2008), http://common wealmagazine.org/women-priesthood-0, accessed March 29, 2012.

20. *Catechism of the Catholic Church*, 1577; Mark 3:14–19; Luke 6:12–16; 1 Timothy 3:1–13; 2 Timothy 1:6; Titus 1:5–9; St. Clement of Rome, *Ad Cor.* 42,4; 44,3: PG 1,292–93; 300. Also, symbolism of Christ being a second Adam and the Church and Mary being the second Eve plays a part in this tradition (1 Cor 15:45; Rm 5). The priest's role is seen as "acting in the person of Christ," and, as a second Adam, Christ's maleness is apparently essential in the symbolism.

21. Recalling the mutual connection between scripture and tradition from last chapter, we can see that this problem is complicated. The common Protestant position, as I generally experienced it, says (1) the scriptures about Orders and priesthood in the Church are not thorough enough to warrant the tradition of male-only ordination. And (2) male-only ordination is a tradition obscuring an egalitarian early Church. It is quite difficult to work through this if *tradition made, edited, and filtered the scriptures.* If one were to appeal to "egalitarian" passages in the New Testament, the traditional position might reply that such verses came through the same tradition filter as the passages about Peter's leadership, bishops, and male apostleship; and that there is no obvious warrant to elevate some parts of the tradition (like some seemingly egalitarian passages) above others. I have thus far found no easy way around this.

22. Chesterton, "The Thing: Why I Am a Catholic," in *Collected Writings vol* 3, 153. Chesterton elsewhere calls Calvinism a reiteration of Manichaeism, an unorthodox dualism that calls spirit good, and matter evil: "Later, again, [Manichaeism] took the form of Calvinism, which held that God had indeed made the world, but in a special sense, made the evil as well as the good: had made an evil will as well as an evil world. On this view, if a man chooses to damn his soul alive, he is not thwarting God's will but rather fulfilling it. In these two forms, of the early Gnosticism and the later Calvinism, we see the superficial variety and fundamental unity of Manichaeism. The old Manicheans taught that Satan originated the whole work of creation commonly attributed to God. The new Calvinists taught that God originates the whole work of damnation commonly attributed to Satan. One looked back to the first day when a devil acted like a god, the other looked forward to a last day when a god acted like a devil. But both had the idea that the creator of the earth was primarily the creator of the evil, whether we call him a devil or a god." *St. Thomas Aquinas: The Dumb Ox* (Seattle, WA: Create Space, 2010), 54.

23. In the history of this break I find some very disappointing missteps on both sides, especially in Roman stubbornness. One great work on the matter is by Steven

Runciman, *The Eastern Schism: A Study of the Papacy and the Eastern Churches During the Eleventh and Twelfth Centuries* (Eugene, OR: Wipf & Stock, 2005 [orig. 1950]).

24. Lohfink, *Does God Need the Church?*, 293.

25. Chesterton, *The Everlasting Man*, 67.

26. Eugene McCarraher identified and corrected some of these historical assumptions prevalent in the work of the late Christopher Hitchens, who argued, "religion poisons everything." See McCarraher's review of *God is Not Great* at "This Book is not Good," June 15, 2007, *Commonweal* magazine.

27. To those who think that progress could only happen after breaking from the Catholic monopoly of traditionalism, Belloc retorts, "The great advantage in our [modern] physical powers over nature and in our knowledge of physical cause and effect is not a product of the Reformation at all: it is a product of the Renaissance." Hilaire Belloc, *How the Reformation Happened* (New York: Robert McBride and Company, 1928), 267.

28. "Catholicism is not ritualism; it may in the future be fighting some sort of superstitious and idolatrous exaggeration of ritual. Catholicism is not asceticism; it has again and again in the past repressed fanatical and cruel exaggerations of asceticism. Catholicism is not mere mysticism; it is even now defending human reason against the mere mysticism of the Pragmatists. Thus, when the world went Puritan in the seventeenth century, the Church was charged with pushing charity to the point of sophistry, with making everything easy with the laxity of the confessional. Now that the world is not going Puritan but Pagan, it is the Church that is everywhere protesting against a Pagan laxity in dress or manners. It is doing what the Puritans wanted done when it is really wanted. In all probability, all that is best in Protestantism will only survive in Catholicism; and in that sense all Catholics will still be Puritans when all Puritans are Pagans." Chesterton, from "The Thing: Why I Am a Catholic," in *Collected Writings vol 3*, 130.

29. Illustrated London News (April 19, 1924).

30. *Aggionamento*, the Italian word used to describe the Second Vatican Council, means "bring up to date," implying an openness to change.

31. Schlabach, *Unlearning Protestantism*, 192.

32. Chesterton, *Heretics*, 21.

33. Perhaps this can give a new angle from which to view Jesus entrusting the care of his aging mother Mary—whom I have previously treated as a symbol of the Church—to his disciple John.

34. Merton, *Conjectures of a Guilty Bystander*, 126.

35. Chesterton writes: "While the two men were thus a contrast in almost every feature, they were really doing the same thing. One of them was doing it in the world of the mind and the other in the world of the worldly. But it was the same great medieval movement; still but little understood. In a constructive sense, it was more important than the Reformation. Nay, in a constructive sense, it was the Reformation" (*St. Thomas Aquinas*, 7).

Further on he writes, "Those who, for other reasons, honestly accept the final effect of the Reformation will none the less face the fact, that it was the Schoolman [the scholastics, like Aquinas] who was the Reformer; and that the later Reformers were by comparison reactionaries. I use the word not as a reproach from my own standpoint, but as a fact from the ordinary modern progressive standpoint. For instance, they riveted the mind back to the literal sufficiency of the Hebrew Scriptures; when St. Thomas had already spoken of the Spirit giving grace to the Greek philosophies. He insisted on the social duty of works; they only on the spiritual duty of faith. It was the very life of the Thomist teaching that Reason can be trusted: it was the very life of Lutheran teaching that Reason is utterly untrustworthy" (11).

36. "Revolutionary subordination" is a term coined by John Howard Yoder in his *Politics of Jesus*, but used in regard to how Christians might relate to political powers, judging from how Jesus submitted to arrest. One might see hints of this subjection to religious authorities in his declaration, "They sit in the seat of Moses. So you must be careful to do everything they tell you. But do not do what they do" (Mt 23:2–3). Or Luke 5:14, in insisting upon reporting to priests and obeying Mosaic code.

37. R. H. Tawney, *Religion and the Rise of Capitalism: A Historical Study, Holland Memorial Lectures* (Piscataway, NJ: Transaction Publishers, 1998 [orig. 1922]). "In one sense the distinction between the secular and the religious life was vanished. Monasticism was, so to speak, secularized. . . . Having overthrown monasticism, its aim was to turn the secular world into a gigantic monastery, and at Geneva, for a short time, it almost succeeded" (98, 115).

38. It is a funny detail to recognize how Church authorities have been reticent to canonize any religious order that wasn't somehow poor, chaste, and obedient—that is, mimicking Jesus' humble position. When a revival movement doesn't mortify the powers of money, sex, and unchecked power, things get even scarier than they already are!

39. Chesterton, *Orthodoxy*, 73.

Chapter Ten: Art and Apocalypse

1. The words, said from St. Veronica to St. Helen, read *Hinc una fides mundo refulgent* ("From here a single faith shines throughout the world"); and from St. Longinus to St. Andrew *Hinc sacerdotii unitas exoritur* ("From here is born the unity of the priesthood").

2. A similar event is recorded differently in Mark, where they are at Simon's, not Lazarus's, house. The woman is not named. The perfume there is poured upon his head, not feet. And instead of Judas complaining, it is a group murmuring about wastefulness, and the group rebukes her. Jesus says, "She has done a beautiful thing to me."

3. Luke 12:33.

4. Deuteronomy 15:4.

5. "I tell you the truth, wherever the gospel is preached throughout the world, what she has done will also be told, in memory of her," (Mk 14:9).

6. Max Weber, *The Protestant Ethic and the Spirit of Capitalism*.

7. Luke 7:33–34.

8. Chesterton, *Utopia of Usurers* (Norfolk, VA: IHS Press, 2002 [orig. 1917]), 17.

9. Berry, *Sex, Economy, Freedom, and Community*, 112.

10. On our short European tour of *Jesus for President* (Grand Rapids, MI: Zondervan, 2008), I was delighted to take a tour up to the top of the central church in Basel, Switzerland. After a long and winding passage past the bell tower, you can find, resting high, near the top of the spire, a stone laid in place which has a tiny mouse sculpted into it. What an expression of a mason's satisfaction and delight!

11. Matthew 6:28.

12. This brings to mind a meditation on gargoyles, from Chesterton, "The Old Greeks summoned godlike things to worship their god. The medieval Christians summoned all things to worship theirs, dwarfs and pelicans, monkeys and madmen. The modern realists summon all these million creatures to worship their god; and then have no god for them to worship. Paganism was in art a pure beauty; that was the dawn. Christianity was a beauty created by controlling a million monsters of ugliness; and that in my belief was the zenith and the noon. Modern art and science practically mean having the million monsters and being unable to control them; and I will venture to call that the disruption and the decay." G. K. Chesterton, *Alarms and Discursions* (Charleston, SC: Nabu Press, 2010 [orig. 1910]), 9.

13. At times, though, the father seems to doubt they really are "the good guys." Who, in these circumstances of constantly choosing between evil choices, can feel "good"?

14. To be true to the text, on one occasion we have the father telling the son "telling him stories of courage and adventure," but these appear in the story as a blip, a grasping Cormac McCarthy. *The Road* (New York: Vintage, 2006, 41).

15. McCarthy, *The Road*, 74.

16. A commendable book that explores this tension is Wes Howard-Brook, Anthony Gwyther, and Elizabeth A. McCalister, *Unveiling Empire: Reading Revelation Then and Now* (Maryknoll, NY: Orbis, 1999).

17. Chesterton, *Orthodoxy*, 77.

18. I love this illustration of the combination: "Monks and nuns stood to mankind as a sort of sanctified league of aunts and uncles. It is a commonplace that they did everything that nobody else would do; that the abbeys kept the world's diary, faced the plagues of all flesh, taught the first technical arts, preserved the pagan literature, and, above all, kept the poor from the most distant sight of their modern despair. We still find it necessary to have a reserve of philanthropists, but we trust it to men who have made themselves rich, not to men who have made themselves poor." G. K. Chesterton, *A Short History of England* (Charleston, SC: CreateSpace, 2011, [orig. 1917]), 18.

19. 1 Corinthians 7:30–31; Philippians 2:11–13.

20. Chesterton, *Orthodoxy*, 106. In another discussion of the monastery-wealth problem, he writes, "It is perfectly true that we can find real wrongs, provoking rebellion, in the Roman Church just before the Reformation. What we cannot find is one of those real wrongs that the Reformation reformed. For instance, it was an abominable abuse that the corruption of the monasteries sometimes permitted a rich noble to play the patron and even play at being the Abbot, or draw on the

revenues supposed to belong to a brotherhood of poverty and charity. But all that the Reformation did was to allow the same rich noble to take over *all* the revenue, to seize the whole house and turn it into a palace or a pig-sty, and utterly stamp out the last legend of the poor brotherhood. "The Thing: Why I Am A Catholic" in *Collected Writings vol 3*, 186.

21. Genesis 3:24.

Chris Haw is a husband, father, carpenter, potter, adjunct professor at Cabrini College, and founder of Camden House, an intentional community. Raised in Chicago's northern suburbs, Haw was baptized Catholic but joined Willow Creek Community Church as a teenager. Here he met and became friends with Shane Claiborne; the two would later become leaders in the New Monasticism movement along with Jonathan Wilson-Hartgrove.

He earned his double bachelor's degree in theology and sociology from Eastern University and his master's degree in theology and religious studies from Villanova. Upon returning from studies in Belize, Haw started an intentional community in an economically devastated section of Camden, New Jersey, which operates in partnership with Sacred Heart Church. This connection fostered Haw's reassessment of his own faith and in 2006 he returned to the Catholic Church. In 2008 he cowrote *Jesus for President* with Shane Claiborne. He has been interviewed by *Christianity Today*, *Sojourner's*, CNN, and Al-Jazeera.

Founded in 1865, Ave Maria Press,
a ministry of the Congregation of
Holy Cross, is a Catholic publishing
company that serves the spiritual and
formative needs of the Church and its
schools, institutions, and ministers;
Christian individuals and families; and
others seeking spiritual nourishment.

———◦◦◦———

For a complete listing of titles from

Ave Maria Press

Sorin Books

Forest of Peace

Christian Classics

visit www.avemariapress.com

ave maria press® / Notre Dame, IN 46556
A Ministry of the United States Province of Holy Cross